FIENDISH
KILLERS

FIENDISH KILLERS

by
ANNE WILLIAMS
VIVIAN HEAD
SEBASTIAN C. PROOTH
AMY WILLIAMS

Futura

A *Futura* Book

First published by Futura in 2007

Copyright © Omnipress 2007

ISBN: 978-0-7088-0725-5

Produced by Omnipress, Eastbourne

Printed in Great Britain

Futura
An imprint of
Little, Brown Book Group
Brettenham House
Lancaster Place
London WC2E 7EN

Photo credits: Getty Images

The views expressed in this publication are those of the author. The information and the interpretation of that information are presented in good faith. Readers are advised that where ethical issues are involved, and often highly controversial ethical issues at that, they have a personal responsibility for making their own assessments and their own ethical judgements.

CONTENTS

PART THREE: WICKED TEAMS

PART FOUR: FIENDISH WOMEN

PART FIVE: FIENDISH DOCTORS

PART SIX: VAMPIRES

PART SEVEN: CHILD FIENDS

PART EIGHT: SCHOOL SHOOTINGS

INTRODUCTION

Imagine a kindly, grey-haired old man walking down the street hand-in-hand with an adorable little girl. Passers-by wouldn't think anything of it, presuming that the six-year-old was simply taking a stroll to the shops with her grandfather. However, envisage a crime of unparalleled revulsion when the body of Grace Budd and many more young children are discovered brutally murdered by possibly one of the most deranged human beings ever encountered – Albert Fish. What drives a person into becoming a psychopathic predator? Although medical research would like to say they have the answers, can you ever really get inside the mind of a fiendish killer?

While the human brain is conditioned into accepting that men commit atrocious acts of murder, it is hard for us to comprehend when the serial killer turns out to be a female or, even worse, a child. Unfortunately, in reality, women have proved to be just as cold-blooded as their counterparts, whether it is out of monetary gain, revenge, pressure or just sheer depravity.

The Countess Elizabeth Báthory is probably the first woman to go down in history as being motivated by bloodlust. She quite openly bathed in the blood of her virgin victims in the hope that she would retain her youthful looks. Hélène Jegado was a French domestic servant and serial poisoner, who murdered at least twenty-three people with arsenic between the years 1833 and 1851. Another female serial killer was Jeanne Weber, who strangled ten children, including her own, eventually killing herself in her own prison cell.

Mary Flora Bell was just eleven years old when she wanted to 'hurt' someone. The product of a broken home, she went through her childhood being angry and the only way she knew how to vent her anger was through killing.

Jesse Harding Pomeroy, dubbed the 'Boy Fiend', was one of the youngest serial killers ever known. Though hardly fourteen, he brutally tortured his victims and took great pleasure in seeing them writhe in agony.

So what turns these people into such barbaric, fiendish killers? We are all born with the capability to hurt other human beings under certain circumstances, but it is hard to understand why one person can control this emotion and another individual doesn't know when to stop. There have been extensive studies and discussions regarding the difference between the normal person (non-killer) and the serial killer, and gradually certain factors arose that seemed to effect behaviour patterns. One disturbing factor is that when a killer is finally apprehended the person who committed such atrocities can appear to be 'normal'. Society would like to think that there is something wrong with a person who displays extreme violence as there are few things more repellent to human nature than the concept of a serial killer.

It is fair to say that serial killers are composed of all types of people from all walks of life. They can be males, females, young or old, single or pairs of killers and from any ethnic background. It could be your next-door neighbour, your best friend, or the nurse that so tenderly looked after you in hospital – history has shown it can be anyone. The serial killer's background seems to play a large part in their behaviour and helps us understand what drives them to inflict pain on others. In the case of many sadistic murderers, their childhood has been a series of abuse at the hands of their parents. Although this is in no way the sole excuse, it is certainly an undeniable factor in many of their backgrounds. Abuse in infancy can often have disastrous results because the child does not learn how to trust, developing traits of insecurity and a lack of social interaction. All they have known from adults, is domination and control, which is something that they carry with them into adulthood. There are usually three common denominators that occur in the childhood of the majority of serial killers: they are bedwetters beyond the age of ten, there is a tendency to inflict suffering on animals and finally there is a pre-disposition to arson.

It could be said that some serial killers are just born 'bad', as in the case of Edmund Kemper. From a very early age he showed signs of sadistic violence by beheading his sister's dolls, taking great pleasure in the art of execution. He said of himself:

> *It was an urge . . . a strong urge, and the longer I let it go the stronger it got, to where I was taking risks to go out and kill people . . .*

Kemper was the product of a broken and abusive home, who was constantly put down by his over-bearing mother. If he failed to do as she wished, she would lock him in the basement of their house for hours on end. He grew up timid and resentful, fearing his own inadequacies, and by the age of ten Kemper had graduated to living targets – he cut the head off the family cat.

The study of serial killers has also shown that many of them suffered severe head injuries at a young age. The case of Phineas Gage in 1848 is a prime example of the drastic changes in character, following a serious accident. Gage worked on the Rutland and Birmingham Railway and, one day in

September 1848, he was tamping down the blasting powder for a controlled charge, when he inadvertently sparked an explosion. The force of the blast blew his tamping iron right through his head. It went in point-first under his left cheek bone, taking his eye out on its way through his brain, eventually coming out through the top of his skull. It landed several yards away, leaving Gage lying on the floor in a convulsive heap. Amazingly, even though the left side of his brain had been completely destroyed, minutes later Gage was able to stand up and speak. His fellow workers watched both horrified and yet amazed, convinced that the accident would have killed him. Within two months Gage was able to walk, speak and appeared normal in every way, with the exception of his character, which had changed beyond recognition. His friends simply said that he was 'no longer Gage'. In place of the friendly, diligent worker, was a foul-mouthed and inveterate liar.

Albert Fish, who was mentioned earlier, also received a head injury when he fell out of a cherry tree at the age of seven. This left him with headaches and dizzy spells but, more significantly, he started to display violent tendencies.

The frontal lobe in the brain is what can simply be termed as the 'stop button', which acts as a conscience in a 'normal' human being. When this lobe is damaged the power of logic is greatly impaired, reducing such actions as self-control, planning, judgement and the balance between right and wrong and good and evil. If only this were the case in all serial killers, it would make the explanation far easier to understand. However, over half of all confessed serial killers state that they knew perfectly well what they were doing – before, during and after their crime. Some even confess to what they were doing was wrong and even contemplated never doing it again. It seems, though, that the thrill derived from murder is comparable to a narcotic fix, which seems to satisfy the killer's senses for a while. But like a drug, the fix wears off and they have the overwhelming desire to kill again.

Statistically, serial killers can be categorised into males from lower- to middle-class backgrounds between the ages of eighteen to mid-thirties. However, there will always be the exception to the rule and many serial killers defy that standard. For example Ray and Faye Copeland were two of the most unlikely serial killers in memory who killed several workers on their farm. Faye was sixty-nine and her husband, Ray, was seventy-five at the time of their killings. Not only did they keep a diary of all their victims, but Faye took pleasure in making a quilt for a bed out of articles of their clothing.

Again, according to standard profile, a serial killer works on his own. However, there have been many examples of killers who have worked in pairs, once again disproving this theory. Perhaps one of the most notorious killer pairs was Kenneth Bianchi and Angelo Buono, also known as 'The Hillside Stranglers'. They were cousins who inflicted terror in Southern California during the 1970s. Martha Beck, an obese woman with a hatred of other females, and Raymond Fernandez, a conman who procured money and valuables from gullible single women, met in 1947 and formed another unique but deadly coupling.

Mass murderers tend to come under a different category to the serial killer in that they are generally apprehended shortly after the event. Very often they will turn themselves into the authorities or, on some occasions, take their own lives. The mass murderer is usually someone who aspires to more than they can achieve and blame other people for their lack of success. They often feel excluded from the society to which they desperately wish to belong, and develop an irrational hatred of that group of people. Very often they choose to die in the violence which is directed at the group they feel oppresses or threatens them. The mass murderer is usually seen as a deranged soul who is out to annihilate their avengers, whether it is through unemployment, loneliness, a family breakup or simply a reprimand from someone in a superior position. Unlike the serial killer, it is very rare that we ever hear of a mass murderer having the opportunity to carry out a second series of killings.

Cannibalism, or the eating of human body parts, has been around for a long time, but when it is done out of sheer pleasure, it makes the thought even more horrifying. The first recorded killer cannibal was a man called Sawney Beane, who lived in the late sixteenth century. He lived in a cave with his wife, fourteen children and twenty-two grand-children, who all survived by eating the flesh of any travellers who passed by. Of course in recent years, cannibalism has been glorified by the film world in the stories of Hannibal Lecter, a psychoanalyst with a taste for human flesh. But perhaps what many people don't realise is that Lecter's story was loosely based around the characters of real-life models – Albert Fish, Jeffrey Dahmer and Ed Gein. It is fair to say that the truth about real-life cannibals is far scarier than their fictional counterparts.

They love the night, they drink blood, they want to meet you . . . yes, real vampires do exist and *Fiendish Killers* gives gory details of their shocking stories. We have all heard about Dracula, but did you know that his character was based on a real-life, fifteenth-century vampire by the name of Vlad 'The Impaler' Tepes, who loved nothing more than to impale his victims on stakes. Arnod Paole, who told his wife he had fears of a premature death, came back to haunt the living in the form of a vampire in the eighteenth century. When his body was exhumed, not only did they find fresh blood on his lips, but when a stake was plunged through his heart, the wound spurted fresh blood and the corpse cried out in pain.

Although there can never be a strictly accurate guideline that can be followed, police investigators try to follow some sort of pattern when trying to track down a killer. It is imperative that they keep an open mind, because it would be too easy just to dismiss a person because he or she didn't fit into their profile. As the police delve deeper into the phenomenon of the fiendish killer, all too often the secrets behind their actions are actually buried with their victims.

PART ONE

CANNIBALS

SAWNEY BEAN

The notorious Alexander 'Sawney' Bean was a Scottish cannibal who, along with his incestuously bred extended family, is reputed to have robbed, murdered, dismembered, pickled and eaten at least 1,000 travellers in the remote part of Ayrshire where the clan lived. After surviving for over twenty-five years in this way, Bean's reign of terror eventually came to an end when he and his evil brood were discovered and captured by an army of soldiers led by King James VI of Scotland (who later became James I of England). They were brought to justice, and their horrific punishment described in the *Newgate Calendar*, a record of criminals that passed through Newgate Prison in London during that period. However, some believe that the account of the Bean clan's crimes is wildly exaggerated, and that although there may be some basis of truth to the legend, it is essentially a myth. Be that as it may, today, the story of Sawney Bean has become part of Scottish folklore, and is certainly illustrative of the barbaric lawlessness of the area at the time.

CANNIBAL CAVE DWELLERS

Alexander Bean was said to have been born in East Lothian, the son of a ditch digger and hedge trimmer. The young boy, nicknamed 'Sawney', followed in his father's footsteps and took up the family trade, but his apprenticeship was short-lived. He had a vicious nature that alienated him from other people, and showed little appetite for regular work. Soon, he felt that the life of an honest labourer was not for him, and decided to make his living in other ways. Having met a young woman, described in the *Newgate Calendar* as equally vicious, they went to live in a cave by the sea at Bannane Head, near Galloway in what is now South Ayrshire. This cave was flooded each day by the tide, and was 183 metres (200 yards) deep, with many passages and corridors extending a long way into the rockface. Because the entrance was so often blocked by water, few people knew it was there, and thus the Beans lived there undetected for many years. Today, the cave has been identified as Bennane Cave, which is situated between Ballantrae and Girvan in Ayrshire.

It was not long before the Beans had children: eight sons and six daughters. Between them, the sons and daughters incestuously produced more progeny: eighteen grandsons and fourteen granddaughters, all of them living in the damp cave together. None of them went out to work, but all survived by a particularly grisly means: they robbed passing travellers and then murdered them, bringing the bodies of their victims back to the cave to rip them apart and eat them. Legend has it that the Beans did not even bother to cook the human meat, but simply tore it to shreds with their teeth, like animals. In a barely more civilised ritual, they took to pickling the leftovers, which sometimes washed up on the local beaches.

LYNCH MOB

Not surprisingly, the local villagers and townspeople began to notice the travellers and others who went missing, not to mention the unsavoury body parts that occasionally appeared on the beach. By this time there were forty-eight mouths in the Bean family to feed, so the death toll of travellers and wanderers who had the misfortune to pass by the cave and were never seen again, was beginning to go up rapidly. However, according to the Newgate source, nobody living in the area realised that there was a tribe of vicious cannibals living in the cave. This was, apparently, because the Beans always stayed at home during the day, and only came out at night to commit their evil crimes.

As the murders increased, the local townspeople began to agitate to find the culprits, and soon several individuals were arrested and charged with murder. A number of innkeepers were accused of the murders, often because they had been the last people to see the victims alive. In some cases, the suspects were even lynched, but to no avail: the murders continued to take place, and the mystery of who was behind them remained unsolved.

BROUGHT TO JUSTICE

Eventually, something took place to shed some light on what was happening. One night, the Bean clan ambushed a married couple returning from a day out at the fair. The man was armed with a sword and pistol and proved himself to be a skilled fighter, holding off the clan for a short while, even though he was only one against many. His wife was not so lucky – the raiders pulled her off her horse and proceeded to disembowel her in front of her husband's eyes, allegedly drinking her blood and ripping her limbs apart with their teeth. It was only a matter of time before the husband met the same fate, but luckily for him, a party of travellers who had also been to the fair were riding along a short way behind and they now came into view. The Bean clan took to their heels, but when the fairgoers came nearer, they saw the bloody work that the bestial murderers had done, and the surviving husband gave them a blow-by-blow account of what had happened. The Bean clan were revealed at last for the gruesome cannibals they were.

News of the dreadful crime made its way to the Scottish court, and it was not long before King James VI himself resolved to put an end to the clan's reign of terror. Assembling an army of 400 soldiers, together with a team of bloodhounds, he rode up to the cave where the Bean family lived. The soldiers poured into the cave, surprising the inmates, and found a hideous scene there. The clan were crouching like animals among piles of human remains, some of them still chewing on the severed, bloody arms and limbs of their victims. It was later estimated that the Beans had murdered and consumed over 1,000 victims, possibly more, during the twenty-five years or so that they had lived there.

The soldiers rounded up all the members of the Bean clan and took them to the Tolbooth Jail in Edinburgh. From there, they were sent on to jails in Leith and Glasgow. So outraged were the public by the story of the murders, that the authorities did not bother to give the Bean family a trial, but decided to execute them in the most cruel ways possible. The men were hung, drawn and quartered; this meant that their hands and feet were cut off while they were still alive, so that they bled slowly to death. The women and children were forced to watch them die, and then burned alive themselves. Thus, the clan met their end as violently as they had lived.

THE 'HAIRY TREE'

There is also a story about one of Sawney Bean's daughters, who is said to have escaped from the cave and set up home in the town of Girvan, hiding her true identity from the local populace and living as an ordinary citizen for some years. However, when the family were captured, her history was made public, and she was pursued by a lynch mob. They hanged her from the branches of a tree that she had planted, known as the 'Hairy Tree'. This tree was apparently situated in Dalrymple Street, and according to local superstition, the corpse of the daughter could be heard swinging from it on windy nights for many years after the hanging.

FACT OR FICTION?

Today, many historians believe that, although there may be some truth to the legend of Sawney Bean, in all probability the story has been much exaggerated. They point out that although the *Newgate Calendar* cites the story, there are no other accounts of him in any other historical records of the period. Also, it has been pointed out that if the entire Bean family had lived only by murdering and eating human beings for twenty-five years, they would have consumed far more than 1,000 people, and would in fact have decimated the population of the area. There is also some dispute as to the date of Sawney Bean's reign of terror; some broadsheets reported it as having taken place during the reign of James VI, while others allege that it was centuries before. Whatever the truth, in all likelihood the story was exaggerated, since the broadsheets – like our own newspapers today – constantly sensation-alised events to entertain their readers.

Because the Sawney Bean story first appeared in British chapbooks, which were like the tabloids of today, some believe that it was made up by English political propagandists in the wake of the Jacobite rebellions, so as to discredit the Scots. However, it has also been argued that as the chapbooks also contained horrifying stories about English criminals, this is unlikely. What does seem to be the case is that, from earliest times, there was a great deal of poverty and lawlessness in the remote rural areas of Scotland, so that many travellers were robbed, murdered and possibly even cannibalised as they passed through, by outlaws such as Sawney Bean and his family.

ALFERD PACKER

Alferd Packer was an American cannibal who was accused of murdering and eating five companions on a trip into the Colorado rocky mountains. He swore that he had only eaten the flesh of men who had already died so as to survive, but he did admit to killing one of them in self-defence. There was a great deal of controversy at the time as to Packer's innocence or otherwise, and nobody really knew what actually happened on the expedition, as he was the only witness.

MINING FOR GOLD

Packer was born in Allegheny County, Pennsylvania, on November 21, 1842. He became apprenticed to a cobbler, but when the Civil War broke out, he enlisted in the army. At the age of nineteen, he headed out west and joined the US infantry in Winona, Minnesota, but was later discharged due to epilepsy. He later returned to the army as a soldier in the Iowa Cavalry, and some believe he was a scout for General Custer, but once again his illness forced him out.

Little more is known of his activities until in 1873, at the age of thirty-one, he joined a group of twenty prospectors who set out from Bingham Canyon, Utah, into the mountains of Colorado to look for gold. The expedition did not go well: the party got lost in bad weather, and soon ran out of food. The members of the group arrived in an Indian camp, where most of them decided to stay put till spring, but five of them pressed on – they were Shannon Wilson Bell, Israel Swan, James Humphrey, Frank 'Reddy' Miller, and George 'California' Noon.

Two months later, they had not arrived at their destination, and their relatives were becoming anxious about them. Accounts vary as to what happened next, but Packer is thought to have appeared at a saloon in the town of Saguache, saying that he had a leg injury and needed some whisky. Observers noticed that he had several wallets on his person. He said that he had become separated from the party, and did not know where they were. However, it was later discovered that there were strips of human flesh on the trail where he had been, and he was questioned once more as to what had happened to his companions.

HUMAN MEAT

This time, he made a formal confession, saying the men had died of starvation and then been eaten by the others, who were crazed with hunger. Israel Swan, aged sixty-five, had died first, and all survivors had fed off his body. The next to go was James Humphrey, and Packer admitted that he had taken his wallet, which had over $100 in it. After that, Frank Miller, known as 'the Butcher', died in an accident searching for wood, and he was eaten too. That left George Noon, who was only eighteen, Shannon Bell and Packer himself. According to Packer, Bell shot Noon, and the two remaining survivors then ate him. Packer then alleged that Bell had attacked him, so he was forced to defend himself. He killed Bell and ate him, then managed to get to Saguache on his own.

The authorities arrested Packer on suspicion of murder, and he was thrown into jail at Saguache. When the trail was inspected further, it became clear that the men had not died one by one. An artist named John A. Randolph discovered five sets of human remains beside the Gunnison River, at a place called Slumgullion Pass. Randolph made a detailed sketch of the bodies, which showed that parts of the thigh and breast had been cut out. Witnesses were brought to the scene, and the bodies were then buried in an area that became known as 'Dead Man's Gulch'.

However, while this was happening, Packer managed to escape from jail, and for the next nine years went on the run, under the name of John Schwartze. Nothing is known of what he did during that time, but in March 1883, a member of the larger party who had stayed in the Indian camp, a man named Frenchy Cabizon, recognised him in a saloon and had him arrested. He was charged with the five murders and made a new confession. This time he said that the men who had left the Indian camp had not taken enough food with them, and had run into a snowstorm, so that they had begun to starve. Some of them, like Bell, began to show signs of madness, and when Packer went on a scouting trip to find food, he returned to find Bell roasting a piece of meat on the fire. It turned out that Bell had killed all four of his companions, in a fit of madness, and was busy cooking a piece of Miller's leg. Then Bell turned on Packer, who defended himself by grabbing the hatchet Bell was using and burying it in his head. He then tried to leave the camp, but was prevented from doing so by heavy snow, so he stayed where he was and began to eat the corpses. Eventually, when the snow began to thaw, he left, taking some pieces of meat with him to eat along the way.

Packer's new story did not convince the jury, and on Friday, April 13, 1883, he was convicted of murder. According to popular legend, the judge called Packer a 'man-eating son of a bitch' and said: 'When you came to Hinsdale County, there were seven democrats. But you ate five of them, goddamn you. I sentence you to be hanged by the neck until you are dead, dead, dead.'

STARVATION AND MADNESS

There was a great deal of controversy about the sentence, and two years later, Packer managed to get a retrial. This time he was convicted to forty years' life imprisonment on a charge of manslaughter. Once in jail, he changed his story yet again, and a local newspaper printed the final version of events. He claimed that the party had run out of food and had been reduced to cooking and eating their moccasins, which were made out of hide. They wrapped their feet in blankets (this detail was borne out by the evidence of the corpses, whose feet were indeed wrapped in this way). Bell had begun to suffer delusions as the result of starvation, and everyone travelling with him had become terrified of him. The party camped by the Gunnison River, and in the morning, Packer went off to see if he could find help. When he came back,

Bell attacked him and he shot him dead, only to realise what had happened after the deed was done. When he realised that Bell had been cooking and eating human meat, he was revolted and threw it away. He tried to cover the bodies of his comrades, and at this point his mind failed. In his madness, he said, he may have eaten human flesh, but he was so disturbed that he could not really remember what happened. Eventually, he wandered into town, dazed and confused by his terrible ordeal.

This version of events did not fit with that of witnesses in the Saguache saloon, who claimed that he had sauntered in looking quite healthy and had shown no signs of madness whatsoever. Clearly, Packer was something of a fantasist, and every time he told the story, it had changed. However, there were those who sympathised with him, arguing that it was understandable that a starving man should eat (though not kill) his companions. To this day, it is still not clear exactly what happened, but the gruesome details of the Packer story made him a notorious figure for many years after the event.

Regarding Packer's name, it is thought that his real name was Alfred G. Packer. However, when he first signed up to the army, he wrote it as Alferd. In addition, this was the spelling that he had tattooed on his arm. (Some believe that the tattoo artist made a mistake, and that Packer subsequently adopted it as a joke.) Also, when invitations to his hanging (which never took place) were sent out, Alferd was the spelling used. It seems likely that even with the spelling of his name, Packer could not be honest, clear and straightforward, but constantly changed his story.

In his final trial, Packer's forty-year sentence was upheld and he was imprisoned. In 1886 he was paroled and went to live in Deer Creek, Jefferson County. Legend has it that he became a vegetarian before he died at the age of sixty-five. In 1981, he was formally pardoned of his crimes. Today, the story of Alferd Packer has passed into folklore, and there is even a ballad written about him, that goes:

> *In the Colorado Rockies*
> *Where the snow is deep and cold*
> *And a man afoot can starve to death*
> *Unless he's brave and bold*
> *Oh Alfred Packer*
> *You'll surely go to hell*
> *While all the others starved to death*
> *You dined a bit too well.*

ED GEIN

Ed Gein has gone down in history as one of the most fiendish killers of all time. This is despite the fact that, unlike many of those remembered for their savagery as serial killers, he was only actually responsible for murdering two of the corpses that were found in his home when police raided it. What was shocking and horrifying about the case was that he was a bizarre necrophiliac, who liked to decorate his house with human body parts. Items such as severed heads made into bedposts in the bedroom, human skin used as lampshades and upholstery for chair seats, skulls fashioned into soup bowls, a necklace of human lips, a face mask made out of facial human skin, a belt made from human nipples and a waistcoat made up of a vagina and breasts stitched together, which he called a 'mammary vest'. In addition to these atrocities, the police were said to have found a human heart bubbling on the stove. It was hard to believe that anyone could be so depraved as to fashion such ghoulish items from human remains, but the evidence was all around the house, for all to see. It appeared that his activities had been going on for years and that, because he was a recluse, nobody knew anything about it. No wonder Ed Gein became the inspiration for many horror stories and films, including the *Texas Chainsaw Massacre* and the Buffalo Bill character in Thomas Harris's *The Silence of the Lambs*.

THE MAKING OF A PSYCHO

Ed Gein was born in La Crosse, Wisconsin on August 28, 1906, the second son of Augusta and George Gein, both natives of the area. His older brother was named Henry. George Gein was a violent alcoholic and was seldom able to hold down a job, but sometimes worked as a tanner and carpenter. His wife Augusta was an extremely religious woman who felt nothing but contempt for her husband but who never considered divorcing him, because of her religious beliefs. To earn the family an income, Augusta ran a small grocery store, in addition to bringing up the two children. Soon after Ed was born, Augusta purchased a small farm in the remote country outside Plainfield, and this became the family's permanent residence.

Augusta had moved to the farm to keep her children away from the rest of society, believing that the influence of others would corrupt her sons.

She made sure that they never had other children home to play, and that they only left the house to go to school. As well as making sure they worked hard at their studies, Augusta made them do many chores around the farm. As a fanatically religious Lutheran, she drilled into young Ed and his older brother Henry that drink was evil, and that all women, other than herself, were sinful whores who would corrupt them and give them horrifying diseases. She taught them that the only justifiable sexual activity was for making babies. Each afternoon, the boys were subjected to long readings from the bible, the passages selected from the Old Testament, to show them how God's wrath would descend on them if they sinned in any way, particularly following any sexual urges.

SEXUALLY CONFUSED LONER

Not surprisingly, Ed grew up with little confidence, and was bullied at school because of his girlish demeanour and the fact that he had a small growth over one eye. His behaviour was strange, and he would laugh at random, which further alienated his fellow pupils. However, although he was not popular at school, he did well at his studies. As he grew up, he began to become critical of his mother, especially when she caught him, as an adolescent, masturbating in the bath and poured scalding water over him. However, he remained working on the farm and grew up as an adult to be a sexually confused loner, with a liking for escapist books and magazines. His existence became extremely isolated and the only human beings he regularly came into contact with were family members. At this stage of his life, he appeared to be strange, yet harmless; it was only when the family members began to die that his behaviour changed.

In 1940 George died, and his sons began to take on odd jobs in town to help make ends meet. Ed worked as a handyman and even as a babysitter, and townspeople found him likeable and trustworthy. Then, in 1944, Ed's brother Henry died under what seemed, with the benefit of hindsight, to be suspicious circumstances. What apparently happened was that Ed and Henry were fighting a fire in the nearby marshes. Then the two got separated and when the fire cleared Henry was found dead. What was strange was that his body was lying in an unburnt area and that there was bruising to his head. The cause of death, though, was listed as asphyxiation.

GRAVE-ROBBING SPREES

With George and Henry gone, Ed was left to keep the farm going with his mother Augusta. But little more than a year later, Augusta died as well. She died of a series of strokes on December 29, 1945, following an argument with a neighbour. Her son's reaction was to nail her bedroom door shut, leaving the room inside just as it was the day she died. He then began to show signs of serious mental disturbance, and it was then that he took up grave robbing. He became fascinated with human anatomy. He was particularly interested in reading about the first sex change operation, undertaken by Christine Jorgensen, and even considered having a sex change himself. Then, together with another disturbed man named Gus, he started visiting graveyards and taking souvenirs – sometimes whole bodies, more often selected body parts. He would scour the obituary column of the local newspaper in order to learn of freshly buried female corpses and, later, at night, pay them a visit.

During these years, Gein started to manufacture his macabre household decorations from the corpses he dug up on his grave-robbing sprees. Eventually, his grave-robbing expeditions failed to satisfy his strange obsession, and in December 1954, he committed murder.

THE MURDERS BEGIN

The police were called when a fifty-one-year-old

woman called Mary Hogan disappeared from the bar she ran in Pine Grove, Wisconsin. As became clear later, the victim had a distinct resemblance to Ed Gein's mother. There was blood on the floor and a spent cartridge was found at the scene. Ed Gein was among the potential suspects but there was no hard evidence to connect him, and the police saw no reason to visit his home.

This was the first of only two murders that can definitely be credited to Gein. The next was three years later. Once again the victim was a woman in her fifties, and once again she looked like Ed's mother. Her name was Bernice Worden and on November 16, 1957, she was abducted from her hardware store in Plainfield. Again, there was blood on the floor. This time, however, the police had a pretty good clue as to who was responsible. The victim's son told them that Ed Gein had asked their mother for a date, and another local resident re-called Ed saying he needed to buy some antifreeze from her store on the day she died. A receipt for antifreeze was found lying in the store and this time the police decided to pay Ed Gein a visit.

MACABRE HOME DECORATION

What confronted them there shocked even the most hardened of the officers. First there were the macabre ornaments in the house, such as the lampshades made of human skin and the skulls made into soup bowls. Worse was to follow when they went into the yard. Bernice Worden's corpse was hanging from the rafters. She had had her head cut off, her genitalia removed and her torso was slit open and gutted. On further investigation they found her head turned into a makeshift ornament, and her heart sitting in a saucepan on the stove. They also discovered a pistol which matched the cartridge found at the scene of the Mary Hogan murder.

On his arrest, Gein immediately confessed to the murders of Worden and Hogan as well as to his grave-robbing activities. His necrophiliac behaviour was so extreme that he was immediately deemed to be insane. For example, he explained the 'mammary vest' that he had stitched together as an attempt to change sex; wearing it, he felt as though he had turned into his mother. A judge found him incompetent for trial and he was committed to a secure mental hospital. Meanwhile, his house was burned to the ground to prevent it from becoming the focus of a macabre cult.

Soon after, Ed Gein's immortality was ensured when local writer Robert Bloch wrote a book called *Psycho*, inspired by the case, and Alfred Hitchcock picked it up for the movies. In 1968, Gein was once more submitted for trial but was once again found insane. He ended his days in the mental hospital, dying of respiratory failure on July 26, 1984. His last words on his deathbed were to curse his mother.

JOACHIM KROLL

Joachim Kroll has gone down in crime history as one of the most prolific serial killers of all time. Over a period of twenty years, he raped and strangled his young female victims, cutting slices from their dead bodies to cook and eat. Amazingly, he was not discovered until he had been killing for more than two decades. This was partly because he lived at a time when poverty and starvation were rife in Germany after the Second World War; even so, it is hard to explain why it took the authorities so long to notice what was going on.

THE FIRST VICTIM

Joachim Kroll was born in the town of Hindenburg, on the German–Polish border, on April 17, 1933. He grew up during the war years, experiencing great deprivation, like many German people at the time. His father was taken prisoner by the Russian Army and never seen again, and after the war, he and his mother were forced to flee East Germany, which was occupied by the Russians. They moved to West Germany, to the Ruhr region, a centre for industry and another very poor, rough area. As a child, and even into his early adult years, Joachim was shy and withdrawn, and had little contact with anyone except his mother. When she died, in 1955, he seems to have experienced a mental breakdown, and within three weeks of her death began a killing spree that was to last for the next twenty years.

His first victim was Irmgard Srehl, a nineteen-year-old girl he raped and stabbed to death in a barn outside the town of Ludinghausen. Not long afterwards he abducted twelve-year-old Erika Schuleter, raping and strangling her in the same way, this time in the town of Kirchellen. Two years later, he moved to Duisburg, another town in the Ruhr district. For a while, he remained quiet, until on June 16, 1959, he raped and murdered Klara Frieda Tesmer. The following month, there was another murder, this time in the industrial town of Essen: that of sixteen-year-old Manuela Knodt. Kroll raped and strangled her, and also cut chunks of flesh from her buttocks and thighs, which he later ate.

RAPED, STRANGLED . . . AND EATEN

Despite his rising toll of murders, Kroll was not caught. In the Knodt case, a man named Horst Otto made a confession, and was later found to be suffering from mental illness. Thus, Kroll was left free to carry on his killing spree. In 1962, he went to where he raped and strangled Barbara Bruder; later that year, on April 23, he raped and strangled Petra Giese. Police noticed that 'the Ruhr Hunter', as the mystery serial killer became known, had taken away parts of his victims' bodies: portions of flesh had been taken from their buttocks and thighs. This horrific cutting out of flesh became Kroll's trademark, and the hunt was now on for a killer who not only raped and strangled, but ate his victims as well.

On June 4, 1962, another young girl was found dead, this time in a cornfield outside the town of Walsum. Her name was Monika Tafel and she was just thirteen years old. But once again, the police got the wrong man for the crime. A thirty-four-year-old paedophile named Walter Quicker was picked up for the murder and held as a suspect. During this ordeal, Quicker hanged himself, and thus the police were no closer to finding the perpetrator of these dreadful murders.

ABDUCTING AND
MURDERING CHILDREN

After the Walsum investigation, Kroll kept his head down for a few years, afraid that his crimes would come to light. But he could not resist murdering again, and so it was that on August 22, 1965, he struck again. This time, his victims were a couple who were parked in their car in a lover's lane. Kroll attacked them with a knife, stabbing the man to death, but the woman escaped to raise the alarm. However, Kroll quickly disappeared, and once again, the police did not catch up with him.

The following year there was another murder, that of Ursula Rohling, who was raped and strangled in a park in Marl. Amazingly, the police got the wrong man again, and accused the girl's boyfriend Adolf Schickel, who – like Quicker – was so traumatised by the accusation that he killed himself. This left Kroll free to prey on his victims once more, and he abducted a five-year-old girl, Ilona Harke. The child was taken by public transport to a wood named Feldbachtal, where she was raped. Afterwards, Kroll drowned her. He was clearly experimenting with new ways to wreak his vengeance on the world. A year later, he lured ten-year-old Gabrielle Puetman into a cornfield where he showed her pornographic pictures; fortunately, some passers-by arrived and saw what was going on. The girl fainted and Kroll ran away. He was pursued, but managed to escape.

DRAINS 'FULL OF GUTS'

Kroll's next victim was not a child but a woman in her sixties, Maria Hettgen. He burst into her home before raping and strangling her. He went on to murder Jutta Rahn, a thirteen-year-old girl who was coming home from school. Once again, police followed the wrong trail, and an innocent neighbour of the girl's, Peter Schay, was arrested and imprisoned for fifteen months before being released. The murders continued with the raping and strangling of Karin Toepfer, also a schoolgirl, in the area of Dinslaken-Voerde. On July 3, 1976, Kroll abducted a four-year-old, Marion Ketter, his youngest victim yet, and murdered her.

The murder of Marion Ketter provoked a public outcry, and the police were forced at last to conduct a proper investigation. Kroll was not covering his tracks very carefully by now, and it appeared that he almost wanted to be caught. He was living in an apartment block, and when a neighbour complained to him about the drains being blocked, he replied that they were 'full of guts'. The neighbour thought he must be joking, but called a plumber, who found that Kroll had been serious when he made this remark. The lungs and innards of a child were found in the drains, and when police searched Kroll's apartment, they found bags of human flesh stored in the fridge. Further investigation revealed a child's hand simmering on the stove, cooked with carrots and potatoes. They immediately arrested Kroll, and he confessed to a long list of murders that he had committed all over the Ruhr area in the previous twenty years. Kroll was charged, brought to trial, and found guilty on eight counts of murder. His sentence was life imprisonment, eight times over. He served his sentence until July 1, 1991, when he died of a heart attack.

A SOCIETY IN CHAOS

In retrospect, it is hard to understand why it took so long to track down and arrest this prolific serial killer, who had left so many clues along the way during his long reign of terror. One reason was, the chaos and turmoil that reigned in Germany during and after World War II made it difficult for normal police investigations to take place. There are many horrific stories of ordinary people starving to death during this dark period in German history, and tales are told of an underground trade in human flesh, which was apparently bought and sold in the markets, and which Kroll may have been involved in.

Not only this, but with the fragmentation of communities and disturbances of populations during the war, disappearances of individuals were relatively common; people often lost touch with their relatives, and human life was cheap. This was a world in which people were struggling to survive, and if a person went missing here or there, there were sometimes few to mourn them; and even if families did raise the alarm, the police were extremely slow to react.

Such an atmosphere of poverty and lawlessness in the depressed industrialised cities of the Ruhr did much to foster crime, violence and brutality, and it is not altogether suprising that a killer like Kroll made less of an impact during that period than he would have done in quieter, more ordered times. Even so, the police record in trying to solve the crimes was startlingly poor, and it was only when Kroll began to abduct very young children that anything systematic was done to try to track him down. By the time that the police caught up with Kroll, he had a long list of violent murders to his name, many of which could have been avoided had previous cases been properly investigated. In addition, two men took their lives as a result of being falsely accused of murders committed by him. Thus it was that the Ruhr Hunter's reign of terror went on, unchecked, for two decades before he was finally brought to justice and imprisoned for the horrific crimes, including rape, murder and cannibalism, that he had committed throughout his adult life.

ANDREI CHIKATILO

Andrei Chikatilo was one of the most prolific serial killers of all time. Known as 'the Rostov Ripper', he murdered over fifty men, women and children during a reign of terror that lasted for years. Like Joachim Kroll, the 'Ruhr Hunter', he was the product of a period of extreme social disturbance, his spate of killings coming at a time when his country, the Soviet Union, was beginning to collapse into disorder. In the early years of his crimes, the extent of what was going on was covered up by the corrupt Soviet government of the time, whose official line was that serial killing was a product of the decadent West, particularly the United States, and did not occur in the Soviet Union. However, because of the ultimate collapse of the Soviet system, Chikatilo's crimes came to international attention when he was arrested in 1990, and shocked the world.

DIFFICULT START

This most fearsome of modern serial killers was

born on October 19, 1936 in the small village of Yablochnoye, which lies in the rural area of the Ukraine. The baby was born with water on the brain and a rather large, misshapen head. Later on, it was found that he had also undergone a certain amount of brain damage. In this respect, he was like many other serial killers, who have often sustained some kind of brain damage, for example through receiving a blow on the head.

This difficult start in life was compounded by the fact that Chikatilo's family were victims of famine, as a result of the forced collectivisation imposed by Stalin. Chikatilo's mother told how her oldest son, Stepan, was kidnapped, killed and eaten by starving neighbours. Whether this was true or not, her tale had the effect of completely traumatising the young Andrei, as well it might.

STARVATION AND MISERY

Chikatilo's early childhood was spent during World War II, when the region's misery grew even worse as privations of all kind were visited upon its people. His father was taken prisoner during the war, then sent to a Russian prison camp on his return. Meanwhile, Andrei was growing up without a father, and with a mother who seemed to take a perverse delight in terrifying her young son. On leaving school, Chikatilo joined the army. He also joined the Communist Party, which was an important step for any ambitious young person who wanted to succeed in Soviet Russia.

When he left the army, Chikatilo worked as a telephone engineer and studied in his spare time to gain a university degree, which eventually allowed him to become a schoolteacher near his home in Rostov-on-Don. His sister introduced him to a young woman named Fayina, whom he married. As it emerged later, Chikatilo's marriage was not happy, and he had lifelong problems with impotence, but he did manage to have two children by Fayina, and for a while the family lived quietly enough together.

RAPE AND MURDER

However, this period of stability was not to last. At the age of forty-two, Chikatilo's past began to catch up with him. In this, he was different from most serial killers, whose impulse to kill usually shows itself in early adulthood, if not before. Chikatilo murdered his first victim in 1979, a nine-year-old girl called Lenochka Zakotnova. He took her to a vacant house in the town of Shakhty, attempted to rape her, failed because of his impotence, and impaled her with a knife instead, stabbing her to death and dumping her body into the Grushovka

River. Her corpse was found there on Christmas Eve. Chikatilo was questioned by police, and persuaded his wife to give him a false alibi. Eventually, local rapist Alexander Kravchenko was beaten into confessing to the crime and put to death, while Chikatilo got off the charges – only to murder again.

Despite his attempts to cover his tracks, Chikatilo's perverted behaviour was noticed by his fellow teachers, and he was accused of molesting boys in the dormitory at the school where he worked. He confessed and was dismissed from his job. However, because he was a member of the Communist Party, he managed to get another job as a recruiting officer for a factory. This meant that he travelled a great deal, and therefore had a lot of opportunity to continue his killing career without being observed. His method of luring his victims to their death was to approach them at a train or bus station and take them into nearby woodland to muder them. In this way, he committed the murder of seventeen-year-old Larisa Tkachenko in 1982. Tkachenko was a poverty-stricken runaway, known locally for her habit of exchanging sexual favours for food and drink. Chikatilo strangled her and piled dirt into her mouth to muffle her screams. He later commented that although his first killing had upset him, this second one had been thrilling for him.

<u>EYE GOUGING</u>

In the same year, Chikatilo killed his next victim, thirteen-year-old Lyuba Biryuk. At this point he committed the act that was to become his trademark as a killer, which was to cut out her eyes. The following year he killed six more times, and this time his murders changed their pattern: two of the victims were young men, which initially confused the police. What the killings had in common was their increasing savagery and the way that certain body parts were always removed. One of the features of Chikatilo's killings was that the genitals of his victims were often missing. It is generally believed that Chikatilo ate the parts he removed; however, he himself only confessed to 'nibbling on them'. Some believe that, in his madness, he was acting out the fate that befell his older brother, to be killed and eaten in the most violent, vicious way imaginable.

Chikatilo's series of gruesome murders attracted a great deal of police attention, but at the time the Soviet media had its hands tied. Journalists were not permitted to publicise the existence of a serial killer in the Soviet Union, as this reflected badly on the political situation there, or so the apparatchiks felt. Thus, the public were not warned to be on their guard and to keep their children safe from harm. For this reason, Chikatilo's crimes became easier, and he continued to kill his victims, in increasingly savage ways. In just one month, August 1984, he did away with eight victims. Despite the increasing death toll, the only clue the police were able to find was that the killer's blood group was AB. This was determined by analysing the semen found on the bodies of some of his more recent victims.

BROUGHT TO JUSTICE

However, it was in late 1984, just as his murders had reached a peak, that Chikatilo was arrested at a railway station where he was trying to seduce some young girls. He was arrested and found to have a knife and a length of rope in his bag but, because his blood group was A, not AB, he was eventually released. This evident mistake by police has never been explained, and it had tragic consequences. Once he was released, Chikatilo redoubled his killings, so that dozens more innocent people lost their lives. In 1988, he murdered eight more times, and in his last year of freedom, 1990, he killed nine people, several of them boys. By then, a new detective, Issa Kostoyev, had taken over the case and was determined to bring him to justice. Kostoyev ordered an army of detectives to wait at train and bus stations in the area and her plan worked.

A detective waiting at a station saw Chikatilo

sweating profusely and breathing heavily, with bloodstains on his clothes, took his name and checked with his superiors to see if there was any information about him. When news came back that he had been a suspect, he was arrested. As it turned out, Chikatilo had just murdered twenty-year-old Svetlana Korostik. After ten days in custody he finally confessed to around fifty-two more murders, many more than the police had been aware of.

MONSTER IN A CAGE

Chikatilo was brought to trial in April 1992. By this time, he was mentally ill and was locked inside a cage. The cage was designed as much to keep him safe from his victims' relatives as to stop him from lashing out. At his trial, it became clear that Chikatilo had completely lost his mind: he was no longer the neat, sober-looking individual he had been when he was arrested, but had become a shaven-headed monster who ranted and raved at the judge and jury.

After a high profile trial that drew many shocked spectators, and that was reported in the media internationally, Chikatilo was convicted of all the murders he was charged with, and received a total of fifty-two death sentences. On February 15, 1994, he was executed by a single bullet to the back of the head. The reign of terror of the cannibal serial killer had finally come to an end.

GARY HEIDNIK

Gary Heidnik was an American killer who abducted a number of women and kept them captive in his basement, murdering two of them and causing extensive injuries to the others. His horrific crimes included kidnapping, murder, torture, sexual abuse of all kinds and cannibalism. A high-school dropout and ex-army soldier with a schizoid personality disorder, he committed numerous crimes, including beating and raping his Filipino wife, abducting and sexually abusing a mentally subnormal young woman, and then, worst of all, abducting five women and holding them in his house, inflicting all manner of torture on them until two of them died. At that point, he dismembered the first victim's body, cooked it and fed it to the surviving victims. Eventually, one of the captives escaped and went to the police, who searched his house and found the scene of horror in the basement. At the trial that followed, Heidnik claimed his innocence, but the jury found him guilty and on July 6, 1999, he was executed by lethal injection.

SCHIZOID PERSONALITY DISORDER

Gary Michael Heidnik was born in November 1943 in Eastlake, a suburb of Cleveland, Ohio. His mother was an alcoholic and his parents, Michael and Ellen, divorced soon after the birth of his younger brother, Terry. First, the boys went to live with Ellen and her new husband, and after that, lived with their father and his new wife. The boys were mistreated by their parents, in particular their father, who would humiliate Gary by hanging his stained sheets out of the window for the neighbours to see whenever he wet the bed. As a child, Gary also fell out of a tree while at school, leaving him with a strangely shaped head, which made him an object of ridicule for his schoolmates. Interestingly, a number of serial killers, torturers and otherwise violent individuals, have sustained serious injuries to the head at an early point in their lives, and there appears to be some correlation between this sort of accident and violent behaviour. Gary's brother Terry, himself a man with serious mental problems, often commented that he believed Gary's extremely violent behaviour started with the head injury he received from his fall as a child.

As a teenager, Gary was keen to join the army, and his father arranged for him to attend Staunton Military Academy in Virginia. He did well there, but after two years he suddenly left and went to live with his father again. At eighteen, he joined the regular army and trained as a medic, but he began to suffer from mental illness and was discharged with a disability pension and a diagnosis of 'schizoid personality disorder'. After this, he tried his hand at various jobs but eventually left all of them, and for the next few years found himself in and out of mental institutions. When his mother committed suicide by drinking poison, his condition deteriorated and he became mute for long periods of time. He also became extremely violent, at one point attacking his brother Terry. When his brother visited him during his period of recuperation, he told him that if he had died, he would have soaked his body in acid to dispose of it.

From this point, Heidnik began to show extreme signs of mental disorder, saluting and rolling up his trousers, wearing the same clothes all the time, and giving up any semblance of personal hygiene. He then decided to start his own 'church', along with his girlfriend, who was also mentally subnormal, and styled himself 'Bishop Heidnik'. Strangely, although he was so crazed, he was good at financial investments, and showed a great deal of skill at making money for the church, amassing a sizeable profit during this time.

ABUSE OF RETARDED WOMAN

In 1976, Heidnik fired a gun at his landlord, slightly injuring the man's face. The police charged him with aggravated assault and carrying an unlicensed pistol, and when the house was sold, the owners found a hole dug into the floor of the basement containing boxes of pornographic magazines. Heidnik's next brush with police came when he took his girlfriend's retarded sister out for the day from the mental hospital where she lived, and kept her prisoner in his apartment for several days. When staff from the home came out to fetch her, they found that she had been raped, vaginally and anally, and had contracted a sexually transmitted disease in the process. Heidnik was arrested and charged with the crime. He conducted his own defence, pleading not guilty, but was given a three- to seven-year jail sentence, most of which he actually spent in mental institutions.

When he was released, Heidnik resumed the sick relationships he had always had with women. He seemed to be attracted to mentally subnormal black women, and had a crazed notion of fathering a host of children by them. Early on in his adult life, he had had a girlfriend who had borne him a child. A little later on he dated a retarded young woman whom he regularly beat and starved. Another woman he had a relationship with, also mentally

58

subnormal, disappeared soon after meeting Heidnik. He then married a mail-order bride, a young Filipino woman named Betty. When she arrived to meet him, in September 1985, he took her to the marital home where a retarded woman was sleeping in his bed. She was disturbed by this, but agreed to marry him, mainly because she could not afford the fare back to her country. However, a week later, she returned to the house to find her new husband having sex with three women in their bed. She demanded to be sent back to the Philippines but he refused, forcing her to stay in the house and cook for his many female guests. He also forced her to watch him having sex with them. Eventually, she escaped with the help of others from the Filipino community in her neighbourhood and went to the police, who charged Heidnik with sexual offences. Later, Betty gave birth to a son by Heidnik.

TORTURE AND CANNIBALISM

Once Betty had left, Heidnik began his career of sexual deviancy and violence in earnest, abducting five women and holding them in the basement of his house in Philadelphia. He chained them up, kept them in filthy conditions, starved them, sexually abused them, beat them and tortured them. When the first woman died of mistreatment, he dismembered her body, ground pieces of it in a food processor and mixed it with dog food, which he forced the surviving women to eat. The victim's arms and legs were kept in a freezer, while her ribs were cooked in the oven. He boiled her head in a pot on the cooker. The next woman died when he electrocuted her in the bath, bound in chains, applying an electric current to the chains. He tortured the remaining women by digging a large pit to throw the victims in when they misbehaved, which he would then cover with planks. Another of his tortures involved hanging the women up by their wrists and forcing metal screwdrivers into their ears, which gave them permanent hearing loss. He also encouraged the women to fight with each other and tell him stories, rewarding them with small privileges when they did so.

After months of this hellish existence, one of the women managed to escape, and on March 24, 1987, she left Heidnik's house, saying that she was visiting her family and promising to return with another 'wife' for him. Over the time they had spent together, she had managed to persuade him that they had a special, close relationship and he believed her when she had said she would recruit another victim for him. However, the minute she was out of his sight, she went straight to her boyfriend's house and then to the police.

SCENE OF DEPRAVITY

At first the police did not believe her story, suspecting that she was suffering from some kind of delusions. However, when she raised the hem of her trousers and they saw the cuff marks on her ankles, they realised that the story was true. The police raided the house and found a scene of depravity that shocked even the most hardened officers. However, despite all the evidence to the contrary, Heidnik maintained his innocence and continued to plead not guilty, even taking to defending himself in court. This time, however, he stood no chance of getting off. He was convicted on an array of charges, including first-degree murder, five counts of rape, six counts of kidnapping, four counts of aggravated assault and one count of deviate sexual intercourse. The jury found him unanimously guilty of the murders of two of the women, Deborah Dudley and Sandra Lindsay, and also of the other charges. After making an attempt at suicide, he was executed by lethal injection on July 6, 1999. When his father was told that his son was going to die, he replied that he wasn't interested. Unsurprisingly, nobody came forward to claim Heidnik's body for burial.

ED KEMPER

The notorious Co-ed Killer, Edmund Emil Kemper, got his nickname by killing and dismembering six young women whom he picked up as hitchhikers in the area of Santa Cruz, California. However, he also committed a number of other murders, including killing his grandparents and his mother. He was only a teenager when he shot both his grandparents dead, having been sent to live with them on their farm. As an adult, he committed a series of murders, mostly of young female hitchhikers and committed gross acts of necrophilia and cannibalism on their corpses. During this time he covered his clues, but as time went on and his madness took hold, he lost all sense of caution. Finally, he murdered his mother and a friend of hers in a fit of furious rage, before finally giving himself up to the authorities. His behaviour was never explained, and at his trial he was seen as a sociopath rather than a psychopath. As a result he was judged to be sane, even though he had spent a good deal of time in mental hospitals as a teenager. The reason he gave for killing the women and the members of his own family, was, he said, 'to see what it felt like'. Words that struck a chill into all who followed his horrific exploits, and persuaded the judge at his trial to give him a life sentence for murder.

KILLING THE FAMILY CAT

Edmund Kemper III was born on December 18, 1948, in Burbank, California, into a troubled family. His father, who went by the nickname E.E., had been decorated in World War II; his mother, Clarnell, a domineering, critical woman, was not happy with her husband, and after a tempestuous relationship the couple parted. His mother took Ed, who was then aged nine, and his sister to live in Helena, Montana. It was here that Ed began to show the first signs of serious mental disturbance. One of the strangest aspects of his behaviour was that he tortured animals in the most horrible way. In an incident that defies belief, he buried the family cat alive in the back garden and when it was dead, cut off its head and put it on a stick. He kept the head on the stick in his bedroom, along with other unpleasant animal parts. How his mother managed not to notice what was going on is still a mystery. He also mutilated his sister's dolls, pulling their heads, arms and legs off and acting out peculiar sexual rituals on them. At this time, he also fell in love with a teacher at his school and confided his feelings to his sister. His sister asked him, as a joke, whether he would like to kiss the teacher, and Ed replied that if he did, he would have to kill her beforehand. Later on, these words were to become prophetic.

Kemper's mother Clarnell seems to have exacerbated the situation, humiliating her son on every occasion that she could and continually berating him in front of others. Eventually, she forced him to sleep in the basement under lock and key, because she was afraid that he would attack his sisters and subject them to sexual acts. She herself was also afraid of him. By this time he had grown into an extremely tall young man, inheriting his height from both parents. His size marked him out from his contemporaries and he was teased at school, but seemed unable to fend for himself and became extremely afraid of being bullied. Thus, although he was a large, violent young man, he was also timid and very awkward with people in general.

Edmund's relationship with his mother soon deteriorated to the point where she declared that she had washed her hands of him. She referred to him as 'a real weirdo' and when his behaviour became completely out of control, sent him to live with his estranged father. His father proved equally inadequate to deal with the situation, and in turn sent him to live with his elderly paternal grand-parents on their farm at North Fork, Carolina.

COUNTRY LIFE – WITH A RIFLE

By now, Kemper was fifteen. To begin with, country life seemed to suit the teenager and he spent his days shooting animals and birds with a rifle. How-ever, tragedy struck when, on August 27, 1964, Kemper turned the gun on his grandparents, shoot-ing his grandmother dead as she put the finishing touches to a children's book she was working on. When his grandfather came home from grocery shopping, Kemper shot him dead as well. Asked later why he had done it, all he could find to reply was, 'I just wondered what it would feel like to shoot grandma and grandpa.'

Kemper was pronounced to be mentally ill and sent to a secure hospital at Atascadero, where he remained for the next five years. He was then judged to be much improved with regard to his mental health and was paroled into his mother's care in Santa Cruz, a college town in San Francisco Bay. Once released, he applied to join the police, but was turned down on the grounds that he was too tall (by now he was 6 ft 9 in). After that, he did numerous odd jobs, never settling for long at any one task. He began to drink regularly at a police bar called the Jury Room, where he befriended numerous detectives and bought himself a car similar to those used by the police as undercover vehicles. He started using the car to pick up young female hitch-hikers, customising the car by making it impossible to open the passenger side door from the inside. In retrospect, it seems clear that he was waiting to claim his next victim – it was just a matter of time until he found the right moment.

MURDER, RAPE AND NECROPHILIA

On May 7, 1972, the next tragedy struck when he picked up two eighteen-year-old students, Mary Ann Pesce and Anita Luchessa, who were hitching to Stanford University. He drove them down a dirt road, stabbed them both to death and then took them back to his apartment. There he sexually assaulted the bodies and took photographs of them, before cutting their heads off, putting the bodies in plastic bags, burying them on a nearby mountainside and throwing the heads into a ravine. Four months later, he killed again. This victim was fifteen-year-old Aiko Koo, whom he strangled, raped and then dissected. The next day, with her head in the boot of his car, he met with court psychiatrists, who declared him to be sane.

Another four months went by, and then Kemper

murdered another student, Cindy Schell. By this time he'd bought a gun, which he used to shoot Schell dead after forcing her into the boot of his car. Now following a pattern, he raped, beheaded and dissected her corpse before disposing of it, burying the head in his mother's garden.

Less then a month passed before he struck again, shooting hitchhikers Rosalind Thorpe and Alice Lin before putting both bodies in the boot and leaving them there while he went to have dinner with his mother. When they had finished eating he decapitated them, taking Lin's headless corpse home to rape.

THE FINAL VICTIM: HIS MOTHER

Clearly, Kemper's madness was now out of control, and over the Easter weekend of 1973 he finally turned on his mother. He lay in wait for her at her home and when she appeared he beat her to death with a hammer. He then decapitated and raped her, before attempting to throw her larynx into the waste disposal unit. In a confused attempt to cover his tracks, he then invited one of his mother's friends over, Sally Hallett, and when she arrived he murdered her as well. Having committed the two murders, he took to his heels and fled, driving west to Colorado. When he got there, he telephoned his buddies on the Santa Cruz police force and told them what he'd done. At first they thought he was joking and did not believe him, but after visiting his mother's apartment, they saw only too well that he was telling the truth and immediately ordered his arrest. He gave himself up without a fight and seemed relieved that his killing spree had now come to an end.

When Kemper was brought to trial, the jury concluded that he was sane and he was found guilty on eight counts of murder. He received a life sentence but apparently asked to be tortured to death. Since that time, he has continued to serve his sentence, appearing to enjoy his notoriety. On one occasion he was interviewed live and asked, 'What do you think when you see a pretty girl walking down the street?' His chilling reply was, 'One side of me says I'd like to talk to her, date her. The other half of me says "I wonder how her head would look on a stick." '

ARMIN MEIWES

The story of Armin Meiwes almost defies belief as a tale that involved a man volunteering to have himself mutilated and killed as part of a sordid sado-masochistic tryst arranged over the Internet. When the case came to court, Meiwes was charged with murder, but he argued that the man he had killed had volunteered to die, and also to be mutilated beforehand. His case was a legally complex one because his victim had chosen to die voluntarily, and initially he was charged with manslaughter. However, it became clear that he was a very dangerous man, and eventually he was convicted of murder and sentenced to life imprisonment.

LURID CANNIBALISTIC FANTASIES

Armin Meiwes was born on December 1, 1961. He grew up with his mother in a large house near the German town of Kassel. He had a very lonely childhood, with few friends, and created an imaginary brother whom he named Franky. Without any real friends to confide in, he told 'Franky' his problems, and fantasised that they were lifelong companions. Later, at his trial, Meiwes explained that as an adult he evolved a desire to eat a man, so that this 'younger brother' figure would become part of him for ever.

According to one of his former schoolfriends, his mother was a domineering figure who often scolded Armin in public. She lived alone with her son until her death, and treated him in a humiliating way. She would accompany him on dates with women, and even went on outings with the troops when he was serving in the German army. It was this experience of being constantly humiliated by his mother that, he felt, had poisoned his relationships with other people in adult life, both men and women.

At the age of forty-two, Meiwes was living quietly in Rotenburg and earning a good living as a computer technician. One woman he befriended at the time described him as 'friendly' and 'sensitive'. Well spoken, smartly dressed and apparently confident, there was nothing to mark him out as a man who engaged in lurid cannibalistic fantasies, but that was exactly what he was. Sadly, it was not long before his desire to see these fantasies acted out in real life got the better of him.

PENIS CUT OFF AND EATEN

He posted an advertisement on the Internet for a 'well-built eighteen- to thirty-year-old to be slaughtered'. A willing victim presented himself in the shape of Brend Jürgen Armando Brandes, who was known to police as having an interest in sadomasochistic male prostitution. According to Meiwes, there were over 200 replies to his advertisement, but this was never verified.

The men met at Meiwes' large, half-timbered house, and decided that they would start the killing ritual by cutting off Brandes' penis. Brandes insisted that Meiwes try to bite it off, but this proved to be too difficult, so instead Meiwes cut it off with a large knife. At this point, the story becomes even sicker. Brandes now decided he would like to eat his own penis, but again this proved difficult to do, as it was 'too chewy'. So, to help him out, Meiwes offered to cook it. Accordingly, Meiwes cooked the penis in a frying pan, seasoning it with garlic, salt and pepper. All the while, the men were recording the scene on a video, which has not been made public.

STABBED TO DEATH

Unsurprisingly, Brandes was not feeling well enough to finish his meal, since he was bleeding to death. Meiwes tried to fortify him with alcohol and painkillers, and then took him to a room he had specially prepared for him, and killed him by stabbing him to death in the throat. After the killing, he hung the body up on a meat-hook dangling from the ceiling, and proceeded to tear bits of flesh from it and stuff them into his mouth. He then froze the remainder of the body parts and over the next few months he ate about 20 kg (2.2 lb) of his victim's flesh.

Meiwes then began to advertise on the Internet again, but this time a student spotted the advertisement and alerted the police. They paid a visit to his house and found the body parts and the videotape of the killing, at which point he was arrested and taken into custody. However, once it was established that his victim had willingly offered to have himself tortured and killed, it became clear that the case was a complicated one. Initially, there was some doubt as to whether he could be tried at all. To confuse matters further, it transpired that cannibalism was not illegal in Germany at the time.

When the case came to court, he was charged with manslaughter, found guilty and sentenced to a term of eight and a half years' imprisonment. However, there was a public outcry and many felt that he deserved a much longer sentence; besides having killed a man, he was thought to be dangerous, since he had advertised again for a willing victim. Thus, in April 2005, he was tried again, after appeals from the prosecution. This time, he was charged with murder, convicted and received a life sentence.

Since then, Meiwes has accepted his guilt and is reported to have regretted his action in killing Brandes. He has spoken of writing his life story, which he hopes will help to deter anyone thinking of following in his path. However, in recent times, a number of websites dedicated to Meiwes have appeared on the Internet, where advertisements are placed to contact willing victims. Meiwes claims there are thousands of victims waiting to be claimed, and estimates that there are about 800 cannibals in Germany.

PART TWO

SERIAL KILLERS

JACK THE RIPPER

Of all the serial killers in history, Jack the Ripper is the most famous. He was one of the first murderers to achieve notoriety by committing a series of gruesome crimes that shocked and horrified the public in London, where he operated; he was also never captured and brought to justice, opening up a continuing debate as to the real identity of the killer. The sheer violence of his crimes ensured that he has not been forgotten: he used to disembowel his victims, remove their internal organs, and drape them round rooms in the most appalling way. The Victorian setting of the murders, in the seedy, rough district of Whitechapel, London, has given rise to endless portrayals of the Ripper in novels, films and on television; and what makes the story even more appealing to modern-day amateur sleuths is that to this day his identity is still unknown. In the new millennium, many books have been written claiming to have found new evidence, most memorably one by crime novelist Patricia Cornwell, who is thought to have spent over eight million dollars of her own fortune in an effort to prove that Walter Sickert, a Victorian painter, was the murderer. However, it is still not clear who the murderer was, and many believe that his identity will never be found.

FRENZY OF RAGE

The story of Jack the Ripper starts on August 31, 1888, when a young prostitute named Mary 'Polly' Nichols was found dead. Initially, the case did not attract a great deal of attention; murders of prostitutes were fairly common in the rough area of London where the Ripper stalked his victims, and Victorian values were such that prostitutes were held in very low esteem, so that their disappearance and murder was not greatly mourned. Poor 'Polly' was, in fact, the third prostitute to have been killed that year in the East End of London. Police did little to follow up the murder, except to note that whoever had committed the crime was extremely violent. There were stab wounds to the woman's genitals, and her throat had been cut. Moreover, her torso had been stabbed, apparently in a frenzy of rage.

At this stage, no one in the police linked the three murders of prostitutes, but before the week was out, another murder was reported. Annie Chapman, who went by the name of 'Dark Annie', was found dead, her throat cut, and this time the murderer had had a field day, disembowelling her and pulling out her entrails, which were draped over her shoulder. Further investigation revealed that the victim's ovaries and vagina had been cut out, and had been taken away. Police were surprised to find that the cuts were very accurate and carefully done. Obviously, this was the work of a trained mortician, or someone who had considerable medical experience in dissecting human bodies.

GRUESOME RITUALS

Pressure was now on for the police to solve the case. The murdered women may have been very low-ranking in the social order, but the general public now began to feel uneasy that such a crazed murderer was on the loose. On September 30, there were another two murders, which further panicked the public: it seemed that, in this case, both of the women had been killed in separate incidents on the very same night. The first unfortunate victim was Elizabeth Stride, known as 'Long Liz', who worked as a seamstress and occasionally supplemented her income by prostitution. It appeared that she had been killed by a knife wound to the throat, but police investigators found no other mutilation and came to the conclusion that the murderer had somehow been interrupted, and had not had time to carry out his gruesome rituals before he was disturbed. It then seemed that he had made up for this by killing another prostitute, Catherine Eddowes, this time making sure that his vile desecration of the corpse was enacted to the full. Strangely, at the scene of the crime, someone had written a message on the wall: 'The Juwes are not the men that will be blamed for nothing.' No one was sure who the message was from, or what the meaning of it was; in any event, it was rubbed off by the police investigating the case, so that there would not be any copycat murdering of Jews, or any other kind of backlash from this horrible incident.

DOUBLE MURDER

What complicated the case was that the newspapers now began to get messages from the killer. The Central News Agency, to whom the messages were sent, was not sure if these letters were genuine; the murders had provoked many hoaxes, and some believed that these new messages were sent by ordinary mischief-makers. However, when a letter came into the agency within hours of the double murder, the newsmen decided it was time to call in the police. The writer of the letter signed himself 'Jack the Ripper' and dropped some clues which gave the police reason to believe that he had personal knowledge of the case. This, of course, made headline news, and soon the case of 'Jack the Ripper' had become famous all over the country.

Then, a fortnight later, another letter was sent to George Lusk, head of the Whitechapel Vigilance Committee, which had been formed to protect ordinary members of the public from this new danger on their streets. The letter was different from the ones that had been sent before. The writer appeared to have difficulty spelling and did not seem very literate. However, the content of the letter was terrifying. The writer put down the provenance of the letter as being 'from hell', and enclosed a fragment of human kidney, which he claimed to be that of Catherine Eddowes. As the police knew, Eddowes had had her kidney removed and taken away. It was impossible to confirm that the kidney really did belong to Catherine Eddowes, but it seemed likely, and the letter had the desired effect of frightening its recipients, who waited in horror to see what would happen next.

WOMB AND FOETUS RIPPED OUT

Less than a month later, Jack the Ripper killed his next victim. This was a prostitute, one Mary Kelly. In this instance, the Ripper committed the crime indoors, rather than out on the street, where his other victims had met their deaths. The room where Kelly was killed was in a place called Miller's Court, a down-at-heel lodging where the Ripper was left free to indulge in his unsavoury rituals without disturbance from neighbours or passers-by. When her body was found, police and investigators were dismayed to see that the body of this unfortunate woman had been completely ripped to shreds. She had been flayed and then disembowelled, her entrails arranged around the room in a parody of domestic decoration. Parts of her body were missing, including her womb and a foetus that was inside it – Kelly was known to have been pregnant when her assailant struck.

The inhabitants of Whitechapel were traumatised, and waited in horror for the next atrocity to take place. Yet, as it turned out, this was the last of the mysterious Ripper's crimes – fortunately for the prostitutes of the area, he vanished as suddenly as he had arrived and no more was heard of him. There were murders of prostitutes in the following few years, but the ritual disembowelling and stealing of body parts did not feature in these murders, and there was no reason to link them to the series of murders that had occurred so close together, and accompanied by such awful mutilations of the dead women's bodies.

AFTERMATH

Ever since the fateful day when the Ripper disappeared, succeeding generations of sleuths – both amateur and professional – have speculated as to who he was. To date, commentators have pointed the finger at Queen Victoria's grandson Prince Eddy, who is argued to have committed the murders in a fit of rage, having contracted syphilis. Other suspects include Sir William Gull, the Queen's surgeon, who was thought to have killed in order to cover up the fact that Price Eddy had conceived an illegitimate child with a working-class girl from Whitechapel. Another theory claims that the Ripper murders were the work of Liverpool businessman James Maybrick, supposed author of *The Ripper Diaries*, published in 1994. None of these theories is very persuasive, since there is a lack of evidence to support them.

Sir Melville Macnaghten, the Chief Commissioner of the Metropolitan Police at the time when the murders took place, put forward what seems a reasonable theory as to the Ripper's sudden disappearance. He argued that the murderer had probably gone mad as the result of his final murder, in which the womb and foetus were taken away, and had most likely committed suicide after the event. Alternatively, he claimed, the murderer's relatives had discovered him in a state of complete mental collapse and had sent him to a mental asylum. Whatever the truth of the matter, to this day we still do not know the real identity of the world's most notorious serial killer, Jack the Ripper.

ALBERT FISH

Albert Fish is one of the most bizarre of all serial killers. At the time of his arrest he looked like everyone's idea of a kind old grandfather. And yet this seemingly harmless pensioner was a paedophile cannibal whose greatest thrill was to eat the flesh of the children he lusted after and strangled. No one will ever know exactly how many children Fish murdered, but there's no doubt that if it had not been for the Herculean efforts of a New York detective, Will King, there would have been many more.

SADISTIC URGES

Albert Fish was born in Washington DC on May 19, 1870. His given name was actually Hamilton Fish, in honour of some distant connection to Washington's famous political family of that name. Later in childhood he adopted the name Albert, which had belonged to a sibling who died young. Albert's parents were relatively well-to-do. His father, Randall Fish, was a boat captain, working on the Potomac River.

However, his father was already an old man and in 1875, when Albert was five years old, he died. His mother was unable to cope with looking after her four children and Albert was placed in an orphanage. There Albert was regularly beaten for being a bed-wetter. Gradually he came to enjoy the beatings and whippings he received. His lifelong sadomasochistic urges had been awakened.

He regularly ran away from the orphanage and, when he was nine years old, his mother was able to take him back home, having found herself a job working for the government. By the time he was twelve years old, however, Albert was engaged in a homosexual relationship with a telegraph boy who initiated him into a whole range of sexual perversions much to the young boy's delight.

By 1890, when he was eighteen, Fish had moved to New York City, where he worked as a male prostitute. Gradually, though, he acquired a more legitimate skill and began to work as a painter and decorator, a trade he would follow for the rest of his life. Indeed, for a long while he seemed to become a respectable citizen. In 1998 he married a woman he'd been introduced to by his mother, and they had six children together: Albert, Anna, Gertrude, Eugene, John and Henry Fish. Later on Fish would claim to have committed his first murder during this domestic period. His family doubted this, suggesting instead that his descent into barbarity only began when his wife left him for a mentally retarded handyman called John Straube in 1917.

EXTREME MASOCHISM

Following this desertion Albert Fish began to behave very strangely indeed. He would eat huge quantities of raw meat every time there was a full moon and began to indulge in acts of extreme masochism. He would drive needles into his genital region, he would place pieces of fabric in his anus and set them on fire and he would burn himself with red hot pokers. He made a wooden paddle and studded it with nails then asked his children to use it to beat him on his naked buttocks.

After a while his children could stand no more of this and his eldest son, Albert Jr., threw his father out of the house. At this point Albert Fish Snr. dispensed with the respectable life. He became a wandering loner, living in flophouses and supporting himself by getting odd jobs as a painter and decorator.

Over the next decade or so, from the early 1920s to the mid-1930s, Fish carried out a huge number of rapes and murders, just how many we will never know for sure. Tragically he was regularly arrested over these years – sometimes for theft, sometimes for vagrancy and on several occasions for sending obscene letters to women – and invariably sent for psychiatric evaluation, but each time the psychiatrists decided that he was an odd bird, perhaps prematurely senile, but basically harmless. And so they let him back onto the streets.

In June 1928, he carried out his most notorious crime and the one that would lead to his eventual arrest. On May 28, 1928, Fish came to the house of the Budd family in Lower Manhattan. The family was struggling financially and their eldest son Edward had placed an ad in the newspaper looking for a residential job in the countryside. Fish claimed to be a farmer called Frank Howard and offered the young man a job at the excellent rate of fifteen dollars a week. The generosity of the offer allowed the Budds to ignore the supposed Mr Howard's rather shabby appearance, and they were happy to accept him as a benefactor. With grossly misplaced trust they even allowed 'Mr Howard' to take their twelve-year-old daughter Grace to a birthday party at his sister's house.

There was, of course, no such party. Instead Fish took Grace to an abandoned house in Westchester. While Grace was outside collecting wild flowers, Fish took all his clothes off, then called out to the girl to come indoors. When she did so, she was horrified by the naked apparition that confronted her. She tried to escape but her abductor was too strong for her. He strangled her, then dismembered her body. Over the next nine days he cooked up and ate as much of her remains as he could, before burying her bones in the yard.

ABDUCTED AND EATEN

When Grace Budd failed to return home by the following morning her distraught family raised the alarm. The story was soon picked up by the newspapers, accompanied by an angelic-looking picture of Grace, and a huge manhunt was launched. It was all to no avail, however. The mysterious Frank Howard had vanished into thin air.

That might have been the end of matters if it had not been for the determination of one man, veteran detective Will King. He became obsessed with the case. Not a day would go by for years without him trying to find some new angle on the case. And finally some six years later, in November 1934, his patience was rewarded in the most grotesque of ways.

During that month Mrs Budd received an anonymous letter. It was clearly written by her daughter's murderer as it contained details of Mr Howard's meeting with the family. The rest of its contents were unspeakably foul. The letter writer talked of being friendly with a sailor who had eaten human flesh while stranded in China. These tales had inspired the writer to embark on his own quest for human flesh and, as a result, he had abducted and eaten Grace. He did, however, assure the grieving mother that he had not raped the little girl. 'She died a virgin' the letter ended.

This bizarre missive must have been unimaginably distressing to its recipient, but it provided Will King with just the fresh piece of evidence he needed. Under detailed examination he noticed that the envelope used bore a minute emblem containing the letters NYPCBA (the New York Private Chauffeurs Benevolent Association). King followed the clue with renewed energy. He assembled all 400 members of the association and checked their handwriting against that of the letter writer. When none of them matched he asked if anyone had ever taken any of the association's stationery for personal use. One member confessed that he had and that he might have left some of it in a lodging house he'd recently stayed in.

King hurried round to the lodging house and discovered that the chauffeur's old room had recently been occupied by a strange old man called Albert Fish. King had a hunch that this might be the guilty man. Fish was no longer staying at the lodging house, but he was in the habit of coming by once a month to pick up a cheque. So determined to catch him was King, that he rented his own room in the lodging house and waited there till Fish finally showed up four days later.

Detective King found Fish talking to the landlady. When he told the apparently harmless old man that he was wanted for questioning, he was amazed to see Fish lunge at him with a straight razor. Razor or not, King was a much stronger man and he quickly overpowered Fish and arrested him.

OBSCENE CONFESSION

Once back at the police station Fish made no attempt to deny his guilt. Instead he embarked on a long, wandering and graphically obscene confession not just to Grace Budd's murder but to a whole string of crimes, most of which the police had no knowledge of. Typically grotesque was his account of the killing and eating of a four-year-old boy called Billy Gaffney in 1929: 'I never ate any roast turkey that tasted half as good as his sweet fat little behind did.'

Just how many people Fish actually killed remained a mystery. He claimed to have killed dozens, but his confessions were often very vague and in the vast majority of cases no body could be found to verify his stories. Apart from Budd and Gaffney there is only one other murder that he is unquestionably linked to, that of five-year-old Francis McDonell in 1934.

In the end he was only tried for the murder of Grace Budd, as that was the case with the most supporting evidence. His defence, the only possible one, was insanity. His defence lawyer simply read out Fish's long confession as evidence that here was a madman. The jury, however, were unimpressed. Mad or not, they clearly wanted Fish to be punished for his crimes and he was duly found guilty and sentenced to death.

This didn't seem to bother Fish in the slightest. When he was told that he was to die in the electric chair he reportedly said that this would be 'the supreme thrill of my life'.

The sentence was carried out in Sing Sing Prison on January 16, 1936. At the first time of asking, the chair failed to electrocute Fish. Legend has it that this was because the metal pins that Fish had inserted into his body had caused the machine to short circuit. At the second time of asking there was no mistake and Fish was duly killed. His career of evil lives on, however, as his life and crimes provided some of the inspiration for Thomas Harris's fictional serial killer Hannibal 'the cannibal' Lecter.

H. H. HOLMES

H. H. Holmes was the alias of Herman Webster Mudgett, an American serial killer who is thought to have been responsible for literally hundreds of murders, although only a few of these were ever confirmed. His most notorious crimes involved entrapping large numbers of mostly female employees and guests at his Chicago hotel and torturing them, before gassing them to death and selling their bodies to medical schools.

THE EVIL ONE

Mudgett was born in New Hampshire on May 16, 1860, the son of an alcoholic father and a timid, submissive mother. He later wrote, 'I was born with the devil in me. I was born with the Evil One standing as my sponsor beside the bed where I was ushered into this world. He has been with me ever since.' As a child, Mudgett was bullied remorselessly by his father, and his mother was too intimidated to intervene. However, the young Herman did well at school, being intelligent, charming, and good-looking. Despite the problems of his home life, he was convinced he would do well in the world and had an ambition to be a doctor. As an adolescent, he took to killing and dismembering small animals, conducting experiments on them, and became fascinated with anatomy.

By the age of eighteen, Mudgett had married a young woman called Clara Lovering and was studying at the University of Michigan Medical School. However, he was expelled from there for stealing corpses, and had to relinquish his hopes of becoming a doctor. He changed his name to Dr Henry Howard Holmes and found work at a pharmacy, which went well until the woman he was working for, a Mrs Holton, disappeared. At the same time, Mudgett remarried, though without divorcing his first wife, and had a daughter with his new wife, Myrta Belknap. The couple named their daughter Lucy. He then married yet again to a woman named Georgiana Yoke, and went on to have an affair with the wife of a colleague, Julia Smythe, who later became one of his victims.

TORTURE ROOMS

Mudgett then murdered the pharmacist and his wife, and with the money he gained, began to construct a large building across the street from the store, which residents of the area called the 'Castle'. It was a block-long, three-storey building and during its construction many of the building contractors were hired and fired. The reason, as it later emerged, was that Holmes did not want anyone to know what the real purpose of the building was. It had many secret rooms and passages, some of them fitted with gas jets. In the basement, there were large vats and secret chutes that led down to torture rooms. Also in the basement there was a dissection table and surgical tools.

While the building was under construction, Holmes was involved in various scams to make money. One of these was to take water from the tap, mix it with vanilla essence, and sell it in the pharmacy as 'Linden Grove Mineral Water'. The authorities found out soon enough and he was banned from selling the water. However, he was not prosecuted and went on to run several other rackets, including selling fresh bodies to the medical schools in the area for students to dissect. Ironically, nobody asked where the bodies came from.

DISMEMBERED BODIES

By the time he was thirty, Holmes was a successful businessman. He owned a pharmacy, a hotel, a jewellery store, a restaurant, a barber's and several other businesses as well. He had many employees, including one named Ned Connor, who had moved to Chicago with his wife Julia and their daughter Pearl, to take up the position of manager in one of Holmes's businesses. Unbeknown to Connor, Holmes was strongly attracted to Julia, a good-looking woman with red hair and green eyes. When Julia invited her eighteen-year-old sister Gertie to stay, Holmes propositioned her as well, promising to divorce his wife so that he could be with her. Gertie, however, was not interested, so Holmes turned his attention to Julia once more. This time, Julia fell in love with Holmes and soon became his lover. Eventually, Connor found out what was going on and the couple separated, after recriminations on both sides.

Sadly, Julia was to suffer a great deal as a result of her attachment to Holmes. She became pregnant with their child and Holmes asked her to have an abortion, but Julia initially refused. Eventually, however, she agreed to let Holmes perform the operation on her, and he took her down to the cellar to do so. But instead of performing the abortion, Holmes murdered her instead, dismembering her body so that all the flesh was cleaned off, leaving only her skeleton, which he sold to a medical school for the sum of $200. Nobody knows exactly what happened to Julia's daughter Pearl, but she was never seen alive again.

GASSED TO DEATH

In 1893, a major exhibition opened in Chicago, bringing visitors flocking to the city, and to the hotel that Holmes had opened there. Over a period of three years or so, he selected his mostly female victims from the guests, took them to the sound-proof rooms and tortured them, before gassing them to death and dissecting them. So that he would not be discovered, he constantly changed the staff who worked at the hotel, firing them every fortnight or so. In this way he was able to carry on his grisly work without detection.

The usual way he operated was to murder his victims, then push the bodies down a secret chute that took them to the basement. There he would dissect them, remove all the flesh from the bones, and assemble their skeletons to be sold to medical schools. He also cremated his victims, throwing their bodies in huge lime pits so that they would be destroyed. In addition, there were two giant furnaces in the building, a torture rack and a huge assortment of poisons and acids designed to dispose of his victims in various ways, as the mood took him.

Not content with this, Holmes decided to make

more money by operating an insurance scam with one of his employees, Benjamin Pitezel. Pitezel took out a life insurance policy for $10,000, citing Holmes as the beneficiary. The idea was that Pitezel would then disappear, Holmes would find a corpse to disfigure, then identify it as Pitezel. Pitezel's children would be roped in to help to identify the body.

THE LONG ARM OF THE LAW

What in fact happened was that Holmes murdered Pitezel, then panicked when the police began to snoop around the hotel. Holmes set the hotel alight and escaped to Philadelphia, taking one of Pitezel's daughters with him. Meanwhile, evidence of what had been going on in the hotel all those years finally came to light. The remains of over 200 bodies were found, and police launched a major manhunt.

Eventually, Holmes was tracked down in Boston and arrested. While in custody, he struck up a friendship with another inmate, Marion Hedgepath, who constantly boasted to him about the various ways that he had made money illegally over the years. Holmes responded by telling Hedgepath about the murder of Pitezel so as to claim the insurance money, and then went on to claim that he had committed many such murders for financial gain. Hedgepath promptly informed the police of

Holmes's story, and Holmes was duly charged with the murder of Benjamin Pitezel. The story that came out deeply shocked the police and, later, the public. Holmes told his captors how he had burned Pitezel alive, despite the man's cries for mercy and his pitiful attempts to pray for salvation when his final end came.

Meanwhile, the police at the Castle in Chicago were tallying up the body count, and found that at least 100 young women, most of them typists and secretaries, had been murdered in the building. The killings had evidently followed a pattern: these young women had caught Holmes's eye, become his lovers and ended up being murdered. Not only did the police find the bodies of the women; there were also children, including Alice, Nellie and Howard Pitezel, whose remains were found in the building. Alice and Nellie had been thrown into a trunk and gassed to death, while their brother had been poisoned and burned before being dismembered.

Despite the mounting evidence against him, Holmes was adamant that he was innocent and continued to plead not guilty to murdering Pitezel. However, when he was brought to trial, the jury did not believe his story and he was convicted of first-degree murder. On November 4, 1895, he was sentenced to death. Before his hanging, he confessed to twenty-seven murders and six attempted murders.

On May 7, 1896, Herman Mudgett, alias Dr H. H. Holmes, was hanged in Philadelphia. According to the *New York Times*, Mudgett told the executioner: 'Take your time; don't bungle it.' However, the executioner did not make a very good job of the hanging. Holmes's neck did not immediately snap and he died slowly, twitching for a good fifteen minutes before he was finally pronounced dead.

PEDRO ALONSO LOPEZ

Pedro Lopez, known as the 'Monster of the Andes', is thought to have murdered more people than any other serial killer in the twentieth century. He himself put the score of people he had murdered at 300, although this has never been clearly established. The only other serial killer to have come anywhere near this number of victims is the British doctor, Harold Shipman, who is thought to have murdered over 200 of his patients.

FERAL CHILD

Pedro Alonso Lopez was born in Tolina, Colombia, in 1949, the seventh of thirteen children born to a prostitute mother. At this time, Colombia was undergoing a time of considerable social unrest, which made his already precarious situation more difficult. By all accounts, Pedro's mother was a harridan who had little love for her children, and in 1957, when she caught Pedro fondling his younger sister, she evicted him from the family home. He was just eight years old.

Lopez did his best to survive on the streets, but was soon picked up by a paedophile who took him to a deserted house and raped him repeatedly. Afterwards, the child was taken back to the streets, where he became so frightened that he hid in abandoned buildings by day, and only came out at night to look for food. Little is known of his subsequent life until an American family saw him begging on the streets of Bogota and took him in. They enrolled him in a school for orphans, but he ran away. The reasons for this are not clear, but it is thought that he may have been molested by one of the teachers. However, the school claimed that he had broken into the office there and stolen money.

KILLING SPREE

Whatever the truth of the matter, Lopez returned to the streets and became a beggar and petty thief. At the age of eighteen, he was caught stealing cars and arrested. He was brought to justice and received a seven-year prison sentence. In jail, he was reported to have been gang-raped by four other prisoners, and responded by killing three of them with a home-made knife. He was given an additional two years to serve, which was far too lenient. By the end of his sentence, he was an extremely dangerous individual, and was leashed on the world to wreak his vengeance.

Lopez was released in 1978. His experiences as a child, and in prison, had made him a very angry man, who had a particular hatred for women. For the next two years, he went on a killing spree, focusing his attention on young girls, mostly between the ages of eight to twelve. Significantly, he chose girls who were in the age range of the sister he had fondled as a child, before being ejected from the family by his mother. He was careful to choose girls from minority Indian tribes, whose disappearance would not be followed up by the authorities, as it would have been if they were white. He also travelled, covering his tracks as he went: he committed crimes all over the Andes, in Colombia, Peru and Ecuador. Later, he confessed to having killed 100 girls in Peru alone, and was eventually caught by a tribe of Ayachuco Indians while attempting to abduct a nine-year-old girl from them. In revenge, the Indians stripped him and tortured him for some while and were about to bury him alive when an American missionary intervened and persuaded them to hand Lopez over to the authorities. The authorities deported him over the border to

Ecuador and let him go. It was the worst mistake they could have made.

HUNDREDS OF VICTIMS

For the next few years, Lopez travelled back and forth between Ecuador and Colombia, killing as he went and never being caught. Families went to the police, and the authorities noticed an increase in the number of girls reported missing, but they explained this as girls being abducted for the slave trade and did not bother to follow up the complaints. It was only when, in April 1980, there was extensive flooding in the Ecuadorian town of Ambato and the bodies of four missing children were washed up, that the authorities realised something untoward was going on. Then a woman named Carvina Poveda, a resident of Ambato, saw Lopez trying to abduct her twelve-year-old daughter. She called for help. Lopez was caught red-handed and taken away by the police.

Once he was in custody, the police had difficulty gaining any explanation out of Lopez. He refused to say a word and ignored their threats. Eventually, they were forced to try another tactic and asked a local priest to talk to him. The priest pretended to be a fellow prisoner and struck up a conversation with him. It did not take long for Lopez to start confessing all, and as his tales of murder came thick and fast, the priest found himself unable to listen any more. He asked to be taken off the job, and reported what he had been told to the police. Lopez was confronted with this evidence and began to confess his crimes to the authorities for the first time.

At first, the police found it hard to credit what Lopez was telling them. It seemed that Lopez had murdered 100 girls in Colombia, over 100 in Ecuador and many more than that in Peru. He expressed a particular liking for girls from Ecuador, whom he described as more innocent and trusting than girls from Colombia. He also remarked that he liked to murder his victims in full daylight, as it was so much more enjoyable to watch the fear in their faces and see the life leave their eyes as he strangled them to death.

THE 'MONSTER OF THE ANDES'

Initially, Lopez's interrogators doubted his story, and wondered whether he had lost his mind. It seemed to them that this account, telling of literally hundreds of murders, was far-fetched and possibly the ravings of a madman. However, apparently preferring to boast about his victims than to be seen as a liar, Lopez claimed that he could lead police to the places where he had buried the girls. He was placed in leg irons, then allowed to lead the police to a site outside Ambato, where the remains of fifty-three girls were uncovered. He then led them to other sites in the area, but most of these were empty: in many cases, the bodies had been eaten by animals, and some had been washed away by flooding. However, despite the lack of corpses in these sites, the first grave had yielded more than enough evidence to convict Lopez, and the authorities were now convinced beyond all doubt that Pedro Lopez was indeed 'the monster of the Andes'.

Lopez went on to make more detailed confessions, and eventually it emerged that he had committed a total of 110 murders in Ecuador alone. He was charged with these murders, brought to trial and convicted. Not surprisingly, he was given a sentence of life imprisonment. At the end of 1998 he was deported to Colombia, where he continues to serve out his sentence to this day. In a recent interview, Lopez described himself as 'the man of the century' and said he was due to be released shortly 'for good behaviour'. Hopefully, this is just wishful thinking on his part.

LUIS ALFREDO GAVARITO

One of the most prolific serial killers in the world is Luis Alfredo Gavarito, a Colombian street trader, who is thought to have murdered over 140 adolescents ranging between the ages of six and sixteen. When he confessed, it emerged that he had made a record of his victims in a notebook that he carried with him as he went on his killing sprees. His victims were mostly street urchins who gathered at his market stall, where he would give them money and food before luring them off to be tortured, murdered and mutilated in hideous ways, including decapitation. His campaign of terror lasted for seven years before he was caught trying to rape a young boy. He was arrested and brought to trial, but received a relatively short sentence in return for co-operating with the authorities. Today, the issue of his possible release in the near future is the subject of much controversy, both within Colombia and internationally.

RAPE AND TORTURE

Gavarito was born on January 25, 1957, in the town of Genova, Quindio, which is located in Colombia's western coffee-growing region. He was the oldest of seven boys, and later told the police that from a young age, his father had sexually abused him. In addition, his father had physically abused him, regularly beating him and his brothers. He also alleged that not only his father, but also two male neighbours, had repeatedly raped and beaten him while he was growing up, so that his childhood had been one of misery and neglect, from his earliest years.

After only five years at school, Gavarito was sent out to work. Finding that he was not wanted at home, he left aged sixteen, and began his working life as a store clerk. Little more is known of his early adult life, except that at a young age he became a serious alcoholic and received medical treatment for depression. He was also, at various times, diagnosed by doctors as having suicidal tendencies.

Eventually, this intensely troubled young man found steady work as a market stallholder, selling religious icons and prayer cards. He began to befriend homeless children living on the streets of Colombia's cities and towns, gaining the nicknames 'Goofy', 'El Loco' (The Madman), and 'The Priest'. He told the children various stories to gain their confidence, such as that he was a monk, or a disabled person. He also gained entrance to schools by saying that he was selling the religious material on his stall in order to make charitable donations to foundations for the elderly and for children's education. This was an unlikely story, but apparently he was believed and allowed into schools on several occasions.

DISMEMBERED CORPSES

In 1992, he killed his first child victim, and after that began to move around the country, covering his tracks as he went. He visited many provinces of Colombia, killing children in each, and also spent time in Ecuador, where he is thought to have committed more murders. He would offer children food and soft drinks as well as gifts and small amounts of money, and gain their trust before luring them off for a walk. When the children grew tired, he would rape and torture them, afterwards cutting their throats. But that was not the end of it: he often dismembered the children's corpses after murdering them. Later, he told police that he always committed these horrific crimes after he had been drinking heavily.

In this way, between 1992 and 1998, Gavarito murdered over 140 children, mostly in Pereira, the capital city of the western state of Risaralda. The police estimate of his murders is actually 172 children, but since some of the corpses were never recovered, Gavarito was only found guilty of 140 of the them.

BLACK MAGIC RITUAL

In 1997, the decomposing bodies of thirty-six boys were discovered in the city of Pereira, prompting an investigation. Up until this time, such was the disorganisation of the Colombian police and government, that no one had realised a serial killer was on the loose in the country. The children were homeless, or from very poor homes, and so in most cases their disappearance was not registered; neither were their relatives taken seriously when they reported the children missing.

The boys' bodies were found in two mass graves, many of them with parts removed and showing signs of torture. The first grave was discovered when a boy walking through a patch of wasteland saw a human skull in the bushes. The second came to light less than a week later, when walkers came upon body parts in a river bed beneath a city highway. After that, more bodies were discovered in over sixty towns in the country.

Investigators claimed that the bodies may have

been evidence of a black magic ritual. There were also rumours that organ trafficking may have been behind the crimes. Another theory was that the murders were a political act: that an individual or group was conducting a campaign of murder against street children as a form of social cleansing. There was much speculation in the press, and a nationwide manhunt was launched to find the killer or killers. As it turned out, of course, there was no organised campaign behind the murders; it was simply the work of one deranged individual, a serial killer who had been on the loose for many years but whose existence had never been noticed.

CAPTURE AND CONVICTION

Gavarito was finally arrested as he tried to lure a small boy to his death. In retrospect, it appears that he had been crying out to be caught, but no one had previously bothered enough about the fate of the street children to pursue him. Gavarito promptly confessed to the murder of many boys over the preceding seven years. He was arrested and taken into custody, where, during a four-hour confession, he produced a notepad and showed police the gruesome tally of his killings. For each murder, he had written a line across the page. The evidence was so compelling that, when he came to trial, he was immediately convicted. He should have received a life sentence; however, because of Colombian law restrictions, his sentence had to be reduced to thirty years; and because he led authorities to the graves of his victims, he also received a further limitation, which reduced the sentence to twenty-two years.

Not surprisingly, this leniency for such a dangerous and prolific killer provoked an outcry in Colombia, and was also widely criticised in the press by foreign commentators. Some argued that Gavarito should have received the death sentence or life imprisonment, but currently, neither of these punishments is available in Colombia, so this was not possible.

In 2006, Gavarito was interviewed on television. The TV host who interviewed him mentioned that Gavarito was now a reformed character who had a desire to help abused children, and was considering a political career when he got out of prison. The interviewer also commented that, due to good behaviour in prison, Gavarito might be eligible for early release. As a response, concerned Colombians began to petition to have the law changed: in cases like this, it seemed essential to bring in life sentences to keep killers in prison, out of harm's way. However, to date, the situation has not changed, and it may be that Gavarito will be released early, much to the anxiety of the Colombian public.

To date, there are still many child murder cases being investigated in Colombia that may or may not be the work of Luis Gavarito. It is thought that continued investigation of these cases may be the only way to detain this terrifying child killer further, and keep him in prison when the time comes for his release.

ANATOLY ONOPRIENKO

Anatoly Onoprienko, nicknamed 'The Beast', is the Ukraine's worst serial killer. He killed at least fifty-two victims in a killing spree that lasted for six years, between 1989 and 1995. He was finally picked up by police, carrying a hunting rifle that he had used to commit murder and, when taken into custody, told police that 'inner voices' had told him to kill.

He was born in 1959 in the town of Zhytomyr in the Ukraine. Little is known of his early life, except that his mother died when he was four, and his father put him in an orphanage. As a young adult, he spent time in psychiatric hospitals and was diagnosed as schizophrenic. According to one account, his doctors knew that he was a potential killer, but nothing was done about the situation – with horrifying results, as it turned out.

KILLING SPREE

Onoprienko's hideous catalogue of crimes came to light when the police received a call from Pyotr Onoprienko, Anatoly's cousin. Pyotr had discovered a large stash of weapons hidden in his house, which belonged to Anatoly. When Pyotr confronted Anatoly, his cousin began to threaten him, saying that he would 'take care' of his family over the Easter period. Afraid of what might happen, Pyotr alerted the police, and a task force was assembled to pay a visit to Anatoly's apartment, where he lived with a hairdresser called Anna and her two children. Luckily for her, she was out at church with her children when the police arrived, and when Anatoly opened the door, thinking it was his girlfriend, the officers were able to arrest him immediately. A sharp-eyed detective, Officer Kryukov, noticed that in the living room was a stolen stereo, matching the description of goods taken after the murder of a local family. When he checked the serial numbers, they matched. In addition, a large stash of items taken from another murder scene was found in the apartment. It was clear that the police were dealing with the murderer.

Realising that his cover had been blown, Onoprienko made a dash for freedom, but was subdued and taken to the police station. At first, he remained silent, but then began to recount the story of how his father had put him in an orphanage, but kept his older brother at home. He had felt that his father could easily have taken care of him, but did not. He then admitted stealing the shotgun police had found in his possession, and went on to confess that he had used it to commit murder. It emerged that his first murder had been committed in 1989. Along with a friend, Sergei Rogozin, he had begun to break into houses, and one night the owners of one of the houses had discovered them. To protect their identity, they had murdered the entire family, including eight children.

INNER VOICES

After that, Onoprienko had developed a taste for killing, and went on the rampage on his own. He killed five people sleeping in a car one night, including an eleven-year-old boy, and afterwards burned their bodies. He then broke into the home of another family, shooting the couple and their two children with a sawn-off shotgun. This time, he took some of their jewellery with him, before torching the place. By now he was hearing voices telling him to kill, and went on to murder a family of four, once again burning down the house after he had done so. He then began to kill indiscriminately, murdering travellers along the highway, including a sailor, a taxi driver and a cook. He described how the murders felt to him like a game, like a form of hunting, and how he had tried and failed to rid himself of the compulsion to kill.

His next victims were five members of a family in Bratkovichi, including a six-year-old boy. Once again, he burned the house down, and as he was leaving, shot two potential witnesses. Two weeks later, he killed a nurse and her two young sons and a visitor to his house. A month after that, he broke into another home and shot the father and son, beating the wife and daughter to death with a hammer. He told the amazing story of how the girl had witnessed the scene and had refused to give up her parents' belongings to him, so he smashed her head in and left her dead.

The killings continued, and he shot a couple, then hacked their two daughters to death with an axe. A witness was also shot and butchered. Onoprienko spoke of how he had 'loved' the children, but had been compelled to kill them by his inner voice. The final murders took place on March 22, 1996, when Onoprienko shot a family of four, once more setting their home on fire. When speaking of his motivation, Onoprienko described how he felt that he needed to do the killings to see how much he could tolerate, to find out if he could 'live with' his crimes. It was as if, in his madness, he was trying to discover the limits of his anger – and was unable to do so.

'I'M A ROBOT'

After extensive interviews, psychiatrists declared that Onoprienko was fit to stand trial, and court proceedings began in November 1998. Onoprienko was brought to court in an iron cage, and was shouted and spat at by onlookers. He refused to make a statement, and when asked his nationality, said 'none'. He later told the court that he had been ordered to commit the murders by the devil and that he was 'a beast of Satan'. Not surprisingly, after only three hours, the jury decided to give him a verdict of guilty, and he was sentenced to death by shooting. After receiving his sentence, Onoprienko said that he was glad he was going to die. 'I've robbed and killed,' he said, 'but I'm a robot. I don't feel anything, I've been close to death so many times that it's even interesting for me now to venture into the afterworld, to see what is there, after this death.'

However, even though the defendant was condemned to death, the ruling was difficult for the authorities to follow up, because the Ukraine had committed itself to abolishing capital punishment as part of its obligation to becoming a Council of Europe member. Even so, many commentators argued that Onoprienko was a special case, and that his situation was exceptional. Later, Onoprienko gave an interview in which he said, 'Death for me is nothing. Naturally, I would prefer the death penalty. I have absolutely no interest in relations with people. I have betrayed them.'

He went on to describe how, when he was in his early twenties, he had shot a deer with a rifle when hunting in the woods. He told the interviewer how, on that occasion, he had felt very upset that he had killed the animal. However, since then, he had never felt any remorse whatsoever for killing any animal or human being. For this reason, he believed that if he was let out of jail, he would continue to kill, and his rampage would be worse than ever before. Onoprienko finished the interview by announcing that if ever he was freed he would find the president of the Ukraine and hang him from a tree by his testicles. Not surprisingly, given this threat and the others that he had made during the interview, the authorities were in no hurry to release him. Today, he lives on death row, and the police are still investigating a number of other murders that took place between 1989 and 1995.

DEATH OF AN INNOCENT SUSPECT

There has been a great deal of criticism about the

authorities' handling of the Onoprienko case. Firstly because it took so long for the culprit of so many murders to be found, despite the fact that whole families had been killed and their belongings stolen, so that whoever was to blame would have had a mass of evidence to show for the killings. Also, the killer did not cover his tracks very carefully, often leaving weapons at the scene of the crime. The murders, in their indiscriminate savagery, were clearly the work of a deranged man, not a careful housebreaker. Secondly, in March 1996, the authorities detained a twenty-six-year-old man named Yury Mozola, believing him to be a possible suspect for the murders. As it later transpired, Mozola was brutally tortured over a period of three days, but because he was innocent, he refused to confess to the crimes. Tragically, he died as a result of the torture. Only a few days later, Onoprienko was arrested, and it became clear that the police had got the wrong man. Mozola had died for no reason, other than that he was in the wrong place at the wrong time.

AHMAD SURADJI

Ahmad Suradji was a sorcerer from a village near Medan, the capital city of North Sumatra in Indonesia. Women of all ages, as well as young girls, went to him to seek advice for marital and other problems, and he would cast spells and administer potions to assist them. However, in 1997 it transpired that, far from helping his credulous clientele, he had actually been murdering many of these innocent women. In all, he admitted to killing forty-two women and girls over a period of eleven years, murdering them in a strange ritual that involved burying them up to the waist in the ground before strangling them with a cable and drinking their saliva.

FATHER'S GHOST

Little is known about Suradji's early life, but he went by a number of different names, including Nasib Kelewang and Datuk Maringgi. Originally a cattle breeder, he developed an interest in sorcery, and eventually came to establish a reputation as a powerful witch doctor, earning a good living from doing so. He was helped in this enterprise by his three wives, all of whom were sisters. After his arrest, he told police that the murders started when he had a dream in which his father's ghost told him to kill seventy women and drink their saliva. His father's ghost had told him that, in this way, he would become a mystic healer, and would be able to help many people with his supernatural powers.

On May 2, 1997, the authorities arrested Suradji after three bodies were discovered in a remote sugar cane plantation near his home in the village of Aman Damai, Deli Serdang, about eighteen kilometres west of Medan. What was particularly bizarre about the discovery was that the bodies had been buried with their heads all pointing the same way – towards the house of Ahmad Suradji. Suradji, at that time aged forty-eight, was brought in for questioning, but initially denied that he had been involved in the murders. However, he eventually confessed and, when questioned further, added an additional thirteen murders to his previous list of crimes.

Horrified by this discovery, the police and authorities went on to search Suradji's house and found further evidence there to incriminate him. Hidden away in the house, they found property belonging to at least twenty-five missing women. Further interrogation revealed that over a longer period of about eleven years, Suradji had murdered a total of forty-two women, all of them customers who had come to him for help. It appeared that his three wives had helped him in this hideous activity. They claimed that they were frightened and embarrassed to let the local community know what was really going on, and so had covered up for his brutal crimes, but there was also some evidence that they had willingly assisted him to lure and murder his victims. Because of this, the oldest of the three wives, Tumini, was arrested to be tried as his accomplice.

LOCAL WITCH DOCTOR

As Suradji's horrifying story of cold-blooded murder unfolded, police learned that the witch doctor had been revered by women in the local community for his supposed extraordinary powers as a shaman, and that he had been a trusted confidant to many of them, discussing their medical, sexual and spiritual problems, and administering spells and potions that he said would help them. The women believed him to be able to help them in many ways, including making their husbands faithful. They also thought that his spells could bring them riches and good health, and that he could also cast evil spells on their enemies. In addition, women flocked to him because they thought he could help them become more sexually attractive. Many of these women were prostitutes, and even those who were not tended to visit him in secret, embarrassed to tell their family and friends about going to him for advice. In this way, he preyed on the gullibility and vanity of his female clients, and was able to continue his ghoulish trade for many years without being discovered.

By the time he was arrested, Suradji was on his way to becoming a rich man, by local standards at least. He had been supplementing his meagre income as a cattle breeder with large fees for his sorcery practice and was now seen as something of a local benefactor and pillar of the community. The reality was a little different. When the women came to him, he charged each of them between $200 and $400, talking to them sympathetically about their problems and casting spells to rid them of their ills. He would then demand that a ritual should take place outside in the sugar cane plantation. His victims, all female and ranging in age from eleven to thirty, followed him, believing that this was part of the treatment. However, once there, the gruesome death rites began.

BURIED WAIST-HIGH IN THE GROUND

First, he would bury the women up to their waists in the ground, telling them that this was part of a magic ritual that would help them solve their problem. Of course, the real reason was to stop them running away when he performed the next step in the ritual. When the women were in the ground, he would take out an electrical cable and strangle them to death. Unable to run away, the terrified women would struggle to stay alive, but there was no hope. All of them met a terrible end, strangled to death by a madman in a field. However, once they were dead, the bizarre ritual continued. Suradji would drink their saliva, pull their bodies out of the holes in the ground, and take all their clothes off. Then he would proceed to rebury the naked corpses with their heads pointing towards his home, apparently thinking that this would give him extra magic powers.

At the time of his arrest, he was hoping to complete his tally of seventy women, as his father's ghost had commanded him, and in this way, to reinforce his reputation as a mystic healer or 'dukun'. Fortunately, police intercepted him by the time he had reached a total of forty-two, otherwise the death toll might have been a great deal higher.

Strangely, although many women in the local

area were reported missing, no one ever accused Suradji. He was thought to be a kind and helpful man, who was known to be willing to help villagers who had fallen ill, and who often made donations to charitable causes. Even though around eighty local families had repeatedly been to the police to report their female relatives missing, for many years Suradji was not brought in for questioning.

THE 'DUKUN' OF INDONESIA

When Suradji and his wife Tumini were charged with the murders and brought to trial, they denied that they had committed the crimes, claiming that they had only made their initial confessions because they had been tortured by police. However, the jury did not believe them, and on April 27, 1998, Suradji was convicted of murder. He was sentenced to death by firing squad. Once in jail, on death row, he admitted to his crimes and became a devout Muslim, praying for God to forgive him for the terrible murders he had committed. According to one source, Justice Affairs Officer Lukas Tarigan, Suradji developed a reputation in prison as a tolerant, kind man – just as he had before his conviction, when he was living in the little village of Aman Damai.

The case of Ahmad Suradji is unusual, involving

as it does a 'dukun', or sorcerer, from Indonesia, where instances of serial killing are relatively rare compared to the West. However, the dukun have long been associated with strange rituals involving death: for example, some of them go to cemeteries to summon up the spirits of the dead. Many Indonesians believe that the dukun, who are also known as 'pawing' or 'bomoh' (meaning shaman), are advised by the wise spirits of the dead, and will go to them for advice about health or romantic problems. The dukun are believed to be able to find out the reasons for bad luck or bad health, and as well as healing ills, are also thought to be able to cause possession by bad spirits, leading to ill health and bad luck. The dukun works by performing incantations and rituals, and also by administering potions. Most of their practices are extremely ancient, and the origins of them are in many cases difficult to trace. Nevertheless, the dukun continue to hold sway in modern Indonesian society, not just in the countryside but even in large cities, where they continue to offer their services in many shopping centres. Many people accept that there is always a risk in consulting a sorcerer, but tend to be unwilling to criticise the dukun, for fear of bringing bad luck on themselves and their families – in Suradji's case, with horrifying results.

PETER MANUEL

Peter Manuel was a serial killer who terrified the people of Scotland with a series of vicious murders in the 1950s. When he was finally arrested and convicted, his callous, arrogant attitude shocked the British nation, for he went to his death without showing any remorse whatsoever. Today, he is remembered as one of the last people to be hanged in Scotland before the death penalty was banned.

BLUDGEONED TO DEATH

Manuel was born on March 1, 1927, in New York. His parents were Scottish, and when he was five years old the family moved to the city of Coventry in England. Growing up in Coventry, young Peter showed signs of becoming a criminal, and was constantly in trouble with the authorities. At the age of twelve, he was arrested for burglary and was sent to reform school. For the next few years he was in and out of reform school, and became known to the authorities as a juvenile delinquent, as young offenders were called then. At sixteen, he was charged with rape and received a jail sentence. In 1953, the family moved to Glasgow, Scotland and when Manuel got out of jail, he joined them there. Birkenshaw, the area where the family lived, was in the rough east end of Glasgow and afforded many opportunities for Manuel to continue his antisocial behaviour. He was jailed for rape several times before beginning a killing spree that lasted for five years until his capture in 1958; by which time people were beginning to lock their doors day and night in the belief that a complete madman was on the loose and would attack them at any moment.

His first unfortunate victim was Anna Knielands, a seventeen-year-old girl that he bludgeoned to death with a length of iron. Her body was found on a golf course in East Kilbride. In 1956 he was pulled in by police for questioning over the murder, but he managed to convince them that he was innocent and was released without charge. Two years later, when brought into police custody on another charge, he confessed to this murder.

NO MOTIVE

His next victims were forty-five-year-old Marion Watt, her sister Margaret Brown, aged forty-one, and Watt's sixteen-year-old daughter Vivienne, who were all found shot at point blank range in their home at High Burnside, Glasgow. At the time, Watt's husband, William, a baker who owned a chain of shops, was away on a fishing trip. Suspicion fell on Manuel and he was taken in to the police station for questioning, but once again he managed to persuade the police that he was innocent. Despite the fact that Manuel had been in the area at the time, and had been out on bail for a burglary at a local colliery, the police were unable to find concrete evidence that he was the culprit.

Two weeks after the incident, Manuel was convicted of the colliery burglary and received a jail sentence of eighteen months. In a pattern that was to become familiar, the murders ceased while he was in jail and started again when he was released. By December 1957, Manuel was at large again, and this time went to Newcastle-upon-Tyne where he shot dead a taxi driver named Sydney Dunn. He then returned to Scotland, where the senseless killings continued, instilling terror into the local population. What puzzled police, and the media, was that unlike most serial killers there appeared to be no pattern to his murders and no motive for his crimes. In most cases, he appeared to shoot or beat to death people who were simply in his way, as if he was killing just for the pleasure of it.

FAMILY KILLING

His next victim, in 1957, was a seventeen-year-old girl named Isabelle Cooke, who set off from her home in Mount Vernon, a district of Glasgow, to attend a dance at a local school, Uddingston Grammar. Her family were alerted when she failed to return, and later her body was found buried in a field nearby. A year later, Manuel struck again. This time the victims were a family – forty-five-year-old Peter Smart, his wife Doris, and their son, ten-year-old Michael, whom he shot at point blank range in their home in Uddingston on New Year's Day 1958. It was impossible to understand what had led Manuel to pick on this innocent family, but one fact was beginning to become clear: that a violent, remorseless murderer was on the loose, who apparently killed at random. The local population were, understandably, terrified and pressure began to build to find the killer and put him behind bars as soon as possible.

After shooting the Smart family, Manuel had stolen a number of new banknotes from their home and used them to buy drinks at a local bar. It was this that led to his downfall. A sharp-eyed bartender became suspicious when Manuel produced the wad of notes and alerted the police, who managed to trace the notes back to Peter Smart's possession. It emerged that the serial numbers of the banknotes matched those paid to Smart before the New Year holiday. The police now had some firm evidence linking Manuel to the murders, and accordingly he was arrested and questioned. Eventually, he was charged with seven murders, although it was believed that he had committed as many as fifteen in all.

BLACK CLOUD OF TERROR

Arrogant as ever, Manuel decided to conduct his own defence, adopting a plea of insanity. However, the jury refused to believe that he was insane, and after a highly publicised trial, he was convicted of all seven of the murders. He received the death penalty, and on July 11, 1958, he was hanged at Barlinnie prison in Glasgow. He was thirty-one years old. He was the second to last person to be hanged at the prison, and the third last to be hanged in the whole of Scotland. It was said that when his body swung from the gallows, the whole of the Scottish nation breathed a sigh of relief and a black cloud of terror was lifted from the land.

The case of Peter Manuel continues to fascinate commentators, since it is still somewhat of a mystery as to why he killed in such a random fashion. Even in the rough world of Glasgow during the 1950s, where gangland violence was common, Manuel was an unusually callous and psychopathic individual. He did not kill for all the usual motives – lust, revenge, or greed – and his victims, most commonly, had no connection with him, so there was no reason for him to kill them. Moreover, each time he was brought in for questioning, the police were taken aback by his audacity and found it hard to believe that he should display such indifference as to the fate of his victims. For example, after murdering Isabella Cooke, he took authorities to the place where he had buried the girl and said: 'This is the place. In fact, I think I'm standing on her now.'

In the same way, when he shot the Smart family dead, he appeared to show no remorse for his crime. In fact, he went back to the house several times after the event, even helping himself to the food that was in the house after the Christmas and New Year festivities. Strangely, he fed the family cat once its owners were dead, and began to drive around in Peter Smart's car, even giving a police officer a lift to work. On that occasion, he casually told the police officer, who was working on the Isabella Cooke case, that the police were looking in the wrong place.

SHEER BRAVURA

On several other occasions, Manuel managed to hoodwink police by a display of sheer bravura. For example, in the Watt case, Manuel's calm, cool demeanour when taken in for questioning convinced police that he was not to blame and, instead, William Watt, Marion's husband, was brought into custody and spent two months in jail on suspicion of committing the crimes. Fortunately, he was released once the true culprit, Manuel, was known.

Writing about the case after the event, the trial judge Lord Cameron commented: 'I saw no sign indicative to a layman of any illness or abnormality beyond callousness, selfishness and treachery in high degree, but I did form the impression that he was even then laying the foundation of a suggestion that he might in the end of the day be presented not as a criminal but as one in need of medical care.'

So calculating was Manuel that even in his initial interviews with police, he took care to show that, should he be found guilty, he could rely on an insanity plea to get him off the hook. However, his plan failed and eventually he was hanged as a common murderer. According to witnesses, his last words before he met his death were: 'Turn up the radio and I'll go quietly.'

JOHN WAYNE GACY

Even by comparison with his fellow serial killers, John Wayne Gacy, 'the killer clown', has become something of an icon of pure evil. This is partly to do with the way he dressed up as a clown to entertain children at parties near his suburban Chicago home – what more sinister notion is there than that beneath the clown's make-up lies a sex killer? And partly it is because of the sheer enormity of his crime – thirty-three young men raped and murdered, almost all of them buried beneath his suburban house.

John Wayne Gacy came into this world on March 17, 1942, St Patrick's Day, the second of three children born to Elaine Robinson Gacy and John Wayne Gacy Sr. He grew up in a middle-class district of northern Chicago and was raised as a Catholic. His childhood was for the most part uneventful. Look a little closer, though, and there were troubles. John Gacy Sr was a misanthropic man who frequently took his anger out on his son through physical beatings and verbal abuse. John Gacy Jr, in turn, became very close to his mother. Aged eleven, he sustained a nasty accident when he was struck on the head by a swing. It caused him to have regular blackouts during his teens. During his teenage years he also complained of heart problems, though this seems likely to be just a symptom of a lifelong tendency to hypochondria – thus whenever he was under pressure he would claim to be on the brink of a heart attack.

Gacy did poorly in high school, left without graduating and headed for Las Vegas in a bid to make his fortune. Instead, he ended up working in a mortuary, where he showed an unhealthy interest in the corpses. He then returned to Chicago and began attending business college. While there, he discovered his considerable ability as a salesman; he was able to talk people into anything.

In 1964, Gacy married Marlyn Myers, a woman he'd met through work, whose father had a string of Kentucky Fried Chicken franchises. Gacy decided to join the family business and became a restaurant manager. The couple had a child and Gacy became extremely active on the local charity and community group circuit around their new home in Waterloo, Iowa.

All this came crashing down in May 1968, when Gacy was charged with raping a young employee named Mark Miller. Gacy was sentenced to ten years for sodomy and his wife promptly divorced him.

He was released from prison after just eighteen months, thanks to his good behaviour while inside. His father had died while he was in prison, but now his mother – whom he had always been close to – stood by him and helped him set up in business again. He bought a new house in the Chicago suburbs and established himself as a building contractor. In June 1972 he remarried, this time to divorcee Carole Hoff. Carole and her two daughters moved into Gacy's house and the family soon became popular in their neighbourhood. Gacy would give big parties with fancy dress themes – often Western or Hawaiian – and was active in local Democratic politics.

BODIES BURIED UNDER HOUSE

Carole Hoff was aware of Gacy's past but under the impression he had put all that behind him. This was far from the truth. In fact, just before they married Gacy had been charged with sexually assaulting a minor, but the case had collapsed when his accuser failed to attend court. However, rumours soon began to get around about Gacy's conduct with the teenage boys he liked to employ in his business. By 1975, his marriage was definitely deteriorating.

Carole was disturbed to find homosexual pornography around the house. Gacy refused to apologise
and even told her he preferred men to women.
The couple divorced in 1976. It later emerged that
throughout their marriage Gacy had been picking
up strangers in Chicago gay bars and had already
carried out several murders, burying the bodies
under the house. The neighbours had even complained about the terrible smell.

Now that his marriage was over, Gacy gave full
vent to his lust for killing. He developed a modus
operandi. Victims, either picked up on the streets or
chosen from his workforce, would be lured back to
the house and given drink and marijuana. Then the
apparently jovial Gacy would offer to show them a
magic trick. The victim would be asked to put on a
pair of handcuffs and would then find out that this
was no trick – the handcuffs were all too real and
they were now in Gacy's power. He would proceed
to torture his victims before finally killing them by
strangling them while raping them.

THE 'KILLER CLOWN'

Time and again, Gacy got away with it. His neighbours suspected nothing, although they persistently
complained about the smells coming from his house.
He carried on giving parties and started dressing up

as Pogo the Clown to visit sick children in hospitals. He became such a valued member of the local Democratic Party that he had his photo taken shaking hands with the then First Lady, Rosalyn Carter.

Finally, in 1978, his secret life began to catch up with him. In February of that year he abducted a young man called Jeffrey Rignall, knocked him out with chloroform, raped and tortured him and then, oddly, dumped him in a park rather than killing him. Rignall went to the police who showed little interest, but, acting alone, he managed to track down his abductor and made an official complaint which the police started to take seriously late that summer.

Gacy had still not been charged with anything when, on October 16, a fifteen-year-old boy called Robert Piest went missing from a Chicago drugstore. His parents discovered that he'd been going to meet John Wayne Gacy about a job. Gacy pleaded ignorance but the investigating officer discovered Gacy's previous conviction for sodomy and decided to press ahead with a search of the house. They discovered an array of suspicious objects, such as handcuffs, pornography, drugs and so forth. They also noted the terrible smell. Gacy was confronted with this evidence and eventually confessed to having carried out a single murder. The police returned to the house and began to dig. Soon they realised there was not just one victim but many more. In all, twenty-eight bodies were found around the house; the five most recent victims had been dumped in nearby rivers, as Gacy had run out of burial space.

Charged with thirty-three counts of murder, Gacy entered a plea of insanity, attempting to use the defence of having a multiple personality, which was a fashionable theory at the time. However, the jury found it hard to believe that a man who dug graves for his victims in advance was suddenly the victim of uncontrollable violent impulses, so he was duly sentenced to death. While in prison he became a grotesque celebrity, giving frequent interviews and showing admirers his paintings – almost always of sinister clowns. In all, he spent some fourteen years on death row. Towards the end of his time there, he began to claim that he had not killed after all, but had been the victim of a mysterious conspiracy. Credulous admirers were able to call a premium rate number to hear his refutation of the charges against him. All to no avail, however. On May 10, 1994, he was put to death by lethal injection.

WAYNE WILLIAMS

The case of Wayne Williams, the Atlanta child murderer, has attracted a great deal of controversy over the years. During the period in which Atlanta suffered a series of child murders, all of black children, there was intense pressure on the police to solve the mystery of who the culprit was. Thus it was that in January 1982 Williams was brought to trial, but no initial connection could be found between him and the children, so he was found guilty of murdering two adults, both men. After this conviction, the police force in Atlanta declared twenty-two of the child murders in the city to be solved (there were twenty-nine in all). Many were not persuaded by this, and the inference was that the police only accused Williams of the child murders because they wanted to clear the crimes off the record. However, after Williams's imprisonment, the murders stopped, which seemed to indicate that he was perhaps behind them. Whatever the truth of the matter, it remains the case that Williams was convicted on a great deal of circumstantial evidence.

Today, many people believe that although Williams was guilty to some degree, the complete facts are still not known, and many aspects of the case are subject to doubt.

TALL STORIES

Wayne Bertram Williams was born on May 27, 1958, the son of two teachers. He grew up in the area of Dixie Hills, Atlanta, which was the neighbourhood from where the child victims were taken. As a young man, Williams was known in the locality as a DJ who worked on a local amateur radio station, broadcasting from his parents' house. He often walked the streets and frequented bars and sports centres in the neighbourhood looking for young musicians to play on his radio station. He was not always well liked by his neighbours because of his habit of telling tall stories about himself so as to impress them, and he was something of a joke in the area. Some believed him to be gay, which further increased his unpopularity among the more homophobic individuals in the community. However, it seemed that Williams was nothing more than a harmless, rather irritating local character. He had no record of criminal activity except that, in 1976, he was arrested for impersonating a police officer, but the case never came to court and the arrest was forgotten. That was his only brush with the law until March 1981, when he became a suspect in the child murder cases that had hit the headlines in the city and nationally.

During the early eighties, Atlanta was in the grip of terror over a spate of child murders that were taking place in the city. The victims were black children, and for a long time police failed to solve the cases, prompting allegations of racism against the police force and the authorities, and fuelling the already tense race relations in many parts of the area. Given the tension of the situation, the police were under a great deal of pressure to find the killer, and when Wayne Williams was seen loitering on a bridge in the middle of the night, close to where a murder had taken place, the police thought that they had found their man.

NAKED BODY IN RIVER

Williams was picked up as he sat on the Jackson Parkway Bridge in a car belonging to his parents. He had turned the lights off, which police thought to be suspicious. Even more suspicious was the fact that police heard a loud splash in the water directly below the car. At the time, the police were staking out the area to discover any clues to the killings, so for once they were in the right place at the right time. Williams was detained by police and asked what his business was there. In response, he gave the name and number of a young singer he said he was going to visit, who lived out of town. However, when police checked the singer's name and address, they found that the details had been invented – no such person existed.

This was enough to arouse their suspicions, and these were confirmed when, only three days later, a naked body turned up in the river. It was that of Nathaniel Cater, a twenty-seven-year-old man who had been reported missing by his family. When the autopsy was performed, the examiner found that the man had probably died from asphyxia, but was unable to be definitive about the matter. He was also unable to determine whether the man had been strangled or not, but the police managed to construct a theory that Williams had thrown the body off the bridge and into the river shortly before they had encountered him sitting in his car there.

CIRCUMSTANTIAL EVIDENCE

A series of investigations were carried out and evidence incriminating Williams came to light. Fibres and hair from Williams's car and home, including dog hairs, were found on some of the child victims' bodies. Witnesses also claimed that they had seen Williams walking about the streets covered in scratches and bruises, which could have been from the victims struggling to escape as he killed them. However, none of this evidence was overwhelmingly persuasive, and accordingly, Williams held a press conference outside his parents' house, declaring himself to be innocent.

The authorities were not persuaded by these protestations and on June 21, 1981, Williams was arrested for the murder of Nathanial Cater. He was also charged with the murder of another man, twenty-nine-year-old Jimmy Payne. He was taken into custody to await trial, amid a tremendous amount of press and public interest because of the link with the child killings. Throughout this ordeal, Williams continued to maintain his innocence and many believed him. However, what made his case seem less persuasive was that while he was out of circulation, the murders of young children that had so terrified the people of Atlanta ceased. Whether this was just coincidence or proof, Williams's involvement is still a matter for conjecture.

THE TRIAL BEGINS

On January 6, 1982, the trial of Wayne Williams began. The prosecution had been hard at work to amass a huge amount of circumstantial evidence, since they were lacking in any other kind. They had taken nineteen types of fibres from Williams' household, including fibres from his bathroom, from his bed, from an unusual kind of carpet he had, from his clothing and from his dog. They claimed that these fibres had been found on several of the child victims, linking him to the murders. They also produced witnesses who said that Williams had been seen with some of the victims, and who alleged that he was a paedophile who preyed on young boys. In addition, they showed that the bloodstains from some of the victims' bodies matched blood found in Williams' car.

During his trial, Williams himself did not help his case. He became aggressive towards the jury, which set many of them against him. Whether it was the frustration of being wrongly accused, or whether this was the behaviour of a man accustomed to violence and to getting his own way through threatening behaviour, is difficult to say. However, on February 27, after a long deliberation of ten hours, the jury found Williams guilty of murdering the two men, Cater and Payne. He was given a life sentence for each murder.

THE ATLANTA CHILD KILLER?

Since that time, Williams has continued to protest

his innocence, and four of the child victim cases have been reopened. Controversy erupted again when Charles T. Sanders, a member of the Ku Klux Klan, was found to have suggested that the killings were a positive step. His actual words to the Georgia Bureau of Investigation were that the killer had 'wiped out a generation of niggers for good'. This meant that suspicion now fell on Sanders, so Williams's defence responded by demanding a new trial for their client. In the weeks that followed, Sanders was cleared of involvement with the child murders, as was the Ku Klux Klan in general, and the case was closed once more.

Today, the identity of the Atlanta child killer continues to remain a matter of controversy, but one positive development remains: since the incarceration of Wayne Williams the child killings have ceased, much to the relief of the people of Dixie Hills, Atlanta, and the rest of the citizens of the USA. Even so, the era in which black families were terrorised by the spectre of the Atlanta child killer remains a vivid memory, one that has been revisited by many film makers, novelists, musicians and other artists in the new millennium.

ARTHUR SHAWCROSS

Arthur Shawcross, also known as the Genesee River Killer, was an American serial killer of children and women, who committed many of his crimes after being released on parole following the murder of two children early in his career. For this reason, the authorities were severely criticised when the facts of the case emerged. In addition, most of his adult female victims were prostitutes, and it appeared that, until he began to kill women who were not prostitutes, very little was done about the murders. During his trial, Shawcross attempted to plead insanity, but the jury rejected this and he was given several life sentences instead.

VIETNAM ATROCITIES

Shawcross was born in Kittery, Maine, on June 6, 1945, and soon afterwards the family moved to Watertown in New York State. Later, his parents and siblings claimed that he had had an ordinary childhood, but he maintained that he had a difficult relationship with his mother, whom he described as domineering, and as a result became a bedwetter. He also claimed that as a child he had been sexually molested by his aunt, and that at a young age he had been involved in sexual relations with his sister. He also said that he had had homosexual relations when he was under age, and even that, as a boy, he had indulged in bestiality. The truth of his claims was never known, as Shawcross was found to be an inveterate liar who tended to change his stories to fit whatever circumstances he found himself in.

At school, Shawcross did not do well. He had a low IQ and was known as a bully. He was also suspected of arson attacks and burglaries in the area. His school work was so poor that he dropped out before ninth grade and then became involved in petty theft. He was put on probation in 1963 after smashing a shop window. The following year, he married his first wife and they went on to have a son. However, Shawcross's repeated brushes with the law caused the breakdown of the marriage and he went into the army, serving in Vietnam in 1967. During this period, he married again but soon afterwards got divorced. Later, he claimed that while in Vietnam he murdered and ate two Vietnamese girls, also killing several Vietnamese children. He also boasted about the number of enemy soldiers he had killed there, but it was later found that this was a pack of lies and he had not killed anyone in the course of his duties.

CHILD VICTIMS

After he returned from Vietnam in 1968, he was imprisoned for an arson attack and served a five-year jail sentence. On his release, he married for the third time and had another child. It was around this time that he committed his first murder, that of ten-year-old Jack Black, who was a member of a neighbouring family. Shawcross had taken the boy out fishing and a few days later he disappeared. Shawcross denied any knowledge of what had happened but after a long hunt, the child's body was found; he had been sexually assaulted and suffocated. It later transpired that the murder had taken place on April 7, 1972, and that Shawcross was the perpetrator of the crime.

A few months later, another child victim was found, an eight-year-old girl named Karen Ann Hill. Mud and leaves had been pushed into her throat and she had been raped before being killed. When she was dead, her body had been thrown under a bridge. Witnesses mentioned that shortly before she died, she had been seen with Shawcross, so suspicion immediately fell on him. On October 3, 1972, he was arrested. Once in custody, Shawcross confessed that

149

he had killed both the children. However, he was only charged with Hill's murder, because there was little concrete evidence – beyond his confession – linking him to Black's. When Shawcross was brought to trial he was found guilty of the murder and given a sentence of twenty-five years.

PROSTITUTE KILLINGS

However, after only fifteen years, Shawcross was let out on parole. While he was in prison, his wife had divorced him. When he went to live in Binghamton, New York State, the news that a child killer was in the area became public and he was forced to move on. By this time he had a new girlfriend, whom he later married but quickly separated from. Meanwhile, the authorities decided to keep his criminal record a secret, to prevent the kind of public outcry that had happened at Binghamton. They could not have made a worse mistake.

Before long, Shawcross was frequenting prostitutes. He later claimed that they had taunted him with his sexual inadequacy, but this was never proved. It has been speculated that he thought people would make less fuss about the killing of prostitutes than the killing of children, and thus targeted the women. Whatever the reason, he murdered his first adult victim, twenty-seven-year-old Dorothy Blackburn, in March 1988, dumping her body in the Genessee River. There were bite marks on her body in the genital region and she had been strangled to death.

Other murders of prostitutes followed, including that of Anna Steffen in September 1989 and Patricia Ives. In another instance, he brutally murdered a homeless woman of fifty-nine, Dorothy Keeler. Around this time, the police, who so far had failed to come up with any solutions to the crimes, began to suspect a serial killer, and the press dubbed the murderer 'the Genessee River Killer'. There was a pattern to the murders: in most of the cases, the victims had been asphyxiated and the culprit had attempted to conceal the bodies. However, because Shawcross's criminal record was sealed by the authorities at the time, he did not come up as a suspect.

THE SCENE OF THE CRIME

The murders of prostitutes continued, but it was only when police discovered the body of a woman who was not a prostitute that a proper search for the murderer was carried out. This was twenty-six-year-old June Stott, who had been strangled and gutted from throat to crotch. Her body showed evidence of mutilation, particularly in the anal and genital area.

The police now came up with a profile of the killer, and prostitutes in the area gave evidence about a man named 'Mitch' who was a regular customer. The murders continued and the mutilations became more and more horrifying: in one case, that of June Cicero, her body had been almost sawn in half after her death. Then came a breakthrough – police in a helicopter saw a man urinating or masturbating on the bridge near where Cicero was killed. They reasoned that he must have returned to the scene of the crime and alerted police patrol teams on the ground to track him down. When Shawcross's vehicle sped away, they noted the registration number and found that it belonged to Clara Neal, who turned out to be Shawcross's latest girlfriend. From there, it was short work to catch up with Shawcross himself and to arrest him.

Once in custody, Shawcross admitted that he had committed the child killings earlier in his career and boasted about his war record. They also discovered that his police record had been sealed. When prostitutes in the area were shown his photograph, they identified him as 'Mitch', the mystery punter. It seemed that, at last, the police had found their man. And not a moment too soon – by this time, Shawcross had claimed eleven female victims and may have been guilty of other murders that were not accounted for.

EATING BODY PARTS

Under questioning, Shawcross admitted all eleven crimes, adding that he had eaten the body parts of many of his victims, especially the genitals, often returning to cannibalise them days after the murders, when the bodies had been rotting in the ground. Such was his perverted behaviour that when the case came to trial, the defence mounted a plea of insanity on behalf of their client. The trial was shown on television and was watched by hundreds of viewers who were fascinated by the hideousness of his crimes. However, the jury were not persuaded that Shawcross was mad and he was found sane and convicted of murder. He was given a series of life sentences for the murders. Today, he continues to serve out his sentence at the Sullivan Correctional Facility in New York State.

The case of the Genessee River Killer became a controversial one after it was revealed that Shawcross's early criminal record for murder had been sealed, and that he had been paroled early, instead of serving out his original sentence. The authorities were criticised for letting him out of prison and for keeping his record a secret thereafter, which allowed him to remain free and commit murders for many years. Had he stayed in jail during that time, at least eleven women would have lived rather than died – and it is also possible that there were other murders he committed that were never solved.

JOHN CHRISTIE

Serial killer John Christie achieved notoriety in Britain during the 1940s and 1950s because of a string of murders that he committed. What shocked the public was the way in which these happened behind closed doors, without suspicion ever falling on the culprit. Christie seemed like a respectable, quiet man, but behind the peaceful facade lurked a violent killer who for over thirteen years had, quite literally, got away with murder.

VIOLENT AND IMPOTENT

Christie was born in 1898 into a large family. He grew up in West Riding, Yorkshire and later claimed to have been abused by his father. The whole family were violent and domineering. Christie recounted that when he was eight his grandfather died and, on seeing the corpse lying in its coffin, for the first time felt at peace. At school he did well and won a scholarship to high school, where he was revealed to have a very high IQ and a unusual talent for mathematics. He also engaged in other school activities such as scouting and singing, but his fellow pupils did not like him and he remained something of a loner. During his adolescent years, his disturbed nature began to come to the fore; his sexual exploits were failures and he discovered he was impotent. This resulted in hysterical rage and constant hypochondria.

After leaving school, Christie pursued a career as a cinema projectionist, following a lifelong interest in photography. When World War I broke out, he suffered a mustard gas attack and had to be taken to hospital. He claimed that the attack had made him blind and mute, but there is little evidence to show that this was really the case. In 1920 Christie married a young woman named Ethel Simpson, but the relationship was not a success as Christie was violently bad-tempered and impotent, visiting prostitutes to fulfil his sexual needs. After four years, during which time Christie terrorised his wife, the couple separated. Ethel went back to live with her family, while Christie moved to London. It was here that his career of crime began. He stole some postal orders while working as a postman, and received a short prison sentence for this, then committed various thefts and received a longer one. Next, he beat up a prostitute that he was living with at the time, and received a term of six months' hard labour for the crime. In 1933, he stole a car and received another prison sentence; on his release, he contacted Ethel and there was a reconciliation. In 1938, she came to live with him in London at his flat with the now notorious address – 10, Rillington Place.

THE FIRST VICTIM

Whether or not Ethel was aware of it, Christie continued to visit prostitutes, often acting violently towards them. He began to show necrophiliac tendencies and started to associate sex with death, just as he had as a boy. When World War II broke out, he made an application to join the police force, and was accepted even though he had served time in prison. He began work at a police station in Harrow Road and did well, before becoming involved in a relationship with a woman working there, whose husband was away serving as a soldier in the war. When the soldier returned, he found out about the liaison and had a fight with Christie, who resigned from his job.

After that, Christie's emotional life took a turn for the worse and he became more violent and aggressive than ever. This culminated in his first murder, of a woman named Ruth Fuerst, in 1943. He had sex with her and strangled her during the encounter, afterwards burying her body in the communal garden that belonged to the flats where he lived. The following year, he murdered a woman named Muriel Eady who he had met at work. He told her that he had a special medicine that cured bronchitis and gave it to her. Unbeknown to her, the mixture contained carbon monoxide. She became unconscious and while in this state, Christie raped and strangled her, before burying her in the garden along with Fuerst.

HORRIFIC DOUBLE KILLING

This was just the beginning of a long string of killings that took place over the next decade. Next to meet their fate were Beryl and Geraldine Evans, the wife and daughter of Timothy Evans who lived in the flat above Christie. When Beryl became pregnant with the couple's second child, soon after the birth of the first, she confided her doubts about the pregnancy to Christie, who offered to abort the child. On November 8, he used gas to render Beryl unconscious, and then raped and strangled her to death. When Timothy Evans came home from work, Christie told him that the abortion had gone wrong and that Beryl had died. At that time in England, abortion was illegal and both men could have been jailed for performing the operation on her. Thus, Christie convinced Evans to help him hide the body. He then told Evans to go away to relatives, leaving Geraldine in his care. Evans was not an intelligent man and apparently had a very low IQ. He did as Christie suggested, but returned to the flat several times to see his baby daughter. Each time, Christie sent him away without seeing her.

Eventually, Evans decided to go to the police in Merthyr Tydfil, where he was staying, and told them that he had killed Beryl by accident, telling them the story of how Christie had said he could perform the abortion, how it had gone wrong and how they had hidden her body. Police went to the house several times and eventually found the bodies of both Beryl and Geraldine in the garden. At this point, Evans confessed to both murders, saying that he himself had strangled Beryl during an argument and had then strangled his daughter before leaving for Wales. In retrospect, it appears that there was a certain amount of police intimidation and that Evans's story was contradictory, but whatever the truth, Evans rather than Christie was charged with the murders. When the case went to trial, Christie was a key witness and blamed everything on Evans. Partly as a result of this, Evans was found guilty. He was given the death sentence and hanged on March 9, 1950, leaving Christie free to kill again.

THREE PROSTITUTES MURDERED

During the trial, Christie's criminal record came to light and he found it difficult to find work after that. In 1952 he murdered his wife Ethel while she was in bed, afterwards claiming to neighbours that she had moved away. He began to sell his wife's belongings and even his own furniture, leaving just bare necessities to survive on. The following year he murdered three women, all of them prostitutes who he invited back to his flat in Rillington Place. These were Kathleen Mahoney, Rita Nelson and Hectorina MacLennan. After this, he moved out of Rillington Place and went to live in a men's hostel, Rowton House. The unfortunate new tenant of his flat found, to his horror, that there were three bodies in the coal hole of his kitchen. He called the police, and when the bodies were examined, it was found that they all contained traces of carbon monoxide poisoning.

By this time Christie was penniless and homeless, and spent his days and nights wandering around London. Eventually, he was arrested by a policeman and gave his name as John Waddington of 35 Westbourne Grove. However, the policeman recognised him from a photograph and asked if he was, in fact, John Christie. Christie, cornered, had to admit that he was.

Christie was charged with the murder of his wife Ethel, and subsequently with the murders of the three prostitutes. He later confessed to having murdered Beryl Evans. He was put on trial first for the murder of his wife and pleaded insanity. However, the jury rejected his plea and found him guilty. He was sentenced to death by hanging, and no reprieve was given so that police could find out the details of what had happened to the other victims. Thus, on July 15, 1953, he was hanged – ironically, on the same gallows where Evans had met his death.

For many years afterwards, there was a great deal of controversy as to whether Evans or Christie had killed baby Geraldine. Many felt it unlikely that two murderers would have ended up living in the same house; others pointed to the fact that Evans was a liar who had a fierce temper. Today, it seems that we will never know the exact truth of what happened.

EARLE NELSON

One of the most horrifying stories in the history of American crime was that of serial killer Earle Nelson, who went on a murderous rampage between 1926 and 1927, and in the course of just one year left over twenty women dead. The victims ranged in age from young to old, and were killed in different cities across the United States and Canada.

BLOW TO THE HEAD

From the start, Nelson's circumstances did not augur well. He was born in Philadelphia in 1897. When he was still a baby, his mother Frances died of syphilis which she had caught from her husband, Earle's father. Not long afterwards, his father died from the same disease and Earle was left an orphan. The unfortunate child was farmed out to relatives and was eventually brought up by his aunt Lillian. Lillian was a devout Christian to the point of madness, and made sure to instil her fire-and-brimstone philosophy into her young nephew, who developed a religious mania that lasted for the rest of his life. To make matters worse, he was a strange-looking boy with a long sloping forehead, which caused others to taunt him. In addition, he had a violent temper and from an early age showed signs of mental disturbance, such as slurping his food like an animal at table and changing his clothes several times a day, often taking off his clean clothes and swapping them for filthy ones. His aunt and grandmother did their best to help him, but they failed to understand the boy, who became wilder and wilder until at the age of seven he was expelled from school.

Not only did Nelson have to suffer his aunt's hysterical religious fundamentalism and his unusual physical attributes, he also had the misfortune to be hit by a streetcar when he was only ten years old. He had been riding on his bicycle when it collided with the vehicle, giving him a massive blow on the head and rendering him unconscious. For a week he was in a coma and afterwards he was severely traumatised. From that point on he began to exhibit seriously violent behaviour and a range of physical and mental problems. One of the symptoms of his condition manifested itself as extreme sexual violence and, as a young man, he attempted to rape a neighbour's daughter. This attack resulted in his being taken to a mental hospital, where he spent several years.

THE DARK STRANGLER

He ran away many times from the home, adopting a variety of pseudonyms each time. As a young adult, he had a voracious sexual appetite, frequenting prostitutes, a habit he had indulged in since the age of fifteen. When he came out of the home and back to his aunt's house, he began to drink a great deal and often talked to himself, reporting that he was hearing voices. He was clearly very disturbed by this time, but his aunt, although she was fond of him, was afraid of him and did not know how to deal with the situation.

Eventually, Earle left his aunt's home and began to wander about the United States on his own. He survived by taking odd jobs and committing petty thefts, sleeping rough in abandoned houses. It was not long before he was arrested and, at the age of eighteen, found himself in the notorious San Quentin jail. On his release, he returned to his aunt's house once more and got married to a fifty-eight-year-old woman called Mary Martin but the relationship lasted only a few months. Nelson had descended into madness, talking to himself and constantly demanding sexual gratification, often masturbating in front of her when she did not comply with his wishes. Soon, he tired of her and set off on his wanderings again – this time with murder in mind.

Nelson's first victim was twelve-year-old Mary Summers, who was playing at her home on May 19, 1921. Pretending to be a plumber, Nelson gained entry to the house and tried to strangle the girl in the basement. However, Mary fought back and screamed loudly so that her older brother came to her rescue. Charles Summers and Nelson went out into the street and fought, until Nelson brought him down with a blow and ran away while he was lying on the ground.

The police were called and before long, Nelson was found. He looked very rough, having scratches all over his face. Once inside the jail, it became clear that the authorities were dealing with a madman. He is said to have plucked his eyebrows with his fingernails, so that there was no hair left, and started to howl at the wall, thinking that he could see faces on it. Not surprisingly, he was sent to the city hospital for psychiatric treatment. When Mary visited him there, she learned that he had been in and out of mental hospitals from a young age, which no one had ever told her before she married him.

While in hospital, Nelson was assessed as being extremely dangerous, both to himself and to his wife. It appeared that he was now suffering from dementia as a result of syphilis. He was ordered to be taken back to the state mental hospital but, as he had done in the past, he escaped.

Between February 1926 and June 1927, Nelson murdered twenty-two known victims in a killing spree that shocked America, becoming known as the 'Gorilla Murderer' because of his tremendous strength and oddly shaped forehead. Another name for the mystery murderer was the 'Dark Strangler'. Most of his victims were landladies in boarding houses. His first victim was Clara Newman, a sixty-year-old woman. Nelson came to enquire about renting a room and ended up strangling her to death. He then quickly moved on and this became his trademark; after killing each new victim, he would move around the country, making it difficult for police to catch up with him. His murders continued until, on June 8, 1927, he went to Winnipeg, Canada, where instead of murdering the landlady of his rooming house, he murdered a girl named Lola Cowan, who was only fourteen years old. He hid Lola's body under a bed in an unoccupied room of the house, following a pattern that he had adopted for hiding his victims.

The night afterwards, Nelson murdered Emily Paterson, hiding her body under the bed in her bedroom. When her husband William returned to the house he could not find her, and noticed that money and clothing had been stolen from a suitcase in the bedroom. Alarmed, he reported her missing to the police but they were unable to help him.

That evening, he knelt down by his bed to pray, only to discover the dead body of his wife underneath it – she had been raped and beaten to death.

GHOULISH FINALE

By now Nelson seemed to be losing sight of what he was doing and leaving clues all over the place for the police to find. The morning after the murder, he went to a second-hand clothes shop to sell the clothes he had stolen from the Patersons, and also visited the local barber's for a shave. The barber noticed that he had blood in his hair. Once again, the police were alerted, but by the time they sent their men out, Nelson had disappeared again. However, they were now on his trail and were able to circulate a description of the killer. Before long, Nelson was recognised and handed over to the authorities. He was charged with the murder of Emily Paterson and went to court in Winnipeg on November 1, 1927, to be tried for the murder.

Nelson's lawyers pleaded his insanity and it was clear that he was far from being in his right mind. His aunt Lillian gave evidence that this was the case, as well as his former wife. However, despite the fact that he was clearly completely insane, after four days of the trial he was found guilty of murder. The death sentence was the penalty for his crime and he was hanged in Winnipeg on January 13, 1928. In a ghoulish ending to the story, he appeared to remain alive for eleven minutes after the hanging, struggling to catch his breath and writhing in agony.

After his execution, the death toll of his victims became clear and it was found that he had murdered women all over the United States, ranging in age between sixty and fourteen. In one case, he appeared also to have strangled the baby of a woman named Germania Harpin in Kansas City. (He also strangled Mrs Harpin.) His killings took place in San Francisco, San José, Santa Barbara, Oakland, Portland, Seattle, Kansas City, Buffalo, Philadelphia, Detroit and Chicago. In Winnipeg, Canada, he killed his last victims. To this day, the extent of the killings, and his travels, which took place over a single year, still remains a shocking story of how one man's rage left a trail of devastation behind him.

PART THREE

WICKED TEAMS

LUCAS AND TOOLE

Henry Lee Lucas and Ottis Toole joined forces to become possibly the deadliest serial murder team ever encountered. However, this title could easily be disputed as they later recanted on their original confessions of over 600 murders. In reality, no one really knows quite how many people they murdered, but there is no doubt that they were both cold-hearted, fiendish killers who were not fit to live in society. They both had childhoods that could only be described as the subjects of nightmares, which would go a long way to explaining their behaviour as adults.

HENRY LEE LUCAS

Henry Lucas was born on August 23, 1936, in Blackburg, Virginia. His parents were both alcoholics, who brewed bootleg whisky as a sideline. His mother Viola ruled the household with a rod of iron and used to prostitute herself to earn some extra money. His father, Anderson, had lost both his legs in a train accident and spent his days trying to drown his misery in alcohol. Henry was one of nine children, although the majority were farmed out to relatives and foster homes over the years, but Henry was not to be so fortunate. He was one of the children that stayed at home but had to put up with the wrath of his mother. For some reason she seemed to despise Henry as soon as he was born and he spent his days trying to avoid the vicious beatings and violent outbursts that he suffered alongside his browbeaten father.

Henry and his father had witnessed a stream of men sharing Viola's bed until Anderson snapped. Finding it too much to bear, he crawled out into the snow where he remained for the rest of the night. The experience killed him as he contracted pneumonia, which left Henry the sole recipient of his mother's cruelty.

Subjected to constant abuse, both verbal and physical, Henry soon learned that life was worth nought. On occasion he would bring a pet home to give him something to love, but his mother would snatch it away and kill it, leaving the young boy distraught. On one occasion Henry gashed his eye while reportedly playing with a knife, but Viola left him to suffer until the withered eye became so bad it had to be surgically removed and replaced with a glass one. Henry lay semi-conscious for three days after he received a severe beating from his mother, and would probably have died had not his live-in 'Uncle Bernie' taken pity on him, driving him to the local hospital for treatment. It was the same 'Uncle' that introduced the young Henry to bestiality. He showed him how to torture and rape the unfortunate animals before they were finally killed.

Henry soon tired of animals and wanted to see what it was like to have sex with a girl. At the age of fifteen he picked up a girl and attempted to rape her. However, she resisted his clumsy fumbling and he had to resort to strangling her and then burying her body in the woods near Harrisburg, Virginia. The disappearance of seventeen-year-old Laura Burnley remained unsolved until Henry eventually confessed to her murder in 1983.

In June 1954, Henry spent a few years in prison following a series of local burglaries, finally being discharged on September 2, 1959. He went to live with his half-sister in Tecumseh, Michigan, but life took another turn for the worse when his mother, now seventy-four years old, turned up on his doorstep in January 1960. She constantly nagged him to return home with her, which was something Henry definitely wasn't prepared to do. One evening the argument reached a climax after a bout of heavy drinking, and Viola struck out at Henry with a broom. For the first time in his life Henry retaliated and killed his mother with a knife.

Henry was arrested five days later and confessed to the murder and even bragged about raping his mother's corpse, which is something he allegedly made up to shock his interrogators. He was given a prison sentence but within two months was deemed to be criminally insane and was moved to Ionia's state hospital. He stayed there until April 1966 and was eventually paroled from prison in 1970, returning to Tecumseh to live with relatives.

Henry was back in prison within the year for molesting two teenage girls but was released back into society in August 1975. While working for a brief spell at a mushroom farm, Henry met and married Betty, who was the widow of one of his cousins. They moved to Maryland but the marriage was doomed from the start, and Betty divorced Henry on the grounds that he had molested his stepdaughters.

PERFECT PARTNERS

According to Henry's own confessions, it was during this period that his 'career' really took off and he allegedly committed murder after murder as the mood took hold. Towards the end of 1976 he met his partner in crime, Ottis Toole, at a soup kitchen in Jacksonville, Florida. Ottis's reputation was no better than his own and the couple hit it off right from the start. Ottis, who had a very low IQ, had been classified as retarded, and had suffered a strange childhood to say the least. His father was an alcoholic, his mother was a religious fanatic, and his sister used to dress him up in girl's clothes because she supposedly wanted a sister to play with as opposed to a little brother. His confusion as to his role in life was further exacerbated by his grandmother who was a Satanist, often being taken as a young boy to graveyards to fetch human body parts for use in her 'magic charms'. Although Ottis repeatedly ran away from home, he always seemed to drift back and as he grew into his teenage years he started to suffer from uncontrollable seizures.

By the time the two men met, Ottis was a homosexual, an arsonist and, according to him, already a serial killer and they spent hours swapping their grisly stories. Over the next six years the two men spent their time together as friends, lovers and murderers, wreaking havoc wherever they went. They picked up hitchhikers along the motorways, all of whom, according to the Henry and Ottis 'ended up dead'.

Finding himself homeless after his divorce, Henry moved in with the Toole family where he was introduced to Ottis's niece and nephew Frieda and Frank Powell. Frieda, who called herself Becky, was only ten years old, but Henry started to form a very strong affection for the child which soon turned into a sexual relationship. When she was placed in a juvenile home with her brother following the death of Ottis's mother, Henry missed her so much he helped her to escape and the four of them spent a few years moving around. Frank reportedly witnessed such evil acts during this time that he went insane and was admitted to a mental institution in 1983. When the authorities came looking for Becky in 1982, she fled to California with Henry, leaving Ottis to go his own merry way.

In Hemet, California, Becky and Henry met up with a couple by the name of Jack and O'Bere Smart and worked as hired hands in return for board and lodging. In May 1982, O'Bere asked the couple if they would be prepared to move to Ringgold in Texas and look after her elderly mother, Kate Rich. They arrived in Texas on May 14, but only lasted four days before being booted out of the house by relatives for cashing cheques from the old lady's bank account. As they hitch-hiked their way out of town, the couple were picked up by Ruben Moore, who invited them to become members of his religious commune, the All People's House of Prayer. The following day Becky made the mistake of slapping Henry round the face during an argument, and she was stabbed on the spot. Henry dismembered her body and scattered the pieces all around the countryside.

Kate Rich went missing on September 16 and police grew suspicious when Henry went missing from Ringgold the following day. His car was found abandoned in Needles, California on September 21 and he was eventually picked up by the police on unrelated charges. Henry confessed to the killing of Becky and Kate Rich and then spent the next few months bragging about a seemingly endless string of murders and atrocities. Ottis, who was serving time in Florida on an arson charge, was implicated in many of the crimes and added to this he had given the police a string of confessions, too.

Many of their alleged victims actually turned out to be alive and well, making their stories even more outrageous. Henry even admitted to committing murders in Spain and Japan, although there is no evidence that he ever left the USA. Henry was finally found guilty of ten homicides and sentenced to death in Texas for the murder of an unknown female hitchhiker who was given the name 'orange socks' for the only item of clothing left on her body. He was granted a stay of execution in September 1995 so that his claims of false confessions could be investigated.

Meanwhile, back in Florida, Ottis was diagnosed as being a paranoid schizophrenic and his death sentence was commuted to six consecutive life terms. Ottis died in a prison hospital on September 15, 1996, of liver failure.

On June 26, 1998, the governor of Texas, George W. Bush, commuted Henry's death sentence to life imprisonment without any possibility of parole, and he died of natural causes in March 2001 without anyone knowing exactly how many murders he actually committed.

The truth about how many people they actually killed has gone with them to their graves, and many feel that the number became grossly exaggerated due to overzealous police officers wanting answers to unsolved murders. It is obvious both men were victims of untold abuse in their youth and, due to their uncertainty as to how to behave normally in society, inflicted their insecurities on innocent victims. There is no doubt they carried out some indescribable obscenities, including cannibalism on some of their victims, but as to the exact extent of their fiendish behaviour, no one will ever know.

THE HILLSIDE STRANGLERS

Between October 1977 and January 1979, Los Angeles was subjected to a particularly brutal series of killings. The women, mainly prostitutes, were found raped, tortured and murdered, and the killers turned out to be two cousins, Kenneth Bianchi and Angelo Buono.

As mirrored by so many of these serial killers, Kenneth Alessio Bianchi had a troubled childhood. He was born on May 22, 1951 in Rochester, New York, to a seventeen-year-old prostitute who had a serious drink problem. At three months of age Kenneth was adopted by Frances Bianchi and her husband, but he soon started to show some bad character traits. He started to throw temper tantrums and also became a compulsive liar, until his parents couldn't believe anything he told them. Added to these problems, his mother was also diagnosed as 'needing help', when she took Kenneth to hospital when he was only three, saying that he wet the bed and had insomnia. Kenneth's problems got worse and by the time he was five, it was back to the doctor because he kept lapsing into periods of inattentiveness with his eyes rolling back in their sockets. The doctor diagnosed the young Bianchi as having petit mal syndrome, or absence seizures which are linked to epilepsy. The physician tried to comfort his mother by saying that Kenneth would probably grow out of the condition, but he was treated again the following year for the same problem.

By the time he was eight years old, Kenneth was being treated for mental and behavioural problems and at school he was finding it hard to concentrate. He was described by his teachers as lazy and in-attentive and he also showed a distinct lack of emotion, especially when his father died when he was thirteen years old.

Things started looking up for Kenneth when he attended high school and began to date girls. His childhood sweetheart was a girl called Susan, but when he proposed to her she turned him down which left him feeling hurt and inferior. After that he showed very little respect for the opposite sex and he was in and out of relationships until he married a girl called Brenda Beck. The marriage only lasted a few months because Kenneth said she failed to meet his accepted standards and in 1970, at the age of nineteen, he enrolled at Monroe Community College to train as a police officer.

Kenneth, with his heart set on his new career, married again but his wife left him after only eighteen months. He applied for a position with the sheriff's office in 1972, but his application was turned down, leaving Kenneth feeling bitter and rejected once again. He went back to his one true love, Susan, and asked her again if she would marry him, but again she turned him down because he didn't have a stable job. He took a job as a security guard but was often in trouble with his employers for stealing and in 1977 he moved out of Rochester, New York, to join his older cousin, Angelo Buono, who lived in California.

Angelo was seventeen years older than Kenneth and had a bad reputation. He worked as a car upholsterer, but he was also a pimp with a very brutal disposition. Angelo was also a sadist and introduced his young cousin to various sexual practices, which Kenneth seemed to get a great thrill out of. In fact, life was starting to look up for Kenneth as he landed a full-time job with the California Land Title Company and his mother sent him enough money to enable him to buy a 1972 Cadillac. He moved into his own apartment so that he could live with his girlfriend, Kelli Boyd, but she soon found out what a violent temper her boyfriend had and worried about their future together.

Kenneth applied for a job with the Los Angeles Police Department in 1977 but was turned down and for a while he became a drifter, turning to marijuana to try and dull the feeling of failure. When Kelli became pregnant, Kenneth proposed to her, but she turned him down even though she continued to live in the same house for a while.

AN EVIL TEAM

When money was starting to get tight, Kenneth turned to his cousin and they came up with the plan to pimp young girls to work for them as prostitutes. They purchased a list of proposed names from a girl called Deborah Noble and her friend Yolanda, but the girls had double-crossed them and gave them a list of fake identities. When Angelo and Kenneth found out they had been duped they sought revenge. They found out that Yolanda worked as a part-time waitress and she went missing on October 19, 1977. Her naked body was found several days later, with the piece of cloth used to strangle her still tied round her neck. Although the autopsy showed she had had sex with two men just before she died, the police did not consider this to be important as she was a known prostitute.

On November 1, 1977, the body of sixteen-year-old Judy Miller was found wrapped in a piece of tarpaulin. There were ligature marks round her ankles, wrists and neck, and her body had been dumped in a residential area of downtown Los Angeles. Another prostitute's body, twenty-one-year-old Lissa Kastin, was found dumped on November 6, showing similar marks to the previous body. However, due to their high-risk lifestyle the murder of these girls was not taken too seriously, but when the murderers moved on to younger prey it made the police sit up and take notice.

The bodies of two schoolgirls, twelve-year-old Dolores Capeda and fourteen-year-old Sonja Johnson, were found by a nine-year-old boy who was taking out the rubbish for his mother. They had both been brutally raped and the ligature marks on their nude bodies indicated that they had been killed by the same person or persons. The bodies of more and more girls turned up and the police set up a thirty-strong team of officers to investigate the murders. They realised that they had a serial killer on the loose, as the murders all showed the same modus operandi, but they were no nearer to solving the crimes. On February 16, 1978, a police helicopter spotted an orange Datsun car abandoned on a cliff edge. When the police investigated, they found the nude body of twenty-year-old Cindy Hudspeth's concealed in the boot. Although Cindy Hudspeth was to be Angelo's last murder, Kenneth moved away to continue his spree of destruction.

Kenneth left Los Angeles to go to Bellingham, Washington, to be with his girlfriend Kelli and their newborn son, Ryan. In May 1978, Kenneth accepted a position with the Whatcom County Sherrif's Reserve and was given the job of guarding a house while the owners were away in Europe. Up to his old tricks, he asked two young girls, Karen Mandic and Diane Wilder to mind the house for him while he went out to get a part to repair the burglar alarm. While he was showing them where everything was, he dragged Karen to the basement and strangled her. He then did the same thing to Diane and dumped both bodies in the boot of his car. He dumped the corpses in a heavily wooded area, but was not very careful and left a trail of evidence, including a note that said '334 Bayside 7.00 p.m. Ken', which led the police straight to Kenneth's house. When they searched the property they found jewellery worn by some of his previous victims.

THE RUSE

Kenneth was arrested on October 22, 1979, in Washington for the rape and murder of two university students. However, having recently seen a movie called *Sybil*, which was about a schizophrenic who suffered from multiple personalities, Kenneth thought he had found the perfect ruse to avoid the death penalty. He immediately claimed that he suffered from multiple personality disorder and that one of these personalities had committed the crimes. Kenneth was careful when talking to his lawyer, to leave large gaps in his stories, and a memory expert, Dr John Watkins, was called in to take a look at him. Watkins put Kenneth under hypnosis and sure enough as soon as he went under, an evil persona emerged calling himself 'Steve Walker'. Walker quite openly admitted to killing in Bellingham in what had become known as 'The Hillside Murders', due to the fact that many of the bodies had been dumped on the side of a hill. He also implicated Angelo Buono in the killings, and Dr Watkins was totally convinced that he did in fact suffer from multiple personality syndrome.

However, the hypnosis session had been video-taped and LA detective Frank Salerno asked if he could study the tape. He watched it over and over again until he found a discrepancy. He noticed that 'Steve' referred to himself as *he* and not *I,* and he managed to convince the court to get a second opinion. The second psychologist was Dr Ralph Allinson, but he was even more convinced than Dr Watkins, and added that Kenneth was in fact scared of his other persona 'Steve'. They sought a third opinion and this time Dr Orne explained to

Kenneth that multiple personality disorders usually involved more than just two personas. That did the trick. In the next hypnosis session, Kenneth quickly introduced the third persona, a man named 'Billy', and also two others. He was exposed as being a fake and, as soon as he realised that things were getting serious, Kenneth turned evidence against his cousin so that he could be spared the death penalty.

Kenneth explained that the two men had found the prostitutes easy prey; posing as police officers with fake identity badges they had had no problem luring them into their car. The victims were then raped, tortured, strangled and dumped, all in a similar fashion.

ATTEMPT TO DECEIVE

While Kenneth was in jail he received a letter from a twenty-three-year-old woman by the name of Veronica Lynn Compton, asking his advice on a play about a female serial killer. The pair continued to correspond over the next few weeks and they formed a strong bond. Compton suggested that she should murder someone in the same way as he had done, proving that the serial killer was still on the loose. She visited Kenneth on September 16, 1980, and took away with her some of his semen hidden in a rubber glove concealed in a book. However, her murder attempt failed and Compton was arrested in California on October 3, 1980, and convicted of attempted murder the following year.

When Compton's ideas failed, Kenneth decided to write a 'letter to the world' in which he stated that he was the innocent party and that Angelo Buono was the true killer.

During his trial Kenneth tried his hardest to confuse the judge by constantly changing his story, but his ploy was seen for what it was. They were both eventually found guilty, Kenneth of five of the murders and Angelo of nine, and they were sentenced to life imprisonment without the chance of parole. Angelo Buono died of heart failure in Calipatria State Prison on September 21, 2002, at the age of sixty-seven. Kenneth Bianchi is still serving his sentence in Walla Walla State Penitentiary in Washington, the sole survivor of a truly evil killing team.

THE HONEYMOON KILLERS

The antics of this bizarre couple had the newspaper reporters in New York City working overtime to try and keep up with a story that was so perverse, the editors even considered taming it down so as not to upset their readers. The couple in question were smooth-talking Raymond Martinez Fernandez and the emotionally vulnerable Martha June Seabrook. The unlikely partnership was ignited through a 'lonely hearts' column in a local newspaper, but it was a love affair that was soon to spiral out of control, culminating in murder.

RAYMOND FERNANDEZ

Fernandez was born on December 17, 1914, in Hawaii, USA, to Spanish immigrant parents. When he was three years old, the family moved to Connecticut, but his father, with his dark complexion and broken English, struggled to find work. Unable to support his family, Fernandez's father took to drinking, which ultimately led to the young boy taking the brunt of his father's anger. A frail, weak child, Fernandez was a deep disappointment to his father who had always wanted a macho son whom he could be proud of, and this left the young boy feeling totally inadequate and fearful of his dominant father.

To try and compensate for his appalling home life, Fernandez took to stealing and by the age of fifteen had served a term in prison. Determined to mend his ways, Fernandez, on his release, decided to try and make a fresh start and went to live in Spain, the country of his ancestors. When the Great Depression hit the USA in 1929, his parents joined him and were astonished at the change in their son. The shy, underdeveloped teenager who had left the USA, had grown into a handsome, self-assured young man, who had many friends. His genial manner won him many favours with the ladies and by the time he was twenty years old he was married to Encarnación Robles, with a young son of his own. Financial problems caused a rift between the couple and Fernandez decided to return to the USA to see if he could better himself. However, a phone call from his wife informing him that his son was very sick, forced him to return to Spain.

Fernandez found Spain torn apart by civil war and decided to enlist in Franco's army. After Franco's victory, Fernandez went back to being somewhat of a drifter, taking menial jobs as a gardener and a dustman, struggling hard to try and support his family. At the onset of World War II, Fernandez came up with the harebrained scheme to travel to Gibraltar and sell ice cream to the troops stationed there. It was while he was selling his wares that he was approached by a man who claimed to be working for the British Intelligence. The man told Fernandez that he felt he would be ideal for espionage, provided he was able to be discreet and obey orders. Fernandez jumped at the chance and assured the man that he had the necessary qualities, and so for a while he became a low-level spy for the Allies. Although it is uncertain what his activities were during this period he received a glowing testimonial for his services and after the war Fernandez found it hard to return to a normal way of life.

Fernandez decided to take employment on board a ship but a nasty accident changed the course of his life. While working on board, a hatch cover slammed shut on top of his head, cracking open his skull. The accident left him with horrific scars and very little of the thick, black hair that he was once so proud of. He started to suffer from severe headaches and everyone close to him noticed a drastic character change. The once calm and controlled man became sullen and flew into violent rages at the slightest provocation. Unable to work, Fernandez decided to return to the USA and went to live with his sister in Brooklyn. She noticed the change in her brother and became even more concerned when he started to practise voodoo worship.

With his marriage now in tatters and his childhood insecurities rearing their ugly heads, Fernandez found it hard to form a meaningful relationship and turned to the column of the 'lonely hearts' advertisements in the local newspaper. Ashamed of his scars and shiny pate, Fernandez took to wearing a thick, black toupee to cover his bald patch. He met several women whom he wooed with his charm, only to swindle them out of their money and jewellery, in fact anything he could get his hands on. This went on until he came across a lonely, well-built nurse by the name of Martha Beck, a woman who was to change his life completely.

MARTHA BECK

Martha Jule Seabrook, as she was born, came into this world in May 1920 suffering from a glandular problem. This illness caused her to be greatly overweight which resulted in her being constantly teased by her schoolmates. To add to Martha's lack of confidence, her father deserted the family while she was still a toddler and her brother sexually abused her when she was still in her early teens.

Martha wanted to make something of her life and dreamed of becoming a nurse. Her dream turned to reality when she graduated top of her class in 1942, but Martha struggled to get a job and ended up taking second best. She accepted a position with an undertaker, helping him to prepare the corpses, and to hide her disappointment she took to reading the lonely hearts columns. Aware that she was grossly obese and fearing she would be totally repulsive to the opposite sex, she fantasised about meeting her perfect man.

When Martha heard that there was a shortage of nurses in California, she decided to take her chances and left Florida, managing to find a job working at a hospital. Spurred on by the romance novels she frequently read, Martha had an affair with a bus driver. However, when she became pregnant and demanded that he marry her, her hapless lover attempted to take his own life and then promptly disappeared into thin air. Martha attempted to track him down, but the shame of being an unmarried mother made her crack and she had to spend a spell in a psychiatric hospital.

After she pulled herself together, she decided to

pretend she was married and bought herself a wedding ring. She also sent herself a telegram saying that her husband had been killed in action. Now a respectable widow with a new baby, Martha met her second love, a man named Alfred Beck. They married, but he divorced Martha after a year and when she was carrying her second child.

Although her home life had taken a downward spiral, her career had taken a turn for the better. She was employed by the Pensacola Crippled Children's Home and impressed them so much with her caring, attentive nature that she was soon promoted to superintendent. Encouraged by her success, Martha decided to take one more chance on love and joined Mother Dinene's Family Club for Lonely Hearts, which is where she met Raymond Fernandez. She was immediately charmed by the thin, black-haired gentleman and she quickly fell hook, line and sinker. Surprisingly, Fernandez, who was used to using and abusing his women, fell for Martha despite her weight problem and they spent many hours of passion in hotel rooms.

However, Fernandez's ardour started to wane when he realised that Martha had very little money and he decided to return to his more 'prosperous' dates and wrote her a goodbye letter. Although Martha was devastated by the news that her new-found lover had dumped her, she was even more distraught when the Pensacola children's home dismissed her on moral grounds, having learned about her illicit liaisons with Fernandez.

Determined that Fernandez wasn't going to slip the noose, she packed up her belongings and went to his house in New York accompanied by her two small children. Although Fernandez was shocked to find them standing on his doorstep, he did not turn them away and allowed them to stay in his house. However, she could only stay on one condition, and that was that she had to get rid of her children. Still besotted with Fernandez, Martha agreed and shipped her children off to live with some relatives back in Florida.

Fernandez decided to be up front about his swindling practices via the lonely hearts route and instead of being appalled, Martha told him that she would help in the deceit by posing as his sister. The first victim to be taken in by this terrible twosome was a schoolteacher from Pennsylvania named Esther Henne. Fernandez started to woo Henne and despite the fact that their dates were always chaperoned by his rather overweight sister, Henne was convinced she had found true love and agreed to marry her suitor. The honeymoon was as strange as the courtship for, instead of sharing a bed with her new groom, Henne had to share her bed with her sister-in-law, too. Although Henne objected to this bizarre arrangement she soon backed down when Martha became intimidating and the threesome returned home. However, back in New York, Henne discovered that her bank account had been bled dry, but rather than have to confront her husband and his very scary sister, she decided to do a runner instead.

For another two years the scary duo continued to attract gullible victims into their web of deceit. They would drain them of all their wealth and then make life so unbearable that they left without making a fuss. However, one day they met a bird that was not prepared to fly from the nest.

A SINISTER TWIST

Myrtle Young of Arkansas was a middle-aged widow who had been looking for someone to fill an empty void. She felt rejuvenated by the love letters she received from the rather dashing Fernandez and when he proposed marriage she eagerly accepted. They married in Illinois but she became outraged when told that she would have to share her honeymoon bed with her sister-in-law. Unable to pacify the situation, Martha forced her to take a powerful dose of barbiturates and then put the semi-conscious Myrtle on a bus heading back home. However, when the bus pulled in to Arkansas, the rest of the passengers realised that the woman was in no ordinary sleep and called an ambulance. By the time Myrtle Young reached the hospital she was already dead.

Fernandez and Martha Beck continued to inveigle their way into women's hearts, homes and back accounts but problems began when Martha made fanatical demands on Fernandez's fidelity. She would go to extreme lengths to make sure that her lover never consummated any of his 'marriages', but Fernandez found it hard to be faithful and became the focus of Martha's violent temper. Added to her obsession with Fernandez, Martha also held a long-felt grudge against women from her constant taunting as a child and so she egged on her partner into more and more liaisons which gradually took a sinister turn.

In December 1948, Fernandez, using the alias 'Charles Martin', befriended a sixty-six-year-old widow by the name of Janet Fay. Before meeting with Fay, Fernandez made the effort to make himself look older by putting white streaks in his hair and adding makeup to give the appearance of facial lines. By New Year, Fay was totally smitten, so much so that she agreed to hand over all her cash, bonds and jewellery to the man whom she believed would soon be her husband. Fernandez invited her to stay at the Long Island apartment that he shared with his 'sister', but the situation became volatile when Fay told Martha that she was going to write to her step-daughter. Martha flew into a rage and started shouting at Fay. Then Martha grabbed a hammer and starting hitting Fay around the head, cracking open the woman's skull. Blood flowed freely from her head and as she gasped her last breath, her mouth fell open and her false teeth fell to the floor. Martha bundled the body into a cupboard, disposed of the dentures and then went to find Fernandez to discuss how best to dispose of the body. They decided to rent another house that had a cellar and Fay was later buried in the basement and covered over with a layer of cement. After the cement had dried, Fernandez returned to the estate agent and told him that they had changed their mind and no longer wished to rent the house.

Their next victim was Delphine Downing, who was a young widow with a two-year-old daughter. She was a war widow and was delighted that her new beau was not put off by the fact that she already had a family. She introduced Fernandez and his 'sister' to her daughter, Rainelle, and invited the couple to stay in her home. Everything went well until Downing returned home one evening to find Fernandez relaxing on her sofa in front of the television without his concealing toupee. When she saw that he was not the young, debonair man she had believed him to be, she called him an imposter and demanded that they left her home. Attracted by the commotion, Martha came into the room and, although there are differing accounts as to how she died, it is believed that Fernandez shot Mrs Downing through the head. When Martha heard Rainelle crying upstairs, she reportedly went up and drowned the child in the bath. Mother and daughter were buried in the cellar covered by a new layer of cement.

Having carried out their deadly deed, Martha comforted Fernandez by telling him he was still young and handsome, and they spent the remainder of the evening at the cinema. When they arrived home, tired and ready for bed, just as they were about to settle for the night they heard a knock at the door. To their astonishment they faced two policemen who wanted to question them about a woman named Janet Fay.

Martha lost her cool and, being ever protective, told the police to leave Fernandez alone. Before she could protest any further she was handcuffed and the pair were taken down to the police station to answer questions.

THE END OF A FINE ROMANCE

The trial of Raymond Fernandez and Martha Beck took place in the summer of 1949 during a heatwave. The court was full of intrigued spectators as the news of the 'Lonely Hearts Killers' hit the headlines. Martha was incensed by the comments made in the press regarding her size, described by one paper as an 'obese ogress'. She protested by saying that she was still a human being and that insults hurt, and became famous for her outbursts in court.

They were both extradited to New York when it was realised that Michigan could not implement the death penalty and the case went to the jury on August 18, 1949. They were both convicted of first-degree murder and were sentenced to death in the electric chair. They were both executed at Sing Sing prison on March 8, 1951, still claiming their undying love for one another. Fernandez and Beck were a truly terrifying twosome who showed complete disregard for their victims but who never wavered in their devotion towards each other.

In the 1970s a film was made of their exploits called *The Honeymoon Killers*, starring Shirley Stoler as Martha Beck and Tony Lo Bianco as Raymond Fernandez. The writer, Leonard Kastle, managed to stick pretty close to the facts and the film became a cult classic for its daring details about the sex and violence carried out by this unconventional union.

LEOPOLD AND LOEB

The friendship between nineteen-year-old Nathan Leopold and eighteen-year-old Richard Loeb began in the Spring of 1920. They both came from wealthy Jewish families and excelled academically, with outstanding IQs. In fact Leopold was a child prodigy and entered the University of Chicago at the age of fourteen, graduating four years later in law, becoming one of the youngest graduates in the university's history earning himself Phi Beta Kappa status. Richard Loeb was the handsome and privileged son of a retired Sears Roebuck vice-president and was one of the youngest graduates, at fifteen, to enter the University of Chicago. When the two met, Loeb was in his first year at Chicago, struggling to form any real friendships due to the fact that he felt superior to all the other students. Introduced to each other by mutual friends, Leopold and Loeb were immediately attracted to one another, but the relationship was both intense and stormy. Apart, the two young men would probably have remained harmless, but together they drove each other to commit the unthinkable act – the murder of a young boy.

THE PERFECT CRIME

Loeb was obsessed with crime and spent many hours with his head buried in detective stories. In his mind he planned crimes, he dreamt about crimes and he actually committed crimes, although none of these involved any physical harm to another person. In a way, crime became a game to the young man and he started to plot how he could carry out the perfect crime without ever getting caught. Although Leopold was doubtful about Loeb's plan, he was obsessed with his friend, describing him as the 'smartest young man in the world', and eventually agreed that it would be an interesting intellectual exercise. He agreed to go along with Loeb so long as he was prepared to become his sexual partner.

The crisis point in their relationship came in 1924 when Leopold was on the verge of going to Europe on holiday and then moving on to Harvard to continue his education. They both decided they wanted to do something drastic to seal their union and to prove their superiority over their fellow students.

The couple started to plot their crime and agreed that the one essential element was to commit murder. They spent hours discussing how they would carry out their plan, which included the kidnap of a child from a wealthy family and then the demand of a hefty ransom. To minimize the likelihood of being discovered they both agreed that it would be necessary to kill their victim after receiving the money. They decided it would be easier to kidnap a boy that was known to either Leopold or Loeb, so that he would willingly get into their car, and their chosen victim was a fourteen-year-old by the name of Bobby Franks.

CARRYING OUT THEIR PLAN

In truth, Bobby Franks just happened to be in the wrong place at the wrong time. The original victim they had had in mind was a boy named Johnny Levinson, a local lad who fitted perfectly into their planned 'profile'. However, when they cruised around the golf course of Jackson Part on Wednesday, May 21, 1924, in their rented grey Willy's Knight, the two teenagers lost their quarry.

At about 5.00 p.m. a boy left a baseball game he had been watching and started to walk south on Ellis Avenue. Leopold and Loeb spotted Bobby Franks and decided to turn the car round and follow him. Loeb knew Bobby quite well because he was a friend of his younger brother, Tommy, and the Franks family lived opposite the Loebs on Ellis Avenue.

Loeb hung out of the window of the car and called to Bobby, 'Bobby, you want a ride home?' Bobby shook his head and told Loeb that he would just as soon walk, as it was only two blocks away. Loeb thought quickly and then said, 'Wait. I want to ask you about that tennis racquet you were using last week. I was thinking of getting one for Tommy.'

Bobby stopped and got into the car, sitting beside the driver in the front seat. Loeb introduced Bobby to Leopold and then asked if he would mind if they just drove round the corner before going home. Bobby said he didn't mind, unaware of the fate that was before him.

The plan was to knock the boy unconscious using a metal chisel which they had previously bound with tape to make it easier to grip. However, the plan started to go horribly wrong when they failed to knock Bobby out with the first hit and he started to scream. They hit him again and again causing the young boy to bleed profusely, leaving blood all over the seats of the car. They stuffed a gag into Bobby's mouth, wrapped him in a blanket and then pushed him onto the floor of the car.

At this point in the proceedings, Leopold lost his nerve and started mumbling, 'This is terrible. This is terrible!' Looking at the amount of blood that had seeped out onto the floor and seats, Leopold was starting to panic, but the ever cool Loeb started to laugh and joke with his friend in an effort to calm him down.

They drove around and decided they would wait until after dark to finish the job. The plan was to strangle him at a predetermined site, each taking one end of a rope so as to apportion the blame, but this part of the plan was foiled because Bobby was already dead. They drove south towards Indiana to their designated spot and then stopped the car, removing Bobby's clothes.

As it would be a little while before it became dark the couple drove round until they came across a hotdog stand. Leaving Bobby on the floor of the car, they sat and enjoyed hotdogs and root beers, seemingly unaffected by the gruesome murder they had just carried out.

As soon as it was dark, Leopold and Loeb headed towards Wolf Lake and the allocated hiding spot, which was a drainpipe under the railway tracks which connected two lakes. They dragged Bobby's naked body from the car and, before placing it in the drainage pipe, poured hydrochloric acid over the boy's face, an identifying scar on his stomach and his penis. Leopold and Loeb were both under the misapprehension that a body could be identified by its genitalia, which is why they tried to destroy Bobby's gender. They had hoped that the body would simply decompose before it was discovered, but the acid actually only discoloured the skin rather than causing any disfigurement.

Leopold put on a pair of rubber waders he had previously purchased, so that he could drag the body into the water without getting too wet. However, as the body hit the water some of it splashed on his clothing causing him some concern. He pushed the head into the drainpipe first, but, overcome by the fumes of the acid, Leopold failed to push the body in far enough and left one foot protruding. This was to be another major mistake in their supposed 'perfect' crime.

After washing the blood off their hands, the two teenagers drove to a drugstore so that Leopold could phone his father and tell him that he would be a little late getting home. While in the drugstore they got the telephone number of the Franks family from the directory and dialled the number. However, the operator took a long time to connect them and Leopold panicked and slammed the receiver down, fearing that the call would be traced.

Instead they addressed an envelope to the Franks and sent a ransom note marking it SPECIAL and mailing it from the Hyde Park Post Office.

On the way home they made another attempt at calling the Franks and this time got through to Bobby's mother. Leopold told Mrs Franks that his name was George Johnson, that he had kidnapped her son, adding that he was safe and that ransom instructions would arrive tomorrow.

Arriving back at Leopold's house, they parked the tarnished rented car on the street in front of an apartment building on Greenwood Street and then Leopold retrieved his own car from the garage where he had left it earlier that evening. Leopold drove his aunt and uncle home who had been visiting his parents, while Loeb stayed and talked to Mr Leopold. When Leopold returned they had a few drinks and then sat up and played cards until about 1.00 a.m. The two young men left and went to Loeb's house, where they burnt the boy's clothing in the furnace and then made a half-hearted attempt at trying to clean the rental car in the driveway.

Another flaw in their 'perfect' crime was the fact that the chisel had been carelessly flung from the car window as they drove around the streets. This action was witnessed by a nightwatchman, who went and retrieved the object which was covered with tape and blood, and took it straight to the police.

Mr Franks, accompanied by his friend and attorney, Samuel Ettelson, went to the police department at around 2.00 a.m. to report that Bobby was missing.

THE RANSOM

The delivery of the ransom note was possibly the most elaborate part of the whole plan, and actually the part that Loeb enjoyed the most.

The following morning the postman brought the special delivery letter written by Leopold the day before. The ransom note assured the Franks that their son was safe and well and would not be harmed provided they followed their instructions precisely. The ransom note instructed the Franks to secure the sum of $10,000 in old bills which were to be placed in a heavy cardboard box and then sealed securely with sealing wax. Finally, it said that they were to have the money ready and wait at home, without calling the police, until 1.00 p.m., when they would receive further instructions. The note was signed 'George Johnson'.

Jacob Franks went to his bank to withdraw the money while Ettelson called a friend of his who was chief of detectives for the Chicago Police Department. In the meantime, the body of a boy had been discovered in a drainpipe near Wolf Lake and the police called Mr Franks with a description of the corpse. Not prepared to accept that the body was in fact that of Bobby, Mr Franks sent his brother-in-law to the morgue to view the corpse.

Back at the Franks' house the telephone rang and

Ettelson answered it. Leopold, still calling himself George Johnson, told him that a yellow taxi would soon be arriving and that he was to instruct it to drive him to a drugstore at 1465 East Sixty-third Street. Ettelson handed the phone to Mr Franks, who asked the caller to repeat the message, but as soon as he put the phone down in their panic neither men had remembered the address to which they were supposed to go. Leopold and Loeb phoned the drugstore several times, but needless to say Mr Franks never arrived and the ransom was never collected.

INCRIMINATING EVIDENCE

Although they had meticulously planned their crime so that their identities would remain a secret, Leopold and Loeb were caught almost immediately because Leopold dropped a pair of eye glasses close to where they dumped Bobby's body. The glasses were easily traced back to Leopold because they had a special patented spring on the frames which had only been sold in one place in Chicago and purchased by only three people.

Once the pair were in custody they both confessed to the crime in lurid details, showing no remorse whatsoever. The public were outraged that two young men from such privileged backgrounds should stoop to such levels and their trial proved to be a media spectacle.

An eminent defence lawyer was hired by the families of Leopold and Loeb, and Clarence Darrow advised the two teenagers to plead guilty to kidnap and murder, thus forgoing a jury. The sentencing hearing was in front of Judge John R. Caverly, and it was Darrow's job to prevent his clients from receiving the death sentence.

The hearing lasted for three months in August 1924, and public interest remained intense throughout. Darrow played on the fact that Leopold and Loeb were still immature and should not therefore be treated as adults. After twelve hours of summing up, Darrow convinced the judge to spare their lives because of their youth and they were both sentenced to life plus ninety-nine years, with no possible chance of parole.

In prison Leopold and Loeb were kept apart and Leopold was devastated when Richard Loeb was murdered in 1936 by a fellow inmate. When Leopold was granted permission to see his friend for the last time, he described the sensation as: 'I felt like half of me was dead.' Loeb's body was cremated at Oaks Wood cemetery in Chicago, but there is no marker and no official burial site.

Nathan Leopold became a model prisoner and published an autobiography in 1958 entitled *Life*

Plus Ninety-Nine Years. Leopold was eventually paroled that same year after spending thirty-three years in prison. He attended the University of Puerto Rico where he earned a master's degree in social work, graduating first in his class. He married Gertrude 'Trudi' Feldman Garcia de Quevado in February 1961 and spent the next ten years living in Puerto Rico away from the glare of media attention.

Leopold died after ten days of hospitalisation on August 30, 1971, with his wife at his side. Right up until the time of his death, he avoided discussing the murder of Bobby Franks, although he always kept a photograph of Richard Loeb where he could see it. For a couple who wanted to commit the perfect crime, they ended up by performing an act that was riddled with flaws.

BURKE AND HARE

With the ever-advancing breakthroughs in medical science, the demand for human corpses grew steadily and in the early 1800s the number of students wishing to study anatomy increased dramatically. Up until the nineteenth century British law forbade the use of cadavers, other than those of recently executed criminals, and so the devious practice of grave robbing became a profitable business. In fact the practice of 'body snatching', as it became known, was so rife in certain parts of Edinburgh that many graveyards had to be protected by large walls and railings, and some even resorted to having watchtowers erected.

Two Irish immigrants, William Burke and William Hare, aware of the growing demand for fresh bodies and that the price paid for these bodies was rising all the time, devised their own sinister scheme for supplying cadavers to the classrooms – with no questions being asked.

Burke arrived from Ulster to work as a labourer on the New Union Canal in Edinburgh. In 1827 the two men met when Burke took up lodgings at

Hare's lodging house in Tanners Close, West Port, and it was from here that they hatched their deadly plan to make some easy money. They started off by simply robbing graves and selling the cadavers to doctors to use in their anatomy classes, but they thought that the digging late at night was too much like hard work. In truth, the two men hit upon their scheme by pure chance when one of Hare's lodgers, an old army pensioner by the name of Donald, fell ill and died. Although Hare was unconcerned about the old man's death, he was annoyed that he had passed away still owing him £4 in rent.

BIG BUSINESS IN BODIES

Shortly after Hare had called the authorities to come and remove the body, he came up with an idea that meant he could recoup his losses. With Burke's help they removed Donald's body from the coffin and weighted it down with logs so the authorities wouldn't be suspicious. They hid the body until the coffin had been removed and then went off in search of Professor Robert Knox. One of Knox's assistants told Burke and Hare that they were definitely interested in taking the body and asked the men to bring it back after dark.

Later that night they took the body round to Knox's rooms in a large hessian sack and, after a couple of his assistants studied the body, Knox offered to pay the princely sum of £7. Burke and Hare were delighted with their night's work and realised how easy it would be to make significant amounts of money with little effort. So, having found a willing buyer for their bodies, Burke and Hare set to work supplying cadavers to Dr Knox on a full-time basis.

A few days later, another of Hare's lodgers, a miller by the name of Joseph, was also taken ill. Although Joseph was not seriously ill, Burke and Hare decided to help him out of his misery once and for all and gave the man large amounts of whisky until he fell into a drunken stupor. With their victim unable to struggle, it was an easy job to suffocate the poor man to death, leaving no obvious marks on the body to cause suspicion. According to his later confession, Burke appeared to nearly always carry out the murder while Hare was the one to negotiate terms with the good doctor.

Needless to say, Joseph was soon on the doorstep of Dr Knox and this was a process that would be repeated time and time again over the next eleven months. Obviously, with the remainder of the lodging house guests in full health, the dynamic duo had to search further afield for their victims. All went well until they murdered a prostitute by the name of Mary Paterson. When the body was delivered to the classroom of Dr Knox, several of his students recognised her – probably because they had taken advantage of her services – and they started to ask Burke and Hare how they had come into the possession of such a fine specimen. Burke and Hare were not prepared to give any details and were not aware that a close friend of Mary's, Janet Brown, was busy making enquiries into the strange disappearance of her associate.

Apart from the close shave regarding Mary Paterson, Burke and Hare's trade in bodies had gone smoothly, and it wasn't long before they started taking uncalculated risks. They even went as far as approaching two local policemen who were carrying a woman who was in a drunken state back to the prison to sleep it off. Burke approached the policemen and told them that he was a friend of the woman and that he would take her home and make sure she was taken care of. Of course the policemen didn't realise quite how she was going to be 'taken care of' and Burke and Hare earned themselves a few more easy pounds that night.

DOCTOR'S DENIAL

Little did Burke and Hare realise quite what an ally they had in Dr Knox until they brought him the cadaver of eighteen-year-old James Wilson, who was known in the neighbourhood as 'Daft Jamie'. He was a popular character who was known for his entertaining stories which kept the street kids highly amused. In October 1838, Hare happened across Jamie who was walking the streets looking for his widowed mother. Hare told the innocent young lad that he knew where his mother was and asked him to go back to his house with him to wait for her. Burke, who had been taking a drink in the local inn, watched the pair go by and realised exactly what was happening and returned to the house.

Back at the house Burke and Hare convinced Jamie to drink some whisky, but he would only take a few sips saying he didn't like the taste. However, before long he was sleeping happily on the spare bed and the two men attempted their usual method of killing by suffocation, but Jamie proved to be too strong for them and fought back. They eventually managed to overpower the hapless boy and that night Dr Knox handed over another £10 for the latest body.

Needless to say, several of Knox's students recognised the popular boy and started to ask questions. Luckily for Burke and Hare, Dr Knox was not prepared to lose his supply of bodies and denied that the body was that of Jamie. He ordered them to carry on with the dissection immediately, and he made sure they focused on the recognisable deformed foot first to destroy any identifiable evidence.

THE FINAL JOB

The Burke and Hare 'body business' was abruptly cut short when they took the life of a recent arrival to Edinburgh, Mary Docherty. Burke started chatting to Mary in the local tavern and invited the woman to come back to his house. That evening Mary spent a pleasant few hours with Burke and mistress Helen McDougal, Hare and his wife Margaret and another couple, James and Ann Gray, who had been staying at the lodging house. After several drinks, Burke convinced Mary to stay the night at the lodging house and the Grays left after Burke promised to pay for alternative lodging so that Mary could use their room. The Grays seemed quite happy with this arrangement and promised to return for breakfast the following morning.

When the Grays returned the next day they were curious why Mary Docherty was not at the breakfast table and started to ask questions. Helen told them she had asked the lady to leave because she had started to become too familiar with Burke. After breakfast, Ann Gray went to the bedroom to get some socks she had left behind and was taken aback when Burke yelled at her to stay away from the bed.

Later on that same day the Grays were left alone in the house and Ann, curious about why Burke wouldn't allow her near the bed, went to have a closer look. When they found the body of Mary Docherty lying there, they both ran from the house straight into the arms of Helen. When they questioned her about the body, Helen panicked and begged them to remain silent, promising them the sum of £10 a week for their loyalty. However, the couple were outraged at her suggestion and went to fetch a policeman.

Aware that they were about to be tumbled, Helen and Margaret ran off to warn their respective partners, so that the body could be removed. By the time the police arrived that night there was nothing to be found. When the police questioned the neighbours, they told them that they had seen Burke and Hare leaving the house that afternoon carrying a large tea chest.

The police decided to interview Burke and Helen separately and, although they corroborated each other's stories, they slipped up on the time that they said Mary left the house. Burke said she had left at seven o'clock in the morning, while Helen claimed that it was seven in the evening, leaving a twelve-hour discrepancy.

Following an anonymous tip-off Mary Docherty's body was traced to the classrooms of Dr Knox and James Gray positively identified her as being the woman they had seen in the Hare household. The police brought the Hares in for questioning and it wasn't long before the whole sorry story started to unravel.

It is believed that Burke and Hare were responsible for the deaths of between twelve and thirty people, but at the end of the day Burke was the only one to be prosecuted and then only for the murder of Mary Docherty. William and Margaret turned king's evidence against Burke, which in turn sent their colleague to the gallows.

Burke was hanged on January 28, 1829, in front of a large, expectant crowd chanting, 'Burke him, Burke him!' His mistress, Helen McDougall, escaped punishment when the charges against her were not proven.

Ironically, no charges were ever brought against Dr Knox, who had so willingly bought the bodies from Burke and Hare. It is alleged that William Hare died a penniless pauper in London in 1859, no doubt haunted by his past. It has also been said that Helen McDougal turned up in the village of Redding, Stirlingshire, but disappeared a few days later. It is alleged that she was burnt to death in a house that mysteriously caught fire in New South Wales.

One strange twist to this macabre story is that Burke's body went the same way as his victims – it was donated to a medical school for dissection!

THE PAPIN SISTERS

In 1933 France was horrified to learn of the brutal double murder that had taken place in the respectable town of Le Mans. Two wealthy women, a mother and daughter, had not simply been killed by their housemaids, but their bodies had been viciously mutilated as well.

The two maids were Christine and Lea Papin, two sisters and their unprovoked crime took place on February 2, 1933. The case attracted a huge amount of public and media interest due to the brutality of the attack. In fact the media had a field day, calling the sisters such names as the Monsters of Le Mans, the Lambs Who Became Wolves and the Raging Sheep. Suddenly the name Papin was known all over France and what made the case even more strange was the reserved demeanour of the two girls throughout the whole scenario.

Because of the odd nature of the circumstances, the case of the Papin sisters attracted many writers, film-makers and artists, including Jean Genet,

Claude Chabrol, and Ruth Rendell, who in their various works discussed the reasons why the murders might have occurred. Moreover, in France, the murders coincided with the rise of existentialist thought as a popular philosophy of the time. Existentialism emphasised the difficulty of understanding motives within human behaviour, pointing to the inequalities in French society, and bourgeois society as a whole, that may – some speculated – have led to this outburst of violence. Thus it was that two obscure maids, who normally would not have attracted the least amount of attention during their lifetimes, came to occupy an important position in French and European literature and the arts during the twentieth century.

RAPE AT AN EARLY AGE

Christine Papin was born on March 8, 1905. Her younger sister Lea was born on September 15, 1911. Little is known about the girls' early life, except that their father was an alcoholic who treated his family brutally, raping at least one of the girls at an early age. In addition, the girls were forced to leave school early, their education interrupted because of their poverty, and had to go into service as maids.

By the time they were aged twenty-eight and twenty-one, they were working for a solicitor, his wife and his daughter in the town of Le Mans. They were hard-workers, and there was little for their employers to complain about. They spent most of their time attending to household duties, and in their free time, they always went everywhere together. They frequently attended church, and were known in the area as sober, prim young women who kept themselves very much to themselves.

Relations in their employers' household were not exactly warm, but there was not a great deal of ill feeling either. The employers were rather lacking in cordiality towards their servants, and the mistress in particular was rather haughty. The maids responded by being rather taciturn and keeping their distance as much as possible. Occasionally, the mistress of the house lost her temper and scolded the maids, but this was hardly unusual behaviour at the time. There was certainly no sign of any major problem that could have explained the terrible bloodbath that was about to occur.

BEATEN TO A PULP

On February 2, 1933, the mistress of the house returned, with her daughter, to find that there had been a power cut. She established that it was the servants who had caused it, by making a mistake of some kind in the kitchen. As usual, the mistress began to complain, when suddenly, the sisters turned on her. One of them grabbed the mistress, and one of them grabbed her daughter, and as though possessed, the sisters proceeded to tear the womens' eyes out from their sockets with the greatest ferocity. Never in the history of crime had such a frenzied attack been recorded.

Next, the servants seized hammers and beat their mistress and her daughter to a pulp, finishing off by carving up their bodies with a kitchen knife. In a bizarre ritual, they transferred the blood of one body to the other, opening up gaping wounds and pouring blood in, especially around the genital area. Later, Christine said she had done this to discover 'the mystery of life'. By now the faces of the victims were so badly beaten that they were unrecognisable, and their bodies were covered in stab wounds and bleeding profusely. But instead of trying to hide their crimes, the sisters simply left the bodies lying on the carpet downstairs, and without clearing up at all, they went upstairs to bed. Before they retired they washed themselves carefully, taking off their bloodstained clothing and removing all traces of blood from their hands. They then got into the same bed together, naked, and huddled together there until they were found. According to the police, who were shocked to find they had made no attempt to hide their crime or cover their tracks, they did not attempt to resist arrest and were immediately taken into custody.

FITS AND HALLUCINATIONS

Naturally enough, considering the spectacular nature of the crime, the French press and public were agog when the case came to trial in September 1933. The sisters gave evidence, but could give no motive for their crimes. They had no grievances to bring against their employers and could not explain why they had suddenly engaged in this brutal attack. In addition, neither of them gave any indication of being insane. They were quiet and decorous, and appeared to understand what was being said to them. Their main objective during the trial appeared to be to ensure that they each took equal blame for the crimes, and they were very keen that they should be sentenced together. They were both convicted of the murders and, eventually, the jury decided that Christine, the elder sister, should be sentenced to death as the instigator of the crimes.

When the pair were sent to prison – Christine to await her death by hanging – they were separated, and it was then that Christine began to show signs of extreme mental illness. She experienced fits and hallucinations, trying to tear out her own eyes and injuring herself in the process. She was restrained by a straitjacket, and after her ordeal, slumped into a fit of depression before beginning to speak deliriously about what had occurred, but in a way that made no sense at all.

THE MYSTERY REMAINS

In the end, because of her delirious condition, Christine Papin was not hanged but instead was sent to a mental hospital in Rennes, where she died only a few years later, in 1937. Her sister Lea remained in prison until 1941, when she was released. She then went to live in Nantes, and her mother came to live with her there. She was thought to have died in 1982 but film-maker Claud Ventura found out, so he claimed, that she was in fact living in a hospice. By now she was paralysed by a stroke and left unable to speak. In his documentary on the case, *En Quete des Soeurs Papin* (In Search of the Papin Sisters), Ventura produced photographs to show that the old woman he found in the hospice was the same person as the young Lea who had committed the murders. However, because of a lack of documentation, it remains unclear whether she really was the Lea Papin who had brutally committed the killings all those years ago.

The celebrated case of the Papin Sisters became a subject for many playwrights, film-makers and writers during the twentieth century. The play *Les Bonnes* (The Maids) by Jean Genet emphasises the sisters' cruel treatment by their mistress and their unhappiness in the household. As ever, Genet's aim in his work was to show the French bourgeoisie at their most despicable, and to make the point that French society was rotten to the core. Other works of art, such as the play *My Sister in this House* by Wendy Kesselman, the film *La Ceremonie* by Claud Chabrol, and the novel *A Judgement in Stone* by Ruth Rendell, take different positions, and it is clear that the strangeness of the event, and the mystery of the sisters' motivation leave the case open to many different readings. In addition, commentators such as the writer Simone de Beauvoir and the psycho-analyst Jacques Lacan have discussed the fact that these were 'women on women' killings, exploring the bizarre relationship between the two sisters that led them to kill their mistress and her daughter.

Thus, instead of having lived out their lives in obscurity as two quiet, unassuming, churchgoing maids in a small French town, the Papin sisters have become emblematic of a complex web of relations between women and society, explored by French intellectuals and others over more than a century of analysis and discussion. Today, their crime remains as mysterious as it was when they committed it in 1933, because although we know the circumstances of what happened, we still remain largely ignorant about why Christine and Lea Papin suddenly decided to murder their mistress and her daughter in such a hideously brutal, violent way; and, moreover, why they took no steps to cover up their crime but simply declared, '*En voila du propre*' (That's a clean job of it), and went to bed, where they were later found naked in each other's arms, waiting for retribution to descend, as it did, in the shape of trial by jury, incarceration, illness and, finally, death.

IAN BRADY AND
MYRA HINDLEY

The case of Ian Brady and Myra Hindley, known as the Moors murderers, was one of the most shocking in British crime history and has remained in the public memory ever since. This is partly because, many years after the murders were committed, there was a great deal of controversy over whether Myra Hindley should be allowed to leave prison. Even though there were many murderers with a worse record than hers, the way in which Hindley and her lover Ian Brady treated their child victims so horrified the general public that there was a tremendous feeling of animosity towards her. There was also a high-profile campaign by an English aristocrat, Lord Longford, to release Hindley, which again attracted a great deal of attention. However, because of the public's attitude towards her, there were fears for her safety once she was let out into normal society, and as a result Hindley was never released. Eventually, she died in prison.

NUMBER ONE HATE FIGURE

Britain has had serial killers who have killed more victims than Ian Brady and Myra Hindley, but none have attracted so much loathing from the public. None have become so clearly the embodiment of evil as this pair of murderers who brutally tortured and killed at least five child victims in the early 1960s. What shocked the public most of all was the role of Hindley. For up to that time, only men had been known to carry out serial sex murders of children in this way. That a young woman should have been involved, as Myra Hindley was, and that the couple would have used tapes of the cruel torture of their victims to enhance their lovemaking, as emerged at their trial, seemed so utterly perverse that for many years, Hindley became Britain's number one hate figure. It was perhaps unfair, but understandable, that she should have been reviled even more than the main perpetrator of the crimes, Ian Brady.

There is no doubt that it was Brady who instigated the plan to murder the children, and that he was an extremely violent, aggressive and disturbed individual. He was born in Glasgow, Scotland, on January 2, 1938. Circumstances did not bode well for the mother and child. Brady's mother, Peggy Stewart, was unmarried at the time and she found herself unable to support her child, so she gave her baby, aged four months, over to the care of John and Mary Sloane, a couple with four children of their own. Inevitably, this arrangement did not offer the baby a great deal of love and attention. Peggy continued to visit her son for a while, though not revealing that she was actually his mother, but then the visits stopped. She married again and moved to Manchester in the north of England, with her new husband, Patrick Brady. By this time her son was twelve years old.

THE LOVERS MEET

Ian Brady was an intelligent child, but had great emotional difficulties as a result of his family problems and had few friends at school. He was a loner, and not easy to get along with. In his teens, despite having passed the entrance examination to a good school, Shawlands Academy, he began to show signs of disturbed behaviour. He became fascinated by Nazi Germany and by Adolf Hitler in particular. He also took to truanting, missing school frequently. In addition, he began to commit petty burglaries around the area in which he lived. By the age of sixteen, he had been arrested by the police three times and pressure was on to send him to Borstal (reform school). He was only saved from this fate when he agreed to leave his home in Glasgow and go to live with his natural mother, Peggy, and her husband in Manchester. His first months there did not seem to be too troubled. When he arrived there, in late 1954, he took his stepfather's name and worked as a market porter, but before long he took to crime again and was jailed for theft. While in prison, he studied bookkeeping and, on his release, he worked as a labourer. However, by this time it became clear that he was now committed to pursuing a life of crime. In the meantime, he got a job as a bookkeeper with a company called Millwards Merchandising. All went well until the following year when a new secretary began work there: Myra Hindley.

Hindley had been born in Manchester on July 23, 1942, the oldest child of Nellie and Bob Hindley. During the war years, while Bob was in the army, the family lived with Myra's grandmother, Ellen Maybury. Later, when Bob and Nellie had trouble coping in the postwar years, Myra went back to live with her grandmother, who was devoted to her. Throughout her school years Myra was seen as a bright, though not overambitious, child, with a love of swimming. In her teens, she was a popular babysitter.

She left school at sixteen and took a job as a clerk in an engineering firm. Soon afterwards, she got engaged to a local boy, Ronnie Sinclair. However, she broke the engagement off, having apparently decided that she wanted more excitement in life. Ominously enough, that desire was granted when she met Ian Brady.

It was not long before Hindley fell in love with sullen, brooding Brady. Brady himself was not much taken with Hindley, however, and it was months before he began to take an interest in her. However, after a year they became lovers, and Brady began to realise that he had found a partner to share his darkest fantasies. For a working-class man, Brady had unusually intellectual tastes: his favourite books were Dostoyevsky's *Crime and Punishment*, Hitler's *Mein Kampf* and the Marquis de Sade's *Justine*. He also enjoyed reading more popular works about sadomasochism. He apparently saw himself as a kind of superman, not bounded by common morality. Myra was extremely impressed by Brady, and tried to transform herself into the Aryan image that he admired, dyeing her dark hair blonde. She cut all ties with friends and began to spend all her time with her new boyfriend. She was completely under his spell, and when he suggested they begin a life of crime together, she was only too willing to join in.

RAPE, TORTURE AND MURDER

In 1964, Brady decided that they should perform a bank robbery. Myra joined a gun club and obtained two weapons for him but then Brady changed his mind. It was not robbery he wanted to commit but murder. Accordingly, they chose their first victim, a sixteen-year-old girl called Pauline Reade who was a neighbour of Myra's. The couple waylaid the teenager on the way to a dance on July 12, 1963 and lured her on to Saddleworth Moor. Brady raped her and cut her throat. They then buried her there on the moor. Having got away with this crime, on November 11 they abducted a twelve-year-old boy, John Kilbride, from a market in Ashton-under-Lyme. He met the same fate. A little more than six months later, in June 1964, another twelve-year-old, Keith Bennett, was abducted from near his home in Manchester. He too was raped, murdered and buried on the moors. The couple struck again six months later, abducting a girl, ten-year-old Lesley Ann Downey. With Hindley's help Brady took pornographic photos of Downey, which he planned to sell, and made a tape of their torture of the terrified little girl. Finally, Brady raped her and either he or Hindley – depending on whose account you believe – strangled her, before they buried her, too, on the moor. Once again, the law did not catch up with them, and they began to believe that they could continue to commit the murders unpunished. Brady even began to brag to friends and family about the couple's exploits. In particular, he told the story of what they had done to David Smith, Hindley's brother-in-law.

At first, Smith did not believe Brady, so Brady became annoyed and asked Hindley to bring him over to their house on October 6, 1965. There, Smith met their latest victim, seventeen-year-old Edward Evans. Smith was horrified and went to the police the next morning, but it was too late: when police raided the house they found Evans' body there. They realised they were on the trail of a serial killer and began to look for the other victims. After a search of the moors, they discovered the bodies of Downey and Kilbride. They also found a box containing the photos and the tape documenting Downey's murder. At the trial both Brady and Hindley tried to pin the blame on David Smith, but the evidence of the tape led to them both being convicted of murder. Brady and Hindley each received a life sentence. Hindley claimed that she was innocent but eventually came to accept partial responsibility. Brady accepted his guilt and later confessed to five other murders, which remain unproven. In prison, he attempted to starve himself to death. In 2002, he wrote a book on serial killers which caused a great deal of controversy in the UK on its publication. That same year, Myra Hindley died in prison.

FRED AND ROSEMARY WEST

Perhaps the most memorable series of murders ever to take place in Britain were those committed by Fred and Rosemary West. These crimes shocked not only the people of Britain but the world. Nine bodies were found buried under their house, one of them belonging to their own daughter, Heather. Nearby, the bodies of Fred West's first wife and child were also found. But what was most bizarre about the whole affair was that for years and years, the Wests had lived as a married couple with a large family in what appeared to be normal circumstances, so that even their neighbours did not know what was going on in the house of horrors in their street. Today, the house has been knocked down, to try to forget what was one of the most horrifying cases ever to take place in British crime history.

SEXUAL ABUSE

How did such a pair come to wreak such violence

on a string of innocent victims? It began with Fred West, who was one of six children born to Walter and Daisy West in 1941, in the village of Much Marcle on the edge of the Forest of Dean. This was a very poor area, a backwater where illiteracy and incest were still common. Fred was very close to his mother, and it is thought that they had a sexual relationship. He also claimed that his father sexually abused his sisters. At school, young Fred was not successful, and even when he left aged fifteen, he was still virtually unable to read and write. However, this did not seem to him a great problem since, like his father and grandfather before him, he worked as a farmhand.

Like many other serial killers, he sustained a head injury at a young age, which seems likely to have contributed to his violent behaviour. When he was seventeen, he had a serious motorbike accident. After this, his behaviour deteriorated until he was arrested for having sex with a thirteen-year-old girl. However, when his case came to trial his lawyer produced evidence to show that Fred suffered from epileptic fits and he was let off. In 1962, he met Catherine 'Rena' Costello, a young woman with a record of delinquency and prostitution. They moved to Scotland, where she came from, and got married, despite the fact that she was already pregnant by an Asian bus driver. The child,

Charmaine, was born in 1963, and the following year they had their own child, Anna Marie.

FIRST VICTIM

At this point, the family moved back to the large town near where Fred grew up, Gloucester, in the south-west of England. However, family life was unstable, and it was not long before the pair split up. Fred began a relationship with a friend of Rena's, Anne McFall, and by 1969, she was pregnant with Fred's child. McFall wanted Fred to divorce Rena and marry her, but he refused and then grew angry. The couple argued and Fred killed her, dismembering her body and that of her unborn child, and burying them near the trailer park where they had been living. Curiously, he cut off the tops of McFall's fingers and toes before burying her. This was to become a Fred West trademark. Then Rena moved back in with Fred. During this period, he is thought to have murdered fifteen-year-old Mary Bastholm, whom he abducted from a bus stop in Gloucester.

It was not long before Fred and Rena split up again, and this time Fred met a young woman who was as vicious as he was. Rose Letts was born in November 1953 in Devon. Her mother, Daisy Letts, suffered from severe depression. Her father Bill was a schizophrenic who had sexually abused her.

A rather unintelligent child, Rose became fat and sexually precocious as a teenager. When she met Fred he was twelve years older than her, but she fell in love with him. Soon after they got together, he was sent to prison for non-payment of fines, and Rose, not yet sixteen, was left pregnant with his child. On his return from jail, Rose went to live with him. She looked after his daughters Charmaine and Anna Marie, and in 1970 gave birth to the couple's own child, Heather. The following year, while Fred was once again in prison, Charmaine went missing. Rose told people that Charmaine's mother Rena had come to take her back, but in fact Rose herself had murdered her. When Fred came out of prison, he hushed up the murder and buried the body of the child under the house. Not long after, Rena came to find Charmaine. Fred killed her too, and buried her out in the countryside.

BLOODY CARNAGE

In 1972, Fred and Rose married and had a second child, Mae, moving to a house in Cromwell Street, Gloucester. There, they began to use the cellar of the house for perverse sexual games, raping their eight-year-old daughter Anna Marie there. Later that year, they employed a seventeen-year-old girl named Caroline Owens as a nanny. Owens rejected their sexual advances but they raped her. She escaped and told the police, but when the case came to trial in January 1973 the magistrate believed Fred's word over Owens' and let the Wests off with a fine. This was to prove a terrible mistake.

The Wests' next nanny, Lynda Gough, was not only raped but ended up dismembered and buried under the cellar. The following year, Rose gave birth to another child, Stephen, and the bloody carnage continued with the murder of fifteen-year-old Carol Ann Cooper. In late December, they abducted university student Lucy Partington, tortured her for a week and then murdered, dismembered and buried her, in one of their most horrifying murders. After that, their perversions became more and more extreme. Over the next eighteen months they killed three more young women: Therese Siegenthaler, Shirley Hubbard and Juanita Mott. Hubbard and Mott had been trussed in elaborate bondage costumes, Hubbard's head wrapped in tape with only a plastic tube inserted in her nose allowing her to breathe.

By now, the Wests' life had descended into one of horror, but the family were still living in their home, and no one in the neighbourhood noticed what was going on. By 1977, Rose was working as a prostitute, and she became pregnant by one of her black clients. At around the same time, their latest lodger Shirley Robinson, an eighteen-year-old ex-prostitute, became pregnant with Fred's child. Rose was angry about this development and decided the girl had to go. In December 1977, she was murdered, and as the cellar was now full, Robinson was buried in the back garden, along with her unborn baby. Two years later, the Wests killed once again. This time, the victim was teenager Alison Chambers, and she too was buried in the back garden. And then, as far as is known, the Wests stopped killing for pleasure. It may be that they carried on killing and that their victims were never found; it may be that they found other sources of sexual excitement; nobody knows exactly what happened.

BODIES FOUND

In the following decade, Rose had three more children, two by another black client, one more with Fred. She continued to work as a prostitute, specialising in bondage. Fred found a new interest in making videotapes of Rose having sex, and continued to abuse his daughters, until Heather told a friend about her home life. Her friend's parents told the Wests about Heather's allegation and Fred responded by killing his daughter, the last of his known victims. And that was that – until in 1992 a young girl whom the Wests had raped went to the police. When police arrived at the Wests' house in Cromwell Street with a search warrant, they found pornography and evidence of child abuse, and arrested Rose for assisting in the rape of a minor. Fred was arrested for rape and sodomy of a minor. Anna Marie made a statement supporting the allegation, as did the Wests' oldest son Stephen; but following threats from their parents, they withdrew them and the case collapsed.

After this, the younger children were taken in to care by the authorities. While there, care assistants heard the children joke about their older sister Heather being buried under the patio. The assistants mentioned this to policewoman Hazel Savage, who sent police to dig up Fred's garden. A day's digging revealed human bones – and not just Heather's. Eventually, a total of nine bodies were found in the garden, and the other bodies the couple had buried nearby were also found. On December 13, 1994, Fred and Rosemary West were charged with murder.

In a sensational development, a week later, Fred hanged himself in prison with strips of bed sheet. Rosemary was charged with murder and tried to put the blame on Fred, but was sentenced to life imprisonment. Today, she is serving out her sentence. She is unlikely to be released before she dies.

ANGELS OF DEATH

BEVERLEY ALLITT

Beverley Gail Allitt was born, one of four children, on October 4, 1968. Overweight and aggressively temperamental as a child, she suffered from an impressive array of ailments ranging from blurred vision and back trouble to ulcers and urinary infections. She also took to wearing bandages and casts over unseen wounds and even persuaded a doctor to remove a perfectly healthy appendix. Doctors suspected these were all just childish attempts at attention-seeking. They were right, but little did they know just how shockingly these seemingly innocent theatrics would later manifest themselves.

With such a personal attachment to infirmity it was perhaps unsurprising that Beverley chose a career in medicine and despite repeatedly failing her nursing exams she finally managed to find employment on Children's Ward Four of the understaffed Grantham and Kesteven Hospital in Lincolnshire.

It was here that Beverley Allitt was to realise her childhood potential and attack thirteen children, four fatally, over a fifty-eight-day period.

It seemed every child entrusted into her care fell foul of a mysterious predisposition to heart failure. Children such as Liam Taylor, Timothy Hardwick and Paul Crampton, all of whom were admitted with comparatively mild, non-heart-related complaints, who had, after being alone with Allitt, deteriorated to such an extent that they went into cardiac arrest.

Yet surprisingly the finger of suspicion failed to point to Allitt. Her eagerness to attend to the children successfully pulled the wool over the eyes of those concerned. This was no more evident than in the case of premature-born twins, Katie and Becky Phillips. April Fool's Day of 1991 was to take on a sickening twist when little Becky was re-admitted to Ward Four with gastroenteritis and into Allitt's care. Two days later, she returned home where she died in her parents' bed. Concerned for their remaining child, the Phillipses admitted Katie to Grantham. Katie suffered two apnoeic episodes while alone with Allitt who raised the alarm each time. In a shocking misinterpretation of events, the Phillipses asked the nurse to be Katie's godmother.

It was only after the tragic death of Claire Peck that an inquiry was eventually held regarding the suspiciously high number of cardiac arrests on the Children's Ward. Case notes tell us that, admitted with asthma, the fifteen-month-old arrested twice in Allitt's company. The inquest found a high level of potassium and traces of lignocaine in her system leading them to suspect foul play. After tests on more of the victims found inordinately high amounts of insulin, they sought a common link. There was only one in all twenty-five suspicious episodes – Beverley Allitt.

In a search for motive, investigators came upon her childhood bouts of attention-seeking and believed this to be a condition called Munchausen Syndrome. With her actions failing to inspire the desired attention, it was believed her condition had developed into Munchausen's Syndrome by Proxy, whereby injury is inflicted on others to receive attention. Prosecutors at her trial used this approach to obtain their conviction. On May 23, 1993, Beverley Allitt received the attention she deserved; thirteen life sentences for murder and attempted murder, the harshest ever for a woman.

GENENE ANN JONES

Dr Kathleen Holland was excited when she opened her new paediatric clinic in Kerrville, Texas, in 1982. She was desperately in need of reliable nurses and, although Genene Ann Jones did not come with very good references, she decided to take her on anyway. Jones had recently worked at the Bexar County Medical Center, but little did Dr Holland know that there was an ongoing investigation into the 'suspicious' deaths of forty-seven children during Jones's four years of employment there.

Parents were pleased to have a new clinic so close to home, but within the first two months of opening, seven children had suffered seizures while under the care of nurse Jones. Dr Holland, saw nothing suspicious in the number of seizures, simply had them transferred by ambulance to the nearby Sid Peterson Hospital. However, the rest of her staff were not so sure.

Some of the nurses approached Dr Holland with their suspicions, but the doctor simply explained that she was at a loss to understand why so many children had been afflicted. She reassured her staff with the fact that none of the children had died, but she spoke too soon. Fifteen-month-old Chelsea McClellan suffered a seizure a few days later and died while being transferred to hospital. Dr Holland was devastated that a child should die under her care and decided to start making investigations to satisfy herself that this couldn't happen again.

During her investigations she learned that a bottle of succinylcholine, a powerful muscle relaxant, had gone missing. Jones's went to Dr Holland's office and told her that she had found the missing drug, but when the doctor studied the bottle she noticed that the cap was missing and the rubber top had been punctured by a syringe needle. Added to this, when Holland had the liquid in the bottle tested, she discovered that it had been replaced with saline. She dismissed Jones's from her employ and then found out about the investigations being carried out in her former place of employment. The drug she had been using was extremely dangerous, which left patients lying inert, aware of what was going on around them, but unable to do anything to get anyone's attention.

Jones was an ex-beautician who had entered nursing in 1977, working her way round several hospitals in San Antonio. On November 21, 1981, Jones was indicted on charges for injuring four-week-old Rolando Santos by deliberately injecting him with heparin, which is an anticoagulant. Physicians managed to save his life, but their resultant investigation pointed towards nurse Jones and she was dismissed from her job. However, she was allowed to continue with her profession elsewhere, allegedly seeking to become a 'miracle worker' by supposedly saving children in near death situations.

On May 26, 1983, Genene Ann Jones was indicted on two counts of murder and charged with injecting lethal doses of a muscle relaxant to deliberately cause the death of Chelsea McClellan. She was also charged with causing injury in the cases of six other children while under the employ of Dr Holland.

Jones was sentenced to ninety-nine years in prison and eight months later a further sixty years were added, when she was convicted of injuring Rolando Santos in 1981. She was suspected in at least ten other homicides, but was spared further prosecution when Bexar County hospital inadvertently shredded medical records, destroying many pieces of evidence that had been under subpoena by the grand jury.

TERRI RACHALS

The early years of Georgia-born Terri Eden Maples paint a benign figure far removed from the label 'murderess of the century' she would later receive. When she was a young child, her parents divorced and after five years' alleged sexual abuse by her stepfather, she began experiencing blackouts, losing hours, sometimes days, at a time.

Life improved, however, and as an adult Terri married Roger Rachals, a local printer in her hometown of Albany. They had a son, Chad, and became a typical American suburban family, attending church every Sunday, with Terri even teaching in Sunday School. It appeared the dark days of her youth had thankfully had little effect.

Seen as a caring, sensitive member of their community, Rachals went into nursing and after two years' training began work at nearby Phoebe Putney Hospital in 1981 where she was soon regarded as one of the best nurses on the staff.

It was not until November 1985 that hospital administrators noticed a sudden rise in cardiac arrests in ICU, the department to which Rachals was assigned. A subsequent review of records showed six suspicious deaths. Police were quietly notified and post-mortems were performed. Traces of potassium chloride were found in the systems of all six; a drug more commonly used on death row inmates. It now became a homicide investigation.

By March 1986 authorities had focused on Terri Rachals as their prime suspect and when arrested she reportedly confessed to injecting five patients with lethal doses of the drug. Later that month, Rachals was indicted on six counts of murder and twenty counts of aggravated assault against nine patients. Many had received multiple injections, some up to six. This Florence Nightingale was more 'Nurse with a Needle' than 'Lady with the Lamp'.

Terri Rachals took the stand on September 23, 1986, at Dougherty County Superior Court where she recanted her earlier confession, saying she did not remember administering the medication. To corroborate this lack of recall, a psychiatrist testified Rachals suffered from chronic depression and other related disorders that made her unaware of her actions.

On September 26, despite strong evidence against the defendant, the jury found Terri Rachals not guilty on all except one count of aggravated assault. On that count the jury found her guilty but mentally ill. Members of the jury later explained that the prosecution had not proved its case and that her defence succeeded in proving she suffered from 'fugue states' – a condition whereby the afflicted would be unable to recall past events. She served her time and 'the murderess of the century' was released from Savannah Women's Transitional Center in April 2003 after seventeen years' incarceration.

BONNIE AND CLYDE

You've read the story of Jesse James
Of how he lived and died
If you're still in need for something to read
Here's the story of Bonnie and Clyde.

The above is part of a poem written by Bonnie Parker in the final weeks of her life. Ironically, the last verse in her poem predicted this couple's demise in a particularly accurate manner:

Someday they'll go down together
And they'll bury them side by side
To few it'll be grief, to the law a relief
But it's death for Bonnie and Clyde.

Bonnie Parker and Clyde Barrow were sweethearts who captivated the readers of the American newspapers in the 1930s with their bungling efforts to rob banks, small grocery stores and petrol stations. Even when their exploits turned to killing, they still had a band of loyal followers, with many people elevating them to the status of heroes as a massive manhunt was launched nationwide.

BONNIE

Bonnie Elizabeth Parker was born on October 1, 1910, in Texas, the second of three children. Her father died when she was only four, which necessitated a move to Dallas, where the family lived in relative poverty with Bonnie's grandparents. Bonnie was an exceptionally pretty teenager with strawberry-blonde hair and freckles, and just under 5 ft tall. By the time she was fifteen she was married to a man named Roy Thornton, but the marriage was doomed from the start and they parted just a couple of years later. Desperate for money, Bonnie took a job as a waitress but quickly tired of the tedious work, knowing in her heart that there was something much better out there.

CLYDE

Clyde Chestnut Barrow was born on March 24, 1909, in Ellis County, Texas, into a poor farming family. When he was still a child, the family moved to Dallas where his father ran a petrol station. He hated the overcrowded conditions they were forced to live in and vowed as he grew older that he would find an improved way of life. Although not very tall, Clyde grew into a handsome young man who was the envy of many of the local girls.

THE TWO MEET

Bonnie and Clyde met in 1930 when Bonnie was still working as a waitress. Bonnie was nineteen and still married to Thornton, who had been imprisoned for stealing. Clyde, who was twenty-one, had never been married and had already gained a reputation along with his brother, Buck, for theft. The police were keeping a careful eye on the Barrow boys, but Clyde was unaware of this when he went to visit one of his friend's sisters who had fallen on some ice and broken her arm. Clyde couldn't believe his eyes when he first caught sight of Bonnie Parker making hot chocolate for her friend. They were both smitten right from the start and talked into the early hours of the morning. Over the next couple of months they were almost inseparable and Bonnie, not wanting to be apart from her lover, even agreed to drive the getaway car while Clyde and his gang robbed the local stores.

On February 12, 1930, the police caught up with Clyde and he was removed to Waco County to face trial for past crimes. He promised to write to Bonnie and in return she promised to wait for him for as long as it took. Although they wrote regularly, Bonnie missed Clyde with a passion and decided to get nearer to him by visiting her cousin, Mary, who lived in the city. From here she was able to visit Clyde on a regular basis and became acquainted with his cellmate, Frank Turner, who had big ideas about escape. He convinced Bonnie to go to his parents' house in East Waco, describing precisely where he had hidden a gun. If she promised to smuggle the gun into the prison, then Turner said he would take Clyde with him.

With the prospect of being reunited with Clyde, Bonnie didn't need asking a second time and convinced her cousin to drive her to the address she had been given by Turner. The two girls broke into the house and found the gun concealed in one of the drawers, just as Turner had said. The following day, with the gun hidden in her purse, Bonnie managed to pass it to Clyde right under the noses of the guards and then returned to Dallas to wait for him.

Bonnie was delighted when she read the headlines about the jailbreak out of Waco, but with police cars constantly patrolling the petrol station owned by Clyde's father, she was well aware that it would be too dangerous for him to return to Dallas. Clyde and Turner fled to Illinois, where they went back to their old ways of stealing.

However, it wasn't long before the police caught

up with Turner and Clyde, when they were too slow to change the number plates on a stolen car. Once again the two men were returned to Waco, Texas, where Clyde waited to hear his fate. Miserable and lonely, Clyde's punishment was worse than he feared. Because of his recent escape, the judge decided to hand out a fourteen-year sentence of hard labour and he was sent to the fearsome Eastham Prison Farm on the Texas plains. Clyde found the life unbearable under the strict rules of Eastham and the only highlight of his days was when he received a letter from his beloved Bonnie.

Clyde was unaware that his mother had caught the attention of a sympathetic judge with her sob story. She told him that she needed an extra hand to help tend their property as she could no longer manage. Meanwhile, Clyde was instigating his own sob story and managed to convince a fellow prisoner to let the axe slip while they were out on work duty, which resulted in him losing two of his toes. Amazingly, the ruse worked and Clyde was released a week later, hobbling on crutches but with a wide grin across his face.

THE GANG

As soon as he was a free man, Clyde headed

straight into the arms of Bonnie and their love affair was reignited. Even though he was happy to be back in the arms of the one he loved, Clyde could not shake the bitter taste that Eastham had left in his mouth and he decided to form a new gang and seek revenge against the prison system. Contacting old friends and former Eastham prisoners Ray Hamilton and Ralph Fults, the gang set about stealing as much money as they could. Determined that she would never again be parted from Clyde, Bonnie went along and at the beginning it was all one big adventure.

Although the first outing with the gang started out as exciting for Bonnie, when she saw that the boys were armed with weapons she became nervous. While she waited outside, the gang rushed into the shop but a nightwatchman had managed to raise the alarm, and Clyde rushed out of the front door motioning Bonnie to climb back into the car. Directly behind Clyde were Fults and Hamilton carrying money bags, nearly tripping over the threshold in their hurry to get away. Inside the car the men were quiet and ashen-faced, nervously looking behind them to see if they were being followed. As soon as they were clear of the town, Clyde turned to Bonnie and shouted at her to get out of the car, stuffing a load of stolen money into her purse.

'I don't want you involved!' he shouted, forcibly

pushing her out of the car, and she stood open-mouthed as the stolen car drove away taking her lover with it.

Bonnie felt rejected and walked back into town surrounded by the sound of police sirens. Clyde, Hamilton and Fults went their separate ways and laid low for a few days. When Clyde met up with Hamilton after several days, he found out that Fults had been arrested, which meant it wouldn't be long before the police were hot on their heels. They decided to make a run for it, but not before taking a share of the takings from a grocery shop run by John and Martha Bucher.

Once again the two men bungled the robbery and ended up by shooting John Bucher in the chest. As he fell to the floor, his wife screamed, and Clyde and Hamilton grabbed what money they could and fled. Clyde made the decision that he was going to run until the police eventually caught up with him, and decided to get a message to Bonnie that she could either join him or stay behind out of trouble.

Although he hadn't wanted to implicate Bonnie in his life of crime, Clyde was beginning to realise that he couldn't live happily without her. When Bonnie managed to dodge road blocks and police cordons to be by his side, Clyde was over the moon and they vowed they would stay side by side until the bitter end.

OVERSTEPPING THE MARK

Huddled beside Clyde in the front seat, Bonnie was unaware that events were about to take a turn for the worse. After driving through the night with Hamilton and another man by the name of Everett Milligan in the rear, the foursome decided they needed to stop for a break. They had hardly stepped out of the car when two patrolmen approached them for drinking illicit alcohol. Of course the desperate men thought their past had caught up with them and pulled out their guns.

The first patrolmen fell to the ground clutching his throat, while the second fell over with a gaping wound to his stomach. Bonnie, Clyde and Hamilton ran to the car, but Milligan in the confusion was grabbed by several angry men, who held him until the highway patrol arrived on the scene.

Even if the killers thought they had a chance of getting away, when Milligan blurted out the name of 'The Barrow Gang', he had helped seal their fate.

Unsure of where to run, Bonnie remembered that she had an aunt, Nettie Stamps, who lived on her own on an isolated farm in New Mexico. Driving as fast as he could towards Carlsbad, Clyde's erratic speed caught the eye of another patrolman, Joe Johns, who had the forethought to write down the number plate. Johns soon found out that the car had been reported stolen several days earlier and spent the rest of the evening driving round the area with his eyes peeled.

Johns noticed the stolen car parked on the property of Nettie Stamps. His suspicions were immediately aroused as he knew the lady well and she had always been a law-abiding citizen. He decided to investigate and went to knock on the front door. As the door opened and he went to speak he found himself staring down the barrel of gun. Clyde and Bonnie bundled the officer into their car and drove away, while her aunt, who didn't like the men that her niece had become involved with, telephoned the police.

The police started an all-out search for Johns, but when they could find no trace they assumed that he had been killed. However, to their great delight he telephoned headquarters several days later from San Antonio in Texas, where he had been released by his kidnappers unharmed. The media soon got hold of the story and the front pages of the news-papers carried the names of Ray Hamilton and the now infamous Bonnie and Clyde.

BIGGER FRY

Ray Hamilton parted company with Bonnie and Clyde to visit his father in Michigan, but was subsequently arrested. Clyde was becoming short-tempered, weighed down with the severity of the crimes that he had committed and his anger was becoming a problem. When he robbed a small grocery shop in Sherman, Texas, with Bonnie at his side, the owner foul-mouthed him and within seconds Clyde had pulled out his gun and shot him dead. However, there were witnesses in the shop who were able to identify the killer, and the names Bonnie and Clyde were once more headline news.

Aware that they would be caught if they spent too long in one place, Bonnie and Clyde were permanently on the move. Clyde was starting to tire of the small change he was getting from his robberies and decided to move on to bigger fry.

His first bank job was at the prosperous Oswego Bank on November 30, 1932. Bonnie had checked the bank out the day before on the pretense that she wanted to open an account and was able to give an accurate description of the layout. However, their first attempt at a bank robbery was a failure when Clyde was confronted by an armed guard and only managed to grab a mere $80 lying on the counter.

The couple took the risk of returning to Dallas to spend some time with their families at Christmas in 1932. While there, Clyde told Bonnie that they needed to recruit a new member into their gang now that Hamilton was out of the picture. He chose an immature sixteen-year-old by the name of William Daniel Jones, who idolised Clyde and had followed their stories in the newspapers.

However, their latest recruitment proved to be lethal. The time had come to steal another vehicle as the one they had been driving was known to the police and they thought it would be a perfect job for Jones. Clyde spotted a Ford Coupe V-8 parked outside a house on a street in Temple, Texas. Clyde drew up next to the car and told Jones to jump out and see if the keys were still in the ignition. Jones's hands were shaking so much he was unable to start the engine and his futile attempts woke the neighbours. Clyde by this time had lost his patience and had pushed Jones out of the way and had managed to start the engine. When the owner, Doyle, looked out of his window and saw someone trying to steal his pride and joy, he rushed out and managed to grab Clyde by his tie, while his other hand tried to get the key out of the ignition.

By this time the rest of the street was awake and was filling up with people coming out to assist Doyle. Bonnie yelled at Clyde to leave the car, while Jones sat shaking and whimpering, not knowing what to do. Clyde took out his gun and went to hit Doyle in the head, but Doyle managed to grab the end of the revolver which caused Clyde to accidentally pull the trigger. The barrel of the gun had been facing Doyle's chest, and he slumped to the side of the car. Clyde wasted no time in accelerating away from the scene, with Jones still crying beside him.

Everywhere the gang turned the streets were literally crawling with police and on one occasion they were caught in a road trap and had to shoot their way out, leaving another police officer dead. They went from town to town, robbing banks, becoming more experienced with each hit.

TWO MORE MEMBERS

Clyde's brother, Buck, was released from prison in March 1933 and, as his parole officers feared, he joined up with his brother to become a member of the Barrow Gang. His highly-strung wife, Blanche, reluctantly accompanied him, having had high hopes that he would now go straight.

Clyde was overjoyed to be reunited with his brother and decided it was time to take a break from their escapades. They rented an apartment over a garage in a quiet area called Freeman Park. However, some of the neighbours who were watching them move in, were concerned when they saw them carrying rather a large number of guns out of the car. They called the police and they decided to put the place under surveillance. As they watched from unmarked cars they were suspicious of the lack of activity inside the apartment, and the fact that the curtains remained closed both day and night.

Occasionally the 1932 Ford Sedan would leave the premises, notably on the night of a local bank robbery. When they realised that the occupants of the apartment fitted the descriptions of the Barrow Gang, the police decided to make their move. They blocked the exits from the apartment and placed cars in strategic positions to stop them from driving away. Clyde heard a sound outside the window and looked out, then turned and yelled to the others that the law were outside.

A gun battle broke out and Blanche ran round the apartment screaming at the top of her voice, completely out of control. Clyde motioned to the others to head towards the garage using an inside staircase. Once inside the garage, Clyde pushed the others into the car, but Blanche managed to escape from Buck's grasp and made a dash for it out of the back door. Clyde yelled to his brother that they would pick her up outside and then drove the car as hard as he could through the garage doors. They rammed the barricade of police who scattered left and right, and as they swerved the corner Buck opened the back door of the car and dragged Blanche inside as she was running, still screaming, down the road. They all escaped unharmed, with the exception of Jones who had been wounded in the shoot-out.

Exhausted, desperate and disconsolate, the Barrow Gang were once again on the run. They were constantly on the search for somewhere to sleep or eat without being spotted, and tempers were frayed.

THE ACCIDENT

With an exhausted Clyde behind the wheel, the occupants of the car all missed the sign warning them of maintenance work ahead. A bridge over a small gully had been removed for repair work, and by the time they saw the gaping hole it was too late. Clyde braked as hard as he could, but the car spun sideways and dropped into the ravine. The car rolled and trapped Bonnie underneath. Within seconds the car burst into flames and the rest of the gang struggled to free Bonnie from the wreckage. Miraculously, they managed to get her out just as the car exploded, but not without Bonnie suffering third-degree burns to her left leg.

A local farmer, Tom Pritchard, had seen the accident and rushed over to help the occupants of the car. He carried Bonnie back to his house and placed her in one of his beds, but as he laid her down he realised the men had guns inside their belts. He then recognised Bonnie's face as being the girl on the wanted poster which had been posted up in the local town hall.

As the farmer's wife attended to Bonnie's wounds, her husband crept out of the house and went to a neighbour's farm to alert the police. Clyde was suspicious and gathered the gang together, stealing the Pritchards' car, despite the fact that Bonnie was still crying in pain.

Back on the road, hungry, with no money and Bonnie in need of urgent medical attention, Clyde realised that he needed to take a major risk. He took Bonnie to a nearby doctor and told him that she had burned herself on an oil stove. The doctor patched Bonnie up as best he could, but advised that she should be taken to hospital as her condition could become critical.

Clyde decided to rent two cabins near Platte City, Missouri, and hold out there until Bonnie was well enough to travel. Although Clyde did everything he could to relieve Bonnie's pain, she continued to cry for her mother and, in desperation, he phoned her sister Jean, who rushed up from Dallas to be by her side. With nursing from Jean and Blanche, Bonnie gradually started to respond, but their trips into town to purchase bandages and atropine sulphate to treat Bonnie's leg had alerted the local sheriff, who decided to put the cabins under surveillance.

Clyde was keen to keep Jean Parker out of any trouble and drove her back to the station. The sheriff moved his men around the cabins with Thompson sub-machine guns directed at the buildings, determined that this time the gang would not get away. Then all hell broke out as a volley of bullets burst through the windows and doors causing shards of glass to fly through the air and large lumps of plaster to fall from the ceiling. Buck stupidly attempted to fire back, but stepped too close to a window and took two bullets to the head. Blanche, who was standing directly behind him, was sprayed with her husband's blood, and managed to catch him in her arms as he fell to the floor.

Clyde, realising that the situation was hopeless, grabbed Bonnie and placed her in the back of their car which was parked in one of the garages. Luckily the bullets had not penetrated the car and, after going back for his wounded brother, shouted at Jones to fire at the armoured car blocking their escape route. Because the police hadn't expected such bravado, they failed to act quickly enough when Clyde drove flat out at their cordon, and once again the Barrow Gang were out on the open road.

However, Buck was dying, Blanche had been blinded from flying glass, Jones was wounded and suffering from a fever, and Bonnie was still moaning and feverish as a result of her burns. The situation for the Barrow Gang was desperate and the prospect of them holding out against further police attacks looked hopeless. Bonnie was really frightened and, although she tried not to show it, she knew that their time was nearly up.

Just after sunrise, Bonnie caught sight of movement in the bushes at the side of the clearing where they had stopped for the night. The gang managed to clamber into the nearest car but every exit seemed to be blocked by armed officers. Clyde was hit in the arm and he lost control of the car and hit a tree. The now pathetic gang literally fell out of the car and Bonnie felt the pain of a bullet tear through a muscle in her arm. Jones was grazed on the side of the head and, unable to reach another car, they had no alternative but to head into the woods. Clyde was unable to reach Buck and Blanche who were huddled together and, with a sad heart, he had to leave them behind.

Buck died three days later in hospital and Blanche was prosecuted and received a ten-year stretch in a women's jail.

Bonnie and Clyde amazingly managed to escape, hiding out in barns and nursing their wounds, until Clyde had the opportunity to steal another car. Jones, who had simply had enough of being in the limelight, decided not to try and find Bonnie and Clyde and went his own way, only to be later apprehended in Houston.

THE END IS NIGH

After several more narrow escapes and a few more robberies, Bonnie and Clyde decided to instigate a jailbreak from Eastham Prison Farm for their old ally Ray Hamilton. However, Hamilton brought a friend with him, a car thief by the name of Henry Methvin, who was partly responsible for the eventual demise of Bonnie and Clyde. During the escape a guard was killed, and when the names Bonnie and Clyde once again came to the fore, the authorities decided that this was the final straw.

A former bounty hunter, Frank Hamer, was hired to track them down. The final shoot-out came on May 23, 1934, on a desolate stretch of road in Louisiana. Bonnie and Clyde had been to see their parents in Dallas for the last time, and Hamer had been informed by Methvin that they were probably en route to visit his father in Acadia, Louisiana. Methvin's hunch was correct and Hamer and his men, hiding in the bushes, soon heard the sound of the stolen Ford V8 approaching them.

As Clyde came over the hill he spotted the truck with Methvin's father standing beside it, all part of Hamer's devious plan. As Clyde slowed down, Hamer yelled 'Shoot!' and his gunmen opened fire, killing Bonnie and Clyde in a hail of bullets.

RUTH SNYDER AND JUDD GRAY

This is the story of a scheming blonde goading her timorous boyfriend into killing her dull, boring and very rich husband. The media relished every gory detail of the case which resulted in Ruth Snyder being the first woman to die in the electric chair at Sing Sing prison, since 1899.

ALBERT SCHNEIDER

In the main Albert Schneider was happy with his life. His job was editor of *Motor Boating* magazine, which tied in well with his true passion in life – fishing, boats and the outdoor life. However, despite being happy in his working life, Albert still felt that there was something missing in his life. At the age of thirty-two, Albert felt that time was slipping by and he was ready to find a wife. His first engagement, to Jesse Guishard, had ended in tragedy, when she died of pneumonia before they even got the chance to tie the knot.

Albert encountered nineteen-year-old Ruth Brown when he lost his temper with a telephone operator after she failed to put him through to the number he had requested. After shouting profanities down the line, he immediately felt sorry for his outburst and, on hearing the sweet, apologetic voice saying, 'Please excuse me', he felt he wanted to make up for his bad temper. He decided to pay a visit to the operator and was completely captivated by the pretty girl with the long blonde hair as soon as he set eyes on her. Albert visited Ruth on a regular basis, and after only a couple of weeks he offered to help her get a job on the magazine that he edited. Ruth felt that it was a step in the right direction and eagerly accepted his help.

Despite his persistent efforts to seduce Ruth, Albert had no luck in winning her over as she was determined to stay a virgin until her wedding day. In the end Albert proposed, and Ruth was quick to accept, with one condition. She asked Albert if he would be prepared to change the spelling of his surname to 'Snyder' as she felt it sounded less Germanic and more American. Albert was so keen to marry Ruth that he agreed to the change.

Ruth never had any real desire to follow a career; she wanted to get married and to someone who would be able to provide for her. She yearned for the finer things in life and, realising that Albert could provide these for her, she happily quit her job at the New York telephone exchange.

Ruth was twenty when she married her new boss, Albert Snyder, but the marriage was troubled right from the outset. Not only was the age difference proving to be a problem, but intellectually Ruth was not a match for her husband and he started to compare her with his beloved Jesse. Ruth soon became jealous of her rival, even though she was no longer alive, and found it hard to accept the pictures, the boat named after her and the tie pin Albert always wore which bore her initials. Everywhere she turned were reminders of the woman who Albert described as 'the finest woman I have ever met'. Once when Ruth removed a portrait of Jesse from the wall, it ended in a huge argument, with Albert demanding that she put the picture back in its rightful place.

When Ruth found out she was pregnant, she thought Albert would at last be pleased with her, but this was not the case. He was not happy about the situation and told her in no uncertain terms that he had never wanted children. Their daughter, Lorraine, was born in 1918, but the trials of having a new baby in the house drove an even larger wedge between the couple.

JUDD GRAY

In 1923 the Snyder's moved into Queens Village in New York City. Ruth had grown into an exceptionally good looking young woman and she wasn't prepared to stay at home and play the dutiful housewife any longer – especially to someone who didn't appreciate her. She invited her mother, Josephine Brown, to come and stay so that she had a permanent babysitter for Lorraine, and Ruth started living the high life. Ruth loved to socialise and started to attend parties and dances and play bridge. Because of her high spirits, her friends nicknamed her 'Gay Tommy'.

Ruth met thirty-three-year-old Judd Gray when she was dining with some friends at a Swedish restaurant. Her friends introduced her to Judd, who was a quiet, bespectacled man who worked for the Bien Jolie Corset Company. Judd was married and could be described as a nice, ordinary man who liked to play golf and bridge. Although they were an unlikely match, Ruth and Judd started to have an affair. Ruth fulfilled the passion in Judd's life, which was sorely missing in his marriage to Isabel. For Ruth, Judd provided a shoulder to cry on and he listened patiently to her stories of belittlement.

The couple met on a regular basis at the Waldorf Astoria hotel, where they were such frequent guests that Ruth was allowed to leave her baby in the lobby while she went upstairs with her lover. They always registered as 'Mr and Mrs Gray' and as the weeks went by Ruth gradually talked about 'doing away' with her husband. She had been astute enough to take out three separate life insurance policies on Albert, which amounted to a payment of $90,000 if his death was accidental.

Over the period of a few months, Albert became 'prone to accidents' but, despite Ruth's efforts to harm her husband through drowning, poison and gas, he survived until March 20, 1927.

Judd was completely against Ruth's devious plans to kill Albert, and her constant demands soon drove him to find solace in alcohol. He started to consume large amounts to try and settle his nerves but on March 19, he finally gave in to her demands.

THE MURDER

Saturday, March 19, was a cold, raw day and Judd had spent most it drinking, trying to pluck up the courage to go through with their plan. He travelled to Queens Village, where the Snyders lived, via Syracuse and hung about for a long time in the street outside their house. He kept taking sips from his hip flask, almost as if he hoped to be picked up by the police for loitering. But there was no such luck and finally he knew he had to go ahead with their plan. He got into the house through the back door, just as Ruth had told him to do. The Snyders were out at a party and Judd planned to lay low in the spare room until they returned. Inside the room Ruth had carefully laid out a window weight, a pair of rubber gloves and some chloroform – the murder tools they had previously talked about.

Albert and Ruth returned from the party at around 2.00 a.m. Ruth went to put Lorraine to bed while Albert went off to bed himself. Ruth told him she wasn't tired and said she was going to sit up and read for a while. After settling Lorraine, Ruth put her head round the spare room door to see if Judd had arrived safely. She returned several minutes later wearing just a flimsy nightdress, and the pair made love while Albert slept blissfully unawares in the other room.

After an hour the couple grabbed the window weight and Ruth led Judd down the hall to where Albert was sleeping in the master bedroom. The couple stood either side of the bed and, as Ruth pulled back the blankets from her husband's head, she placed a cloth soaked in chloroform over his face. When they felt Albert was in a state of semi-consciousness, Judd clumsily crashed the weight down onto his skull. Possibly, due to his advanced state of drunkenness, Judd's first hit simply glanced off the side of Albert's head causing him to cry out loud and he lurched to grab his attacker. Ruth, keeping a clear head and exasperated at her lover's feeble efforts, grabbed the weight out of Judd's hands and brought it crashing down on her husband's head, killing him instantly.

When the deed was done, the couple went downstairs, poured themselves a drink and then discussed how to carry out the remainder of their plan. They decided they would fake a robbery and set about knocking over furniture and opening drawers and cupboards, scattering their contents over the floor. Then Judd tied Ruth's hands and feet loosely, leaving her enough movement to enable her to reach Lorraine's room, and finally placed a gag in her mouth before leaving the house. Waiting until Judd was safely out of the way, Ruth went up to her daughter's room and knocked loudly on the door. Lorraine opened the door and then removed the gag from her mother's mouth. Ruth told her to run to the neighbours and ask them to call the police.

BUNGLED JOB

Although Ruth and Judd felt they had covered their tracks after carrying out the 'perfect murder', the investigating officers were far from convinced. When they arrived at the scene of the crime they found Albert Snyder in the bedroom, bound at the hands and feet and lying in a pool of his own blood, with a piece of picture wire tied tightly around his neck. On the floor were three bullets and a revolver lay on the top of the bed. Ruth told the police that there was money missing from her husband's wallet, and that her jewellery had also been stolen.

All of the items that Ruth told the officers had been stolen, were soon found to be hidden under the mattress. Added to this they found a pillowcase covered in bloodstains, a five-pound sash window weight and a cheque made out for $200 to H. Judd Gray. Also, after leaving the Snyder house, the police discovered the life insurance policies taken out on Albert secreted in a safety deposit box registered to a Ruth Brown. Not surprisingly, it wasn't long before Ruth confessed. However, she was not prepared to take the entire wrap and tried to blame the whole thing on Judd Gray.

Gray was found hiding out in his hotel room in Syracuse, having taken several shots of illicit liquor to settle his shaking hands. Although he emphatically denied having been in New York, he had carelessly thrown his train ticket stub into the waste paper basket. He also acted with stupidity when he walked away from the Snyder house, by approaching a policeman to ask him when the next bus was due to take him back to the station. With all the odds against him, Judd could do nothing but confess. Just like Ruth, however, he tried to place all the blame on his accomplice, and by the time the case went to trial, the two former lovers were at each other's throats.

THE TRIAL

Ruth and Judd both had separate attorneys arguing their cases. One said that Ruth had been driven to it by living in a loveless home, blaming her lover Judd for pushing her into killing her husband.

Judd, when asked to take the witness stand, played the downtrodden husband and lover, saying that he had been drawn into Ruth's devious plan because of his weakened mind due to an over-powering lust for his lover.

Ruth's attorney tried to say that Judd had taken out the insurance policy on Albert, thus encouraging her to kill for monetary gain. On the other side, Judd's attorney argued that the insurance policy had been all Ruth's idea and added that this was not the first time that she had attempted to kill her husband.

Despite all the play-acting and tears on the part of Ruth, the jury only took ninety minutes to reach their verdict. They were both pronounced guilty and sentenced to death.

THE DAY OF EXECUTION

The case of the two lovers had not only attracted a large media following but it had also encouraged 1,500 applications to witness the electrocutions. The death chamber at Sing Sing Prison could only hold twenty, so many people were disappointed not to witness the end of such a notorious murder case.

Judd Gray was the first to be led down to the death chamber on January 12, 1928, having spent the previous few hours quietly reading the Bible. He went peacefully, happy in the thought that his wife had written him a heart-wrenching letter in which she said she forgave him for what he had done.

Ruth Snyder was led down just minutes later but, unlike her lover, she broke down in floods of tears. She had to be forced into the chair by a pair of prison matrons and she cried out loud as the executioner flicked the switch, 'Jesus have mercy on me, for I have sinned.'

Although cameras were forbidden in the death chamber, the following morning a ghostly picture appeared in the *New York Daily News*, taken at precisely the moment the current entered Ruth's body. This had such an enormous impact on Sing Sing Prison that from that day on, any witnesses were searched before being allowed to enter the prison.

The case received so much publicity that it led to James M. Cain writing a novel called *Double Indemnity* about the Snyder–Gray case. Billy Wilder took the book and turned it into a film, with Barbara Stanwyck playing the part of the murderous wife.

PART FOUR

FIENDISH WOMEN

VELMA BARFIELD

Velma Margie (Bullard) Barfield, the first woman to be executed in the United States since the 1976 reinstatement of the death penalty, was a woman with deep-rooted physiological issues. Although there was some dispute as to her sanity, Velma showed no remorse when tried for her crimes.

Velma was born on October 29, 1932, in North Carolina in the United States. She was born into a large family, the second eldest of seven siblings and the couple's eldest daughter. Although Velma achieved high grades scholastically, she was rejected by her peers. Velma claims that her childhood was marked by rape and abuse, but this was of course strongly contested by her relatives. Velma dropped out of high school and by the age of nineteen was a mother of two children by a man named Thomas Burke. Velma married Thomas and, for a while, it looked like her married life was going to be a normal one. In 1963 Velma underwent a hysterectomy which was physically successful but left her mentally scarred for life. In 1966, after

Thomas was rendered unable to work from a horrific car accident, Velma was forced to find work in a local shop to support her family. It was not long before Thomas became an alcoholic and Velma's stress level shot sky high. She, in turn, took to drugs and set a collision course for a nervous breakdown. Velma's emotional state worsened and she was placed on antidepressants. In 1969, in what later turned out to be very suspicious circumstances, Thomas was killed in a house fire.

Not long after the death of her husband, Velma started to date Jennings Barfield. Jennings had also lost his spouse around the same time, and it is probable that their union began by mutual comforting during their grieving stage. They were married in August 1970, but Jennings was not a healthy man and suffered from diabetes, emphysema and heart disease, causing him to take early retirement. Jennings was also unhappy with Velma's unyielding drug addiction and on more than one occasion he had cause to take her to the hospital after she had overdosed. He eventually left her because she seemed unable to free herself from the vice, but they reunited when Velma promised to cut down on her intake of pills. Unable to maintain her promise, Velma struggled with her addiction and it seemed likely that the couple would soon divorce. A divorce, however, proved unnecessary because on March 21, 1971, Jennings died of apparent heart failure. His death was not viewed as suspicious at the time because of his long-term health problems.

Velma's emotional state had never been so precarious, but it was about to get worse. Her son decided to enlist in the army to fight in Vietnam. The war that was raging in Vietnam was akin to the one that Velma was fighting with her own psyche. Her condition worsened as her drug addiction increased and she educed strife at work. Her boss assigned her to the stock room so that she didn't offend customers. As if her problems were not large enough, her son expressed interest in getting married, a notion that Velma bitterly rejected. She said that he would never be interested in having her around anymore, despite his arguments to the contrary. Her mental condition was so poor that she had doctors attempt to stop her son from being sent to Vietnam, but the pleas were unsuccessful and he was ordered into active duty. Her life spun out of control, and to top off all her compounded problems, her home caught fire for a second time.

Following the sudden death of her mother, Velma became a nervous wreck and she moved in with an elderly couple by the name of Mr and Mrs Edwards. Montgomery Edwards was a sickly man and died shortly after Velma started to cook for them. Dollie Edwards was a healthier woman but was struck down by a mysterious illness after repeated arguments with Velma. She died after serious stomach and back cramps.

This theme of death seemed to be following Velma wherever she went. If that were not enough, a man that she was dating died in a car accident. Velma did well out of his death as he had made her the sole beneficiary of his life insurance which amounted to $5,000. Just when Velma thought her life was improving with the news of her son returning from military service, she lost her job. It was around this time that Velma was arrested after forging a prescription and she got into further trouble with the law when she attempted to cash forged cheques. Velma started caring for another elderly couple, eighty-six-year-old farmer, John Henry Lee and his seventy-six-year-old wife, Record. Velma reportedly grew tired of Lee's conversation and he died after a short illness of the same description as her previous landlords. The doctors assumed that he had died from an airborne virus and never suspected foul play. Never once did the police suspect that Velma had anything to do with the suspicious string of deaths, and a short time later she moved in with Stuart Taylor.

Taylor was a tobacco farmer and was quite wealthy. He was aware of Velma's criminal past and assumed that because she had recently become a better Christian that she was back on the path of righteousness and the law. Even though Taylor enjoyed Velma's company a great deal, he had no interest in marrying her. They spent most of their time attending church functions and during one of the sermons Taylor had to leave and lay down in his vehicle. He was suffering from extreme stomach cramps and died a few days later. His sudden death puzzled doctors and his family and the doctors recommended that an autopsy be performed on him. The autopsy revealed that Stuart had been killed by the lethal drug arsenic and, as always in a murder investigation, the partner was the first suspect.

Before the autopsy results were in, a call was received at the police station from someone who was claiming to be Velma's sister. She told the police that Velma had murdered her husband and several other people, naming the elderly couple who had died as well as John Henry Lee. The police became suspicious immediately and questioned Velma. She denied that she was capable of such a horrible act. Later that week, Velma made a private confession to her son that she was only trying to make Stuart ill and did not intend for him to die. He encouraged her to turn herself in to the police. Velma Barfield confessed to the killings of the Edwards, John Henry Lee and her mother, Lillie Bullard. Later she admitted that the only reason for killing them was to cover up that she had stolen money from them to support her drug addiction. Velma was arrested and tried for murder in the first degree.

The prosecutor, Joe Freeman Britt, was an advocate of capital punishment and wanted Velma tried for the first-degree murder of Stuart Taylor. Velma's defence maintained that she only wanted to make Taylor ill so the crime should be murder in the second degree, which would of course commute the death sentence. The judge allowed further evidence from her previous marriages and the case soon closed around Velma's neck like a hanging noose. No defence was strong enough to prevent the jury from finding Velma guilty of murder in the first degree. Velma showed no remorse at any time during the court proceedings and went as far as to applaud the closing arguments. The sentence was to be death by lethal injection. It was only later in prison that Velma admitted that she was responsible for the deaths of her husbands Thomas Stuart Burke and Jennings Barfield. She had carried out these killings in the same way she had with the elderly couple, John Henry Lee and of course Stuart Taylor. All in all, Velma was responsible for the deaths of at least seven people. There is the possibility that she killed others whose deaths were never suspected as unnatural.

Velma Barfield was sent to prison in North

Carolina to await her fate. During the six years before her execution she became a born-again Christian and even counselled the other inmates. She became famous and many lobbied to have her sentence reduced to life imprisonment. The appeals were denied and soon Velma became comfortable about her impending forced demise. The day before she was executed she ordered all appeals be dropped as she 'wanted to die with dignity'. Velma denied her final meal and, dressed in her favourite pink pyjamas, was wheeled strapped to a stretcher into the execution chamber at 2.00 a.m. Three volunteers activated the lethal injection that was done in two parts with one a placebo. This was done so that no one actually knew who adminis-tered the lethal drug. She asked that her organs be made available for transplant and said the following words:

I want to say that I am sorry for all the hurt that I have caused, I know that everybody has gone through a lot of pain – all the families connected – and I am sorry, and I want to thank everybody who has been supporting me all these six years. I want to thank my family for standing with me through all this and my attorneys and all the support to me, everybody, the people with the prison

*department. I appreciate everything – their
kindness and everything that they have
shown me during these six years.*

Velma was pronounced dead at 2.25 a.m. on
November 2, 1984, in her home state of North
Carolina. She was the first woman ever to die of a
lethal injection and the body was removed by the
ambulance service shortly thereafter. All that
remains of Velma Barfield today is a book of her
memoirs that she co-wrote in prison, *Woman on
Death Row.*

Velma was the subject of many forms of torment
in her life, from self-drug-induced hysteria to the
constant subjection of unrelenting pain. The kind of
pain that she knew would only end with her death.

AUDREY MARIE HILLEY

Audrey Marie Hilley was a master of disguise and deception. Living manufactured lives, posing as non-existent family members and deceiving the people who cared for her most, was all in a day's work for this criminal mastermind. Her crimes were those of someone who could not bear to be out of control and it was only after she lost it completely that she was captured.

Audrey Marie Hilley was born in 1933 to Lucile and Huey Frazier in Blue Mountain, Alabama. Her family was not a rich one but, as most parents do, the Fraziers did their best for their children. Marie was known to be a spoiled child and delivered torrents of tantrums when she didn't get what she demanded. Her parents held high hopes for her and they pressured her to achieve in school. It was not until 1945 when the family moved to Anniston, Alabama and Marie entered high school that she really started to excel scholastically. She began to fit in with her peers far better than she had in their previous town of Blue Mountain, and eventually joined the 'Future Teachers of America' club in school. It was also during this time that she was pursued by the boys for her looks and envied by girls. She was voted as the prettiest girl at the school one year but Marie was only interested in the affections of one boy.

Frank Hilley, a native to Anniston, held Marie's affections and had done since she was around twelve years old when he was still a junior in High School. Frank was not afraid to prove his point with his fists but was for the most part a nice young man. Marie's parents were not happy when she returned Frank's affections even though his family was not dis-respected; they wanted better for their daughter. Marie ignored her family's distaste and continued seeing Frank. Because of the attention that Marie got from the other boys in school, Frank doted on her hand and foot, anything to protect his prize. When Frank graduated from High School he joined the US Navy and while away on assignment his infatuation with Marie increased and during a period of leave in May 1951, Frank and Marie were married.

They moved around the country from California all the way back to the East Coast and back down south to Alabama. It was not long before Frank was

discharged from the navy and shortly afterwards
Marie became pregnant. Michael Hilley was born
on November 11, 1952. Marie was a big spender
and, her husband now working at a local mill, was
struggling to support her zealous buying habits.
Problems came to a head when Frank had planned
a trip for Marie and Michael and there was no
money to buy the tickets with! Their daughter
Carol Hilley was born in 1960 around the same
time that Frank was promoted to foreman at the
mill. It was also at this time that Marie started having problems at work. She was not a team player,
but always managed to be pleasant to her boss. Due
to her unpopularity with her workmates, Marie was
forced to find new work quite frequently, but didn't
have any trouble getting re-employed due to her
excellent references. Frank became a respected
member of the community, joining clubs, while
Marie became active in the local church. Many
people thought Marie was odd because she would
make unpleasant remarks and play power games
when she didn't get her way.

Marie favoured her first child, Michael, and left
Carol out of many things. She didn't like Carol's
tomboyish approach to life and she didn't measure
up to what Marie expected of her daughter. When
Frank noticed this, he went out of his way to spend
time with Carol and they developed a strong bond.

LEFT: *William Hare and (below) William Burke were possibly two of Scotland's most gruesome serial killers. Starting with grave robbing, their 'business' escalated to murder as they sold cadavers to medical schools on an 'ask no questions' basis.*

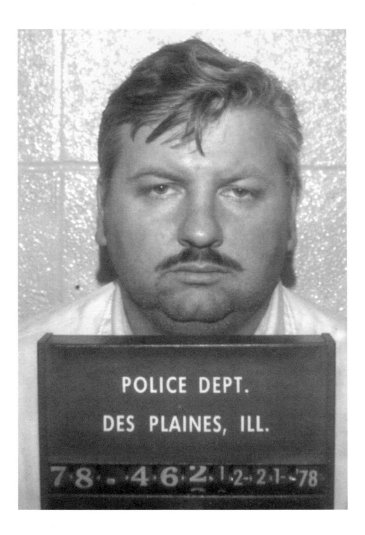

ABOVE: *John Wayne Gacy was an American serial killer who was convicted and later executed for the torture, rape and murder of thirty-three males, twenty-seven of whom he buried in a crawl space under the floor of his house.*

ABOVE: *Andrei Chikatilo, dubbed the Ripper of Rostov, preyed on adolescent boys and girls and maimed them in unspeakable ways, often violating and cannibalising their bodies.*

ABOVE: *Kristen Gilbert was a nurse with grisly motives. Jokingly called the 'Angel of Death' by her workmates, little did they know that she was killing her patients by injecting them with epinephrine, causing them to have heart attacks.*

ABOVE: *It is hard to imagine anyone who spread so much fear as Peter Kürten, the Düsseldorf Vampire. From an early age Kürten relished the taste of blood and this turned into a murderous obsession as he reached adulthood.*

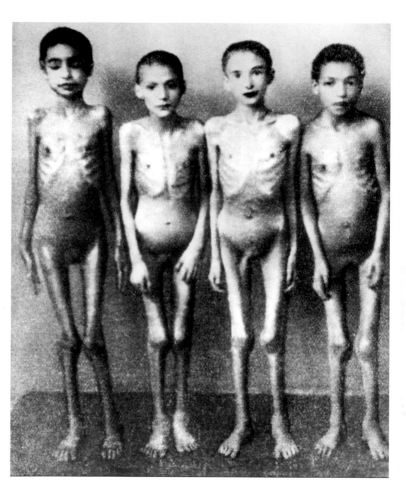

LEFT: *German Nazi doctor and war criminal Josef Mengele (1911–1979) and (above) child prisoners of the Nazi concentration camp Auschwitz, who were used by Mengele for inhumane experiments.*

ABOVE: *Eric Harris (left) and Dylan Klebold (right) examine a sawn-off shotgun at a makeshift shooting range. Just six weeks after this video was made, the two boys killed thirteen people at Columbine High School, the worst school shooting in US history.*

Marie became a great worry to her husband when she started to suffer from panic attacks. Marie loved to play power games with her husband and never ceased to spend their money like water. Frank's concern jumped sky high when he was told of the debts his wife had accumulated. This was not the only embarrassment, as one day Frank came home from work sick and found his wife in bed with her employer!

Throughout 1974 Frank's overall health declined dramatically. In 1975 as his health continued to get worse, he told his sister that he thought that he was dying. The doctors treated him for stomach cramps, but a short time later Frank was taken to the emergency room where they found that his liver had failed. He was diagnosed with hepatitis. Several months later on May 25, 1975, Mike found his father dead in their home, and the cause of death was thought to be hepatitis. Marie collected on Frank's life insurance at a value of $31,000. She was not a happy woman even after showering her family with gifts funded by her late husband's life insurance. Marie complained that her family did not love her and continued to blame her daughter for a multitude of other problems.

It was around this time that Marie asked her son Michael and his wife Teri, who had recently been diagnosed with cancer, to come and live with her.

Teri didn't get along with her mother-in-law and there were frequent arguments. Michael and Teri decided to find somewhere else to live. They found an apartment and the day before they were to move in Marie's house caught fire and they all had to move into the new apartment together. They lived there for some time while Marie's house was being repaired and the bickering continued. The night before Marie was to move back into her own home the apartment next door to Michael and Teri's caught fire and they all had to move back into the house together. This was obviously an intolerable situation for the couple who were doing their best to get away from Marie and her strange behaviour.

Throughout 1977 the police became familiar with Marie Hilley. Michael and Teri finally escaped Marie's clutches and Marie's mother, Lucile, died in January 1977. Marie started to call the police on a regular basis complaining of minor incidents such as a burglary or, on one occasion, a fire in her closet. Marie's neighbour Doris Troy also reported similar occurrences, but had no idea who was responsible. Marie's tales of woe gained her favours from certain police officers who called at her home. Officer Billy Atherton fell for her and the couple began an intense sexual relationship. A short time later Marie and Carol moved in with Mike and Teri in their new home in Pompano Beach, Florida. Marie used

Mike's money in the form of borrowing on his credit card with promises of paying him back later, but it soon became clear that her spending issues still existed.

After a few months of living with her son, Marie and Carol moved back to Anniston. It was during this time that Marie had been buying life insurance for her children. She insured Carol for $39,000 and during the next few months a series of strange occurrences took place. There were incidents such as small house fires and damaged telephone wires, but most worrying of all was that more people were getting sick! Marie became more than just a chronic spender, she also committed fraud, telling a friend that she had cancer but didn't have enough money to cover the treatment. Problems in the Hilley household started to reach a climax in 1979, when Carol became really sick. Her symptoms were horrible stomach cramps, vomiting and fainting. Marie continued to nurse her even after she moved into her own apartment. Doctors were contacted many times during this period and after a series of tests, concluded that Carol's problems must be mentally induced and referred her to a specialist in Birmingham.

Michael Hilley became suspicious of his mother's activities when the bank contacted him advising that she had attempted to cash forged cheques.

Mike started to become concerned that perhaps his father might not have died naturally and decided to take his suspicions to the police. It wasn't long before Marie was under investigation for the murder of her husband and the attempted murder of her daughter. The doctors had found Aldrige-Mees Lines under Carol's fingernails, which are the tell-tale signs of arsenic poisoning, while Marie was being held in custody for passing the bad cheques. The tables now turned on Marie, who was charged with the attempted murder of her daughter. The investigators came to the conclusion that she had been poisoning her daughter for quite some time. The investigation gave cause for Frank Hilley's body to be exhumed, as well as Marie's late mother, Lucile. The forensic team soon discovered that both bodies had indeed been subject to arsenic poisoning. Marie Hilley was bailed to await trial, but ran away on November 18, 1979, on a day that she was supposed to meet with her attorney. She left a note and most of her belongings and was gone. The FBI started a manhunt but the trail went cold very quickly. There was nothing for them to find, it was like she had vanished from the face of the Earth.

For the next three years Marie lived a manufactured existence under an assumed name. She took the name Robbi Martin and married John Harmon in New Hampshire. She told him and her co-workers that she was dying from a rare disease. Her lies were so involved that she even left town for treatment at one point. While she was away she started living the life of Robbi's twin sister, Teri. She got work as Teri and told her co-workers that her sister Robbi was very ill. It did not come as a surprise to her boss or co-workers when she told them that Robbi had died. Teri (Marie) called Robbi's husband to tell him of Robbi's death and that she would be coming to New Hampshire.

It was a downhill road for Marie from there. Her lies didn't add up and even though she managed to find work as Teri, she hadn't anticipated that people around her would start to doubt her stories. The police arrested her at her place of work, following information from a work colleague, and became suspicious about a series of discrepancies in her story. She told them she was really Audrey Marie Hilley, and they suddenly became aware that they had the woman who was wanted for murder.

The trial started, and it didn't take long to determine that Marie had killed her husband and attempted to kill her own daughter Carol. The defence tried to claim that Carol could have been trying to poison herself and discredit her mother in a number of ways. This did not help Marie, however, as the jury did not believe her story, and she was sentenced to life in prison for the murder of her husband, and an additional twenty years for the attempted murder of her daughter. She was sent to the Wetumpka Women's Prison in Alabama. Just three years later she was granted permission to leave the prison for a day and she disappeared.

Audrey Marie Hilley eventually died following a gruelling manhunt that left her very weak. She had gone to a friend's house and collapsed on the doorstep. She died in hospital on February 28, 1987, from a heart attack. There is much controversy surrounding the life and exploits of this black widow, and she continues to attract interest from all kinds of people even after her death. One thing is for certain however, Marie Hilley was a mistress of disguise.

KRISTEN GILBERT

Kristen Gilbert is a woman with deep-rooted psychological issues which spread throughout her life like poison ivy. Once her problems surfaced they manifested themselves in a variety of ways, from stealing to lying and finally to murder.

Kristen Strickland was born on November 13, 1967, in Massachusetts, USA, to Richard and Claudia Strickland, and was the eldest of two sisters. Before Kristen entered High School she seemed to be like any other teenage girl and had the respect and admiration of her friends. She made friends and socialised easily. However, as she started to mature she became abusive and dishonest in all her relationships. After Kristen graduated from High School she attended medical school at Greenfield Community College in Massachusetts. While here her social problems worsened and ex-boyfriends described her as abusive and controlling in their relationships. If that wasn't enough, Kristen took to petty theft, something which she denied when confronted about a stolen blouse that she had the gall to be wearing at the time. It was clear to all that knew her that Kristen had some serious issues.

Kristen married Glen Gilbert whom she had met in Hampton Beach, New Hampshire, and graduated from Greenfield College as a Registered Nurse in 1988. A short time later she began work at the Veterans Administration Medical Centre in Northampton, Massachusetts. While working in Ward C, Kristen got along well with her co-workers who described her as thoughtful and very sociable. Her work performance was rated as top notch according to management, and it seemed that Kristen had found her calling working at the hospital. Settling in with her new husband in their new home and a new job seemed like a dream come true, life couldn't get any better than this!

In 1990 Kristen and Glen had their first child. It was only after Kristen returned to work that the problems in Ward C started to occur. Since returning to work Kristen had transferred to the night shift which was 4.00 p.m. until midnight. Ward C, as if possessed by evil spirits, started experiencing an unusual number of deaths. Kristen was always on duty when these sudden deaths occurred and offered her expert medical attention. This kind of sudden death was occurring with patients throughout Ward C and even with patients who were not in the hospital for life-threatening conditions. The cause of death was determined for many of these deaths as cardiac arrest, but most of the patients didn't have a previous risk of heart problems. Kristen's co-workers dubbed her the Angel of Death but they remained silent and kept their suspicions to themselves for many years.

In 1993, Kristen and Glen had their second child but their marriage was becoming strained. Kristen was enjoying a friendship with another man, James G. Perrault. He was a security guard at VA Medical Centre and was called whenever a patient required resuscitation. He worked during the same hours as Kristen and they became familiar, often going for drinks after work. It was also around this time that Glen Gilbert became very suspicious of Kristen. He told his friends he thought that his wife was trying to poison him. Shortly afterwards James told Kristen that they could not continue to see each other unless she left her husband. In December 1994, Kristen Gilbert decided that her relationship with James was more important than the one she had with her husband or the obligation she had to her children. She moved out of their home and moved into an apartment. Now that Kristen was free of family ties James was quite happy to escalate their relationship and they became more intimately involved. Meanwhile, the body count at the hospital continued to mount. Kristen's co-workers began to talk about the sheer number of deaths that were occurring during her watch.

When the nursing staff of Ward C started to investigate for themselves they made a startling discovery. Vials of the synthetic adrenaline heart medicine Epinephrine were missing from the supply closet. Epinephrine is a drug used under very controlled dosage to regulate the beating of the heart. If wrongly administered it can cause the heart to beat with an abnormal rhythm, even beat too fast to be effective and cause heart failure. On one occasion when a co-worker was experiencing breathing difficulties due to asthma, Kristen produced a vial of Epinephrine from her pocket and offered it as a bronchodilator. Other events of note included a time that Kristen, eager to meet up with her boyfriend James, asked her supervisor if the patient she had in Intensive Care died, would she be able to leave early. When the boss told her yes, the patient died in a matter of hours. In February 1995 after a patient suffering from AIDS collapsed under Kristen's care, the medical staff decided to make their suspicions known. At this time Kristen had been working at the hospital for around seven years and 350 deaths had occurred during her watch.

The police were brought in and they began to investigate Kristen Gilbert, her reputation and work practices. It did not take long to work out her motive and Kristen's carefully maintained house of cards fell around her. The prosecution maintained that Kristen overdosed her patients with Epinephrine so that they would go into cardiac arrest and her lover James Perrault would be called. She did this so that she could impress him with her nursing abilities and to be near to him. As soon as Kristen was suspended from the hospital, the death rate in Ward C returned to normal. It was also during this time that Kristen's relationship with James hit the rocks, and James decided to end their relationship by mid-1996. In response to his decision Kristen took an overdose and had to be admitted to hospital for psychiatric evaluation. During the time she was in care she called James, who was still working for the hospital, and confessed to the murders. James immediately contacted the police about her confession.

'You know I did it. I did it. You wanted to know. I killed those guys,' Kristen told James.

Kristen landed herself in jail after she bought a voice changer and called the hospital with a bomb threat. Once traced and apprehended she was sentenced to fifteen months and it was during this time that investigators started exhuming many of the bodies of Kristen's patients who had died under her care. By 1998 the investigators had enough evidence and charged Kristen with murder. It was a very lengthy trial in which US Attorney Welch II maintained that Kristen had killed to make it easier to spend time with her lover, James Perrault. Once James Perrault testified, David Hoose, Kristen's defence attorney, claimed that there was not enough evidence to convict her. His efforts were in vain because on March 14, 2001, the jury returned their verdict – guilty. The malicious nurse was convicted on three counts of murder in the first degree, one count of murder in the second degree and the attempted murder of two more. Because her crimes were committed on federal property the death penalty was applicable but it was commuted in favour of a sentence to life in prison.

Kristen Gilbert, at the age of thirty-three, was neutralised behind bars but her victims were not so fortunate. It is entirely possible that a good number of the 350 deaths that occurred in Ward C of the Veterans Administration Medical Centre between 1990 and 1995, were directly due to the ministrations and whims of this twisted nurse. Kristen Gilbert is now serving her life sentence with no possibility of release.

DOROTHEA PUENTE

Dorothea Puente is a woman whose life consisted of failed marriages, deceit, forgery and murder. Underneath a benevolent, grandmotherly guise was a woman who would rob from the defenceless and infirm and murder the innocent.

Dorothea Helen Gray was born on January 9, 1929, in Redlands, California into a home that was already a ticking time bomb. Her childhood had barely started when her father died from consumption and less than two years later her mother died in an accident. After her parents' death and before the age of ten, Dorothea had lived with multiple members of her family in and around southern California. Dorothea's teenage years were turbulent ones as she began showing character traits that would remain with her for the rest of her 'professional career'. In 1945, at the age of sixteen, she escaped her foster parents and fled to Washington State where she changed her name to 'Sheri'. It was around this time that she met and fell in love with Fred McFaul. She told McFaul that she was thirty years old and they married soon after in Nevada. During their marriage Dorothea and Fred had two daughters. Shortly after the birth of their second daughter, Fred left Dorothea after he became aware of her habitual lying and the children went into care. Dorothea was again on the run.

Dorothea got her first taste of prison when she was jailed for three years after stealing a series of government cheques. Her life of sudden relationships and marriages continued when she married sailor Axel Johansson. Because of the nature of Axel's work he was hardly ever at home. This gave Dorothea ample opportunity to be unfaithful to him, an opportunity that she exercised frequently. Axel was often told of the strange men who came to their house while he was away on assignment. Despite their difficulties Dorothea and Axel remained married for fourteen years. Like so many marriages, the years were not happy ones and, as if set on a perpetual collision course with failure, Dorothea and Axel's marriage finally crumbled.

In 1968, after the split with Axel, Dorothea opened up a halfway home and soon began an affair with another man. Dorothea married twenty-one-year-old Robert Puente after they decided to go into business together in the half-way home. For multiple reasons, most prominently the fact that Robert was half Dorothea's age, there was constant distress and this eventually led to total business failure in less than a year. The business was not the only casualty, however, as their marriage self-destructed around the same time. Puente's disturbing behaviour continued when, although deeply in debt from her failed boarding home business, she moved into yet another halfway house and took the position of manager. Before long, she married one of the residents, fifty-two-year-old Pedro Montalvo. Pedro quickly realised his new wife was high maintenance and later complained about her extravagant spending habits. By 1978 Puente was back in court for trying to cash forged cheques. On this occasion the judge was more lenient and gave her five years of probation and ordered her to seek counselling.

Dorothea Puente went back to work at her boarding house and a short time later a resident by the name of Ruth Monroe died of a drug overdose. Ruth was known to be a little mentally unstable and the coroner decided that her death was the result of suicide and did not pursue it. Puente was emboldened and continued to steal from the elderly after drugging them heavily. One man later described watching her through a drugged stupor as she pilfered his belongings while he lay paralysed. Around a month after Ruth's death Puente was arrested for these crimes and was sentenced to five years in prison of which she would serve four.

Upon her release Dorothea had no plans to discontinue her spree of murder, theft and deceit. While in prison she had corresponded with Everson Gillmouth, a seventy-seven-year-old who believed that Puente and he were in love. Everson wrote to his family telling them of his lover and that he and Puente were to be married. Within a short time Gillmouth made Puente a co-signer on his bank account. It was not long before Gillmouth had met the same fate as Ruth Monroe and was dumped at the side of the Sacramento River in a makeshift coffin. Gillmouth's body would remain undiscovered for three months and unidentified for a further three years.

Puente's strange fascination with the elderly led her to continue breaking her rules of probation which stated that she was to have nothing to do with the elderly or handle any government cheques. When social services brought more of the elderly, infirm and substance abusers to Puente she accepted her latest victims with open arms. She never bothered to tell social services that it was against her parole and as many as nineteen people were placed under her care in 1987–88. Social services were more than happy with Puente as she was accepting many of the more difficult residents to house, such as the verbally and physically abusive. Unfortunately, Puente continued to take drugs and steal from her home's occupants. Social services only stopped sending the needy to her after she was overheard and reported for being verbally abusive to a client.

Investigators arrived at Puente's boarding house in November 1988 looking for a previous occupant, Alvaro Montoya, who had been placed in the home by social services. After looking in the backyard, one of the detectives, John Caberra, stumbled on what appeared to be a tree stump. On further investigation it was revealed to be a human leg bone. When Caberra informed Puente she pretended to be totally shocked, but she knew exactly what had been uncovered in her back garden. The investigators returned the next day with heavy digging equipment, county officials and numerous coroners. They began to excavate the entire garden, including the area at the side of the house. Puente's carefully buried bodies began to resurface all around her. In the following hours seven bodies were recovered from various places in the yard. During the excavation Puente asked the police if she could go to a local hotel to have a cup of coffee. Not only did the police allow her to leave but they escorted her through the crowd of spectators and press to freedom. Only hours later did investigators realise that Puente had not returned; little did they know she was already hundreds of miles away! The police entered the boarding house and found more evidence that pointed to Puente's guilt. This included expensive clothes, perfume and a roster of how much money she was collecting from the boarders she had killed. Her profits were adding up to around $5,000 a month.

Dorothea Puente, armed with some $3,000 and the need to escape and lay low, fled to Los Angeles without incident. It was not long before she was looking for another victim and found herself in a bar. Puente got talking to a man but aroused his suspicions when she asked about his personal finances – specifically how much he received in social security a month. Although it was not immediate, the man recognised Puente from the 'Wanted' bulletins on the news and he called the police. That night police surrounded the hotel where Puente was staying and arrested her with no difficulty. A few days later she was taken back to Sacramento to await trial. Puente pleaded innocent to the nine charges of murder for which she was a prime suspect. In court Puente played the role of the benevolent grandma by altering her hairstyle and dress. The prosecutor's case was weakened as there were no witnesses to these crimes but the State was given a second wind when laboratory tests revealed the presence of tranquillisers in all of the exhumed remains. As the evidence mounted against Puente the prosecution was only able to maintain beyond a reasonable doubt that she had definitely killed one of her victims. The other bodies were too heavily decayed to make an exact determination as to the cause of death. Former residents of Puente's halfway house testified against her, speaking of how she would try to get them to take drugs while they resided in her home. The case began to close around Puente's neck like a noose. Six years after the bodies were discovered in the yard, after a long investigation and a gruelling trial, the verdict for the murderous grandma was ready.

On December 10, 1993, Dorothea Puente was found guilty of murder on three counts and the judge sentenced her to life imprisonment with no possibility of parole. She was sent to a women's prison in central California at the age of sixty-four. She remains incarcerated to this day.

KARLA FAYE TUCKER

After a childhood that was full of abuse and neglect, and her early years spent in a haze of drugs and immorality, it is not surprising that Karla Faye Tucker went off the rails. By the age of nine, marijuana had become Karla's 'friend', someone she could turn to when life became unbearable. But soon her 'friend' was not enough and she embarked on a downward spiral, injecting herself with heroin. Consequently, at an age when most young girls were still playing with dolls, Karla went out with her older siblings and became part of their orgies.

By the age of fourteen, encouraged by her mother, Karla had become a prostitute and life became a whirlwind of drugs, men and concert tours as she followed her groupie mother from tour to tour.

When Karla was sixteen she met and married a mechanic by the name of Stephen Griffith. Although externally the marriage seemed to work well, underneath Karla wasn't happy and felt restricted by the confines of marriage. She decided to leave her husband and resorted to her old trade as a prostitute, which she felt offered the freedom she was so used to.

Shortly after leaving Griffith, Karla, now twenty-three, was introduced to thirty-seven-year-old Danny Garrett. Danny became a close friend; not only did he allow her to continue her chosen 'career' but he also supported her drug addiction. They lived together in a small brick house in Houston, Texas, and in June 1983 they decided to throw a party for Karla's older sister, Kari Ann.

The party became infused with drugs, drink, music and sex, and soon reached fever pitch. Karla at one point sat talking to her friend Shawn, who was going through a bad time with her biker husband, Jerry Lynn Dean. Shawn was angry; she had arrived at the party with a broken nose and split lip, following a violent argument with her husband. As the party progressed and the drugs and alcohol took hold, Karla's anger rose and she told her friend that she should get her revenge.

Danny had to leave the party half way through the evening because he had a job working in a local bar. Karla drove him to work and promised to pick him up again at around 2.00 a.m. When Karla arrived back at the party she found Shawn in an even worse state, crying openly about her husband, whom she claimed she still loved desperately despite the constant beatings. Karla, who had never liked Jerry Lynn, had quite openly had several arguments with him in the past, leading to him banning his wife from ever seeing Karla again. Shawn had ignored him which had made the whole situation even more volatile.

REVENGE

Karla left the party just before 2.00 a.m. with a man named Jimmy Leibrant, who said he would accompany her to pick up Danny. When Danny got into the car, Karla was still angry and told him about the state that Shawn had got herself into over Jerry Lynn. Danny said he had an idea and he suggested that they steal his motorbike, which was the ultimate insult to a biker. The other two agreed that it would be sweet revenge and decided to go and find Jerry Lynn.

First they called back at the party to see if Shawn could tell them where her husband was likely to be. She told them that he would most probably be sound asleep at that time of night having smoked a few joints. When they told her about their plan to steal his bike, she thought it was a good idea and wished them luck. Before they left the house Danny

grabbed a shotgun, which he kept concealed underneath the sofa, and gave Jimmy a .38 which he had
in the glove compartment of his car. He told Jimmy
and Karla that it was a good idea to carry weapons
because they were about to go into a neighbourhood that was renowned for trouble.

When the trio arrived at Jerry Lynn's house they
found it in darkness. Danny told Jimmy to wait
outside while he and Karla cased the joint to see
how easy it would be to steal the bike. Danny
managed to open the front door without too much
trouble and they walked into the hall trying to adjust
to the dark. They could smell petrol and realised
that they had found the bike, as Danny put his hand
on the cold stainless steel of the handlebars. They
stood quietly to see if they had disturbed Jerry Lynn
when they had forced the door, but when they
heard nothing, Danny took a torch out of his pocket
and shone it onto the gleaming Harley Davidson.

Karla was disappointed to see that Jerry Lynn
had taken the bike to pieces and so it would be
impossible to simply wheel it out and ride it away.
Just as they were considering what to do next, a
shaft of light came from a door to the side of them
and a voice bellowed, 'Who the hell is out there?'

Karla froze and clenched her hands into tight fists.
Danny, on the other hand, had already reacted to
the situation by grabbing a hammer out of the

toolbox in the hall. Holding the hammer aloft he ran into the bedroom and Karla could see by the shadow against the wall that Danny was striking Jerry Lynn, who had managed to get half out of bed. Karla stood in the doorway and felt a thrill go through her loins at the sight of so much blood, as Danny hit his victim time and time again over the head.

Karla was sorry that she couldn't take part in the action, she would have liked to have taken out her own revenge on Jerry Lynn. Just as she had accepted the fact that she would only be a spectator, she spotted a female figure cowering under the covers. Karla felt the anger rise, knowing that not only had he beaten Shawn up but he was cheating on her as well. She ran back into the hall and grabbed the first thing that she saw – a pickaxe.

This time it was Danny who stood and watched as his girlfriend swung the axe over the body of the quivering girl. 'Let her have it!' Danny yelled and Karla brought the axe down over her body, suppressing the scream that was about to come out of her mouth.

Soon the killing became a game, as Danny threw a blanket over Karla and told her to try and strike while she was blindfolded. She got more and more excited as she could hear the squish of the blood as the axe hit the body of the girl, who was later named as Deborah Thornton.

PROUD OF THEIR ACTIONS

Back at the party Danny and Karla quite openly bragged about what they had done and by the morning it had become a sort of blur. They hadn't bothered to try and cover their tracks; they were so blinded by drugs and drink they simply felt they had killed two worthless individuals.

When the landlord discovered the two mutilated bodies he immediately called the police. It didn't take the brain of a genius to work out who had carried out the act – word had spread fast. Added to the fact that their fingerprints were all over the handle of the axe which was embedded in Thornton's chest. When they interviewed Jimmy Leibrant, he agreed to turn state's evidence in return for his freedom.

It was a cut and dried case and both Danny and Karla were found guilty and given the death penalty. Danny died in prison of liver disease shortly after hearing his conviction, cheating the system out of getting its justice. Karla, on the other hand, had to endure a waiting game as she appealed time and time again against the death penalty.

After fourteen years in prison and becoming a born-again Christian, Karla Faye Tucker lost her last appeal. On February 3, 1998, she was taken from death row at a prison in Gatesville, Texas, and flown to Huntsville which was eighty miles north of Houston. Karla was given a lethal injection at 6.01 p.m. after a final meal of banana, peach and salad.

SUE BASSO

The crime committed by Suzanne Basso was made even more horrendous by the fact that her victim was a good-natured, retarded man by the name of Buddy Musso. She lured this happy, but simple man into her web and treated him in such a way that by the time his body was found he was barely identifiable as a human being.

IN SEARCH OF LOVE

Buddy was a gentle-hearted man who craved love and companionship but somehow it had eluded him for more than two decades – that is until he met Sue Basso. The couple met in early 1997 at a church bazaar near his home in Cliffside Park, New Jersey. Sue was just visiting the town from her home in Houston and Buddy found her easy to talk to. Buddy was smitten and asked if he could keep in touch when Sue returned home. He waited excitedly for the phone to ring and told his friends and family about his 'new love'.

Although Buddy's friends were pleased for him, they were also worried due to his diminished mental capacity. They wondered why a woman would want a relationship with a man who had the intellectual level of an eight-year-old boy. Buddy worked at a local grocery store as a bagger and lived in a warden-assisted home in Cliffside Park. The other residents in the home were very protective of their friend, due to the fact that he had a very affectionate nature and became very attached to people in his desperate search for love.

Buddy loved to dress as a cowboy and could often be heard singing western songs in his slightly off-key way. He had the ability to make people laugh and nearly always wore a bright smile on his face. Buddy had married when he was a young man but his wife had died tragically of cancer in 1980, just two years after giving birth to their son, Tony. This experience had left Buddy even more insecure and his friends doubted Sue Basso's motives when she asked him to move to Houston to be with her. Sue was exceptionally overweight and at forty-four years old, was fifteen years Buddy's senior.

Paying no heed to his friends' warnings, Buddy started to pack his things and prepared to move to Sue's home in Jacinto City, Texas. He bought an inexpensive engagement ring using his social security cheque, said goodbye to all of his friends and boarded a Greyhound bus on June 14, 1998.

LOVE AT A PRICE

When Buddy arrived in Houston, his buxom woman greeted him warmly and led him off to her house – a place that would offer no love, only pain.

Ten weeks after Buddy left New Jersey, a jogger noticed a body lying in a ditch close to Jacinto City. He called the police who were appalled at the state of the body – it had numerous cigarette burns, contusions and a fractured skull. In fact they had to look closely to make sure that it was in fact a human being. The corpse bore no sign of identification, and it appeared as though it had been cleaned up and dressed in fresh clothing before being dumped in the ditch.

A few hours after the discovery of the body, the police were compiling a list of details to start their investigation, when an obese woman waddled into the station. She gave her name as Sue Basso and said she would like to report that a simple-minded man by the name of Buddy Musso had gone missing from her house. The body found in the ditch was quickly identified as being that of Buddy and a seven-page autopsy report revealed that he had in fact died the most horrendous death. Due to the amount of injuries found on his body, it was apparent that he had been tortured for days, possibly even weeks, before he finally died from a blow to the head.

THE MISFITS

Sue Basso lived a strange existence with a house full of people who could only be described as misfits. One of her housemates was her own son, James O'Malley, who had a fixation with anything to do with the army and wore full military regalia both day and night. James accompanied his mother to identify the body as their missing friend and it was his lack of reaction that gave the police reason to be suspicious. When Sue looked into the ditch she broke down into a false hysteria, while James just stood there expressionless as if he knew exactly what he was about to see.

Aware that Sue was the dominant force, the police took James to one side and asked whether he knew what had happened to Buddy. Without even stopping to think, he replied, 'Yeah, we killed him'. The 'we' he was referring to were Sue Basso, himself, fifty-five-year-old Bernice Ahrens Miller, Miller's son and daughter, twenty-five-year-old Craig and twenty-two-year-old Hope, and finally, Hope's fiancé twenty-eight-year-old Terence Singleton.

Once back at the police station James sung like a

bird and gave full details of exactly what had taken place. He explained that the fatal blow to Buddy had happened at Bernice Miller's flat in Houston. They had forced Buddy to kneel down on a child's play mat for several days because he had accidentally broken a toy. He was beaten severely which caused him to soil himself, and then he was beaten even more for making a mess. Not only had he been constantly beaten, but they had burned him with cigarettes, scrubbed his body with a wire brush and dumped him in a bath full of bleach and kitchen cleaner. When they had eventually sapped the last bit of life out of his body, they re-dressed him and dumped him in a ditch in Galena Park.

James eventually led the police to a dustbin where they had dumped Buddy's bloodstained clothing, towels, a child's mat and a pair of rubber gloves. Inside the house the police had to hold their hands over their faces as the stench brought bile to their throats. There was dog, cat and ferret faeces everywhere and also a soiled mattress where Buddy had been forced to sleep on the floor. There was junk everywhere, plastic bags full of old clothing, a computer, but more significantly, they found a $15,000 life insurance policy taken out on Buddy Musso. An additional clause to the policy boosted the payout to $60,000 if death was from a violent cause. In a drawer the police discovered a will signed by Buddy and witnessed by Sue and three of her friends, naming Buddy as the sole heir to his property. A copy of the will was dated 1997, but the original document file was found to have been created on the computer just twelve days before Buddy's death. The computer also contained a restraining order, that barred Musso's family from getting in touch with him, leaving Sue and her 'family' to carry out their regime of torture. The police also found evidence that Buddy had been turning his social security cheque over to Sue each month, so it became quite evident that Buddy Musso had been killed for monetary gain.

With so much evidence to hand the police were able to arrest all six of the suspects and charge them with the murder of Buddy Musso.

THE TRIAL

Throughout the trial Sue Basso sat unkempt and morose, demanding that she be led into the court in a wheelchair, faking temporary paralysis. As each of the suspects stood in the witness box, they made it clear that Sue was the primary culprit. Even her own daughter, Christianna Hardy, painted a black figure of her mother. She described a miserable childhood that was marred by sexual and physical abuse, something which Sue herself had been subjected to as a young girl. James was treated even worse and was forced to have a sexual relationship with his mother. He was often locked in the house for days on end, and forced to eat scraps of food off the floor like an animal.

The prosecutor said of Sue Basso: 'I've seen a bunch of evil in my job as a prosecutor, but she exhibits so many different demonic traits that it's hard to see her as anything but an evil-minded person.'

Sue Basso received the death penalty for her part in the murder of Buddy, while her associates were given maximum jail sentences. Hope Ahrens was the only one of the six killers who has a realistic chance of parole, having been sentenced to twenty years.

Sue Basso now lives on death row with eight other condemned women at the Mountain View Unit Prison in Gatesville. She will not be missed when her execution day finally arrives, as even her daughter is counting the days. When they announced the death penalty, Christianna cried tears of joy and said, 'She was never a mother. She doesn't have any mothering instincts. She threw us away and left us out there to fend for ourselves. Now, let her do a little fending for herself.' The description of a truly fiendish killer.

CELESTE BEARD

Celeste Beard was married to millionaire business tycoon Steven Beard and life should have been idyllic and free from care. Steven Beard had made his money as the co-owner of a local television station, and was a rich, powerful and well-liked member of the community. To friends and family theirs was a fairytale marriage, but the Beards' world was turned upside down in the early hours of the morning on October 2, 1999.

Steven woke with excruciating pain in his stomach and put it down to a recent hernia operation. However, when he looked down at the bed sheets they were soaked in blood and as he peered under the covers he was horrified to see a mess of innards where his stomach should have been.

Steven was alone in his room, as Celeste and her twin daughters from a previous marriage were sleeping in another wing of the large mansion. He managed to reach the phone and dial the emergency services, who struggled to understand exactly what had happened. Steven told the operator that he was in awful pain and that he needed an ambulance. When he tried to describe what was wrong he said, 'My guts just jumped out of my stomach.' When asked how it happened, he simply replied, 'It just happened. I woke up. I just woke up.'

The operator, who could not make head nor tail of the conversation, decided to send an ambulance and the police, having ascertained where the caller lived. She decided to keep him talking until the ambulance arrived, but when they got there they found the house in complete darkness and all the doors and windows shut tight. The police peered through the windows and eventually saw Steven lying on a bed. As they hadn't managed to rouse anyone by ringing the front doorbell, they decided to break in via a patio door.

When the paramedic studied the wound he surmised, like Steven himself, that the hernia incision had probably burst open. It wasn't until they lifted him onto a stretcher that the Deputy Sheriff, Russell Thompson, noticed something lying on the bedroom floor. It was the shell casing from a 20-gauge shotgun which had only recently been fired. All of a sudden the emergency had taken on a completely new perspective.

Steven was flown to Brackenridge Hospital in Austin, Texas by a medical helicopter, while his wife and two daughters, who had been woken by all the fuss, were driven to the hospital by police car. At the hospital the twins' boyfriends arrived and the five of them sat and waited, with Celeste pleading with the doctors, 'Please don't let him die.'

Back at the house the police were proceeding cautiously, with guns at the ready, searching thoroughly from room to room. The bathroom was in a terrible state and clothing had been pulled out of the drawers and laid scattered on the floor. Although Steven's wallet was missing, strangely the remainder of the couple's valuables had been left undisturbed. The police were suspicious as they had seen enough burglaries to realise that this looked as though it had been done deliberately.

Steven Beard survived the attack and was allowed to leave hospital after emergency surgery, but four months later he died as a result of his wounds. Celeste was devastated and went into a state of severe depression. The burglary turned into a murder enquiry and when Steven's adopted daughters were questioned the name 'crazy' Tracey kept cropping up.

TRACEY TARLTON

Several months before Steven's death, Celeste had befriended the manager of a bookstore, Tracey Tarlton. She was thirty-five years old, rather plain looking and slightly overweight. Her life had been marred by psychological problems, resulting in drug and alcohol abuse. Tracey was quite open about the fact she was a lesbian and felt comfortable working with the open-minded friends she had made at the bookshop. However, despite being very good at her job she suffered a mental breakdown in February 1999 which caused her to make a scene in public, shouting obscenities and threatening violence. With the encouragement of her family and friends, Tracey checked in to St David's Pavilion, a mental clinic, to try and get her life back on the straight and narrow.

THE FRIENDSHIP

Despite having a stable marriage, Celeste was having her own kind of problems, one of them being the amount of money she was spending. Steven was a very generous man and gave her a $10,000 allowance each month – but for Celeste this wasn't nearly enough. In their four years of marriage she had managed to work her way through well over $1 million dollars of her husband's wealth. This caused arguments and when Steven considered his wife's spending to be totally out of control, he threatened to destroy her credit cards. Celeste couldn't stand the thought of having no money and even threatened suicide, until Steven decided to take drastic action and sent her to St David's Pavilion for some counselling.

It was inevitable that Celeste and Tracey should become acquainted, taking solace in each other's problems. They formed a close sexual relationship which worried many of the nurses at the hospital, but it would appear that nothing would tear them apart. Even when they both returned home they were caught kissing on several occasions by Celeste's two daughters and on another by Steven, who banned Tracey from his house.

When the news of Steven Beard's shooting hit the headlines, quite a few people indicated that Tracey Tarlton might be involved, everyone that is except Celeste Beard. When Tracey was pulled in for questioning they asked her if she owned a 20-gauge shotgun, to which she replied 'yes' and quite willingly handed it in for ballistic testing.

The tests proved positive, which confirmed that the shell found at the Beard house came from the shotgun the police found at Tracey's house. Six days after the shooting Tracey was arrested and charged with assault.

When Steven died, Tracey was indicted for murder and the police put two and two together that she had murdered Celeste's husband out of sheer jealousy. Although the police were convinced that Celeste was somehow involved in the shooting, no amount of persuasion would get Tracey to implicate her lover. That was until she read an article in a newspaper saying that Celeste had married Cole Johnson, a bartender and musician, in a beautiful ceremony high in the mountains of Aspen.

Tracey was enraged that she had been dumped for a man and decided to change her story, telling the police that 'I did it for Celeste'.

She told the police that Celeste had confided in her that the marriage was not happy and that Steven was the only person who stood in the way of her inheriting a fortune. Celeste was well aware that Tracey owned a gun and they made plans for her to creep into the house and shoot Steven.

Celeste was arrested on March 28, 2002, and charged with Steven's murder, with bail set at $8 million. Several months later she was indicted for a second felony, that of attempting to hire her friend Donna Goodson to murder Tracey Tarlton.

In court, Tracey was angry and told the judge that both she and Steven had been tricked by the same scheming woman. Celeste went down the track that Tracey was lying, saying that she had never had a lesbian relationship with the woman, despite the evidence of several people to the contrary, including her two daughters.

The jury deliberated for twenty-three hours and Celeste was given a mandatory life sentence. By

Texas law she will have to spend at least forty years in prison, which means she will be eighty before she is eligible for parole. Tracey, on the other hand, who turned state's evidence, could be free as early as 2009. Celeste never did inherit her ex-husband's money. It was divided up between his blood children and Kristina and Jennifer, his adopted daughters. Mind you, money wouldn't be much good to Celeste now anyway, as she has nowhere to go on her extravagant shopping sprees.

WINNIE RUTH JUDD

The daughter of a reverend, the wife of a doctor, and the subject of one of the most sensational news stories to rock the depression-hit United States.

Winnie Ruth Judd had been married to Dr William C. Judd, a morphine addict, for seven years. His drug habit, which commenced initially as treatment of a wound sustained during the Great War, contributed to his failing practice and the marriage in general was not what Winnie had expected. The plans they had made for their future and the dreams they had shared were affected in the early days of their union by two failed pregnancies and Winnie's contraction of tuberculosis, which resulted in her husband's placement of her in a Californian sanatorium while he continued his medical duty in Mexico, travelling through poverty-stricken towns. Upon regaining her health, his wife joined him on several occasions, but the conditions in which he was working only worsened her frail condition. Unable to endure this, she moved back to the United States, to Phoenix, and her husband with whom she remained in frequent contact continued his work and travels in Mexico.

Perhaps predictably, the relationship suffered from the distance and it was not long before Winnie's attentions were diverted by a charismatic man named Jack Halloran, the married neighbour of a family for whom she worked as governess and a well-known local figure. Despite the continuation of her correspondence and declarations of love to her husband, an affair quickly began.

Soon Winnie gave up work as a governess and took on a job as a medical secretary in a private clinic. By this time, her husband had been admitted into a rehabilitation clinic in California to cure his drug habit. Her salary was an improvement, and enabled her to send what was left over after rent and living to Dr Judd for his care.

In her new place of employment, Winnie became acquainted with Anne LeRoi and Hedvig Samuelson ('Sammy'). Anne and Sammy were a lesbian couple who loved to party, and who frequently invited Winnie and Jack to gatherings at their place. In spite of their own relationship, the girls displayed a keen interest, not only in Jack, but in the married colleagues who would frequently accompany him to their parties (while their wives assumed they were working late) and leave significant amounts of cash on their departure. On occasion, Jack himself visited the two girls alone, and Winnie could have been in little doubt as to the purpose of his visit. However, she never attempted to stop him.

Soon, Winnie moved in with Anne and Sammy, but it was not to last. The two girls, meticulously tidy, were ill at ease with Winnie's sloppy habits and regular arguments ensued. Winnie moved out, but the experience had damaged the friendship. Added to grievances which had resulted from living together, Winnie was beginning to feel uncomfortable regarding the girls' relationship with her precious lover, Jack.

On Thursday October 15, 1931, Jack picked Winnie up and they drove to the house of Miss Lucille Moore, a colleague of Winnie's at the clinic. Winnie had arranged the meeting with Lucille as the young nurse came from the White Mountains of Arizona, an area where Jack had arranged a deer-hunting party with his friends. Winnie felt that Lucille would be able to inform Jack further on the wildlife of the region. They were due to go to Winnie's house for dinner, but on the return journey Jack declared that they would stop in on Anne and Sammy, who were entertaining friends of Jack's who he wanted to see. As Anne had previously declined a dinner invitation from the two girls, she was reluctant to pop in. Opinions differ however, regarding Winnie's hesitation. Some believe that Winnie anticipated the jealousy that would surface in the two girls if they knew that Jack was being introduced to the pretty, young nurse. Yet, they arrived at the house, Jack spoke to his friends, and the four women appeared to chat amicably. Appearances, however, can be deceptive, as the events of the following night would testify.

Having been left waiting by Jack, who was supposed to be taking her out to dinner on that fateful Friday night, Winnie decided to take the bus to Anne and Sammy's. She knew that they were hosting a bridge game, but when she arrived it was all over and their other guests had left. Nonetheless they asked her to stay the night, especially as Winnie and Anne would be going to work in the clinic together in the morning. But for Anne, the morning would never come. Whilst preparing for bed, Anne began to criticise Winnie for having introduced Jack to Lucille. The nurse, she claimed, was being treated for syphilis, and Winnie therefore was putting Jack's life in danger. Winnie replied that Jack had no interest in Lucille and reminded Anne that regardless of that, clinic information should be confidential and she was not at liberty to be discussing Lucille's condition. An argument erupted in which Anne and Sammy united against Winnie.

Insults and threats flew between the women, each party hell bent on destroying the other.

Breaking away, Winnie walked to the kitchen, but turned back again to see Sammy pointing a gun directly towards her chest. She pushed it away and reached for the kitchen knife. A struggle ensued in which Winnie was shot through the hand. As Sammy re-aimed the gun at Winnie's chest, Winnie lurched forward with the knife and slashed Sammy across the shoulder. The women fell to the ground, and another bullet was fired. This one hit Sammy in the left shoulder but she continued to fight. Until that is, Winnie managed to wrestle the gun towards Sammy's chest and pull the trigger.

As quickly as this was happening, Anne was upon the two women, attacking Winnie's head with an ironing board and encouraging Sammy to fire. There was no movement from Sammy so Anne continued her assault on Winnie with the board. Despite this, Winnie managed to stand, gun in hand, and shoot Anne until she fell lifeless to the floor.

Winnie dressed herself, and returned to her home. According to her, the time was about 11.30 p.m. A drunken Jack Halloran was already there, and Winnie told him of the events and requested his help. He refused to believe her and insisted on returning to the girls' house, which they did. After surveying the scene, Jack began to move the bodies, dropping Sammy's corpse on to Anne's bed and in doing so, scattering small droplets of her blood across the nearby wall. Winnie attempted to clean the floor but a combination of emotion, and pain from the bullet-wound in her hand, rendered her incapable of doing so. Jack took over. He also refused to let her talk to the police as she wanted to do, telling her instead to trust him and speak to no-one. In fact he went one step further and drove her home in order that he could return on his own, dispose of the bodies in a packing trunk he had found in the garage and drop it somewhere in the desert. Winnie dropped the murder weapon into her handbag and agreed to Jack's plan.

Jack did not make contact with Winnie until later the following afternoon when he asked her to take public transport to the girls' place where he would meet her. When she walked in, her heart dropped at the sight of the packing trunk, still there. Jack explained that it was likely to be found if he simply deposited it in the desert and that Winnie would be an obvious suspect having been a friend and flat-mate of the girls. He suggested instead that Winnie board a train to Los Angeles with the trunk, thereby taking it far away from Phoenix, where he promised that she would be met by an acquaintance of his. With the added incentive of visiting her husband, who could both attend to her hand and serve as an alibi for her trip, Winnie agreed to the plan. She did query the size of the trunk and its capacity to hold both bodies, to which Jack replied that Anne had fitted but that Sammy had been 'operated on'. He told her that he would arrange for the train ticket to be waiting for her at the ticket office and that she was to call the 'Lightning Delivery Service' to take the trunk to the station and load it on to her train.

None of Jack's plans or promises materialised.

Winnie contacted the 'Lightning Delivery Service', but when they turned up they informed her immediately that the trunk was too heavy to be loaded on to the train. She asked them instead, to their puzzlement, to deliver it to an alternative address – hers. Clearly she would need to divide the load into two cases. Jack was no longer anywhere to be found so Winnie began the nauseating task herself, frequently having to leave the house to take some fresh air, away from the stench of decomposing flesh.

The next morning, unable to transport the heavy cases to the train station, Winnie enlisted the help of her landlord and his son, and they willingly cooperated. The larger case was significantly overweight, but to Winnie's relief the porters accepted a fee to cover the surplus, gave her a receipt to sign, and took the cases out of her sight. With the trunks being taken care of, as she was sure

Jack had arranged, Winnie boarded the train and looked forward to meeting Jack's acquaintance at her destination twelve hours later. However, there was nobody there to meet her, and when Winnie phoned Jack for confirmation, she was told that he was away and would be for some time.

In desperation, Winnie tracked down her brother Burton and explained that she had just arrived in LA with heavy luggage and that she needed his help. He obliged, and drove her to the train station to collect the cases. But the baggage handler had been alerted by the foul odour emanating from the trunk, and had become suspicious of a liquid seeping out, which looked much like blood. He told Winnie she would have to open the trunks in front of him. Thinking quickly, Winnie replied that her husband held the key so she would need to find him and return with it in order to do so. Winnie fled the station. Burton was growing suspicious of his sister's behaviour, anxiety and her reluctance to answer any of his questions. When she eventually asked him for money and told him she needed to get away, he stopped the car, told her he thought maybe that was for the best and wished her luck as she disappeared into the crowd.

Police were soon scouring the city for the woman who had been labelled 'The Trunk Murderess'. Both her husband and Burton were found and questioned but quickly dismissed as having had no involvement in the crime and no knowledge of Winnie's whereabouts. A media frenzy erupted and a full-scale manhunt to find Winnie was launched. It didn't last long. She was found on October 23, and gave herself up immediately. She tearfully claimed self-defence from the start, telling police and reporters that she 'had to do it', and this confused the baying public who had been expecting someone as cruel and vicious as her crimes suggested. LA was left in a state almost of sympathy for Winnie Ruth Judd. Unfortunately for her, Phoenix, Arizona, was not.

Winnie was sent back to Phoenix, to a much more hostile reception. The court believed that Winnie had killed her two victims in cold blood and during their sleep, a belief supported by the absence of the mattress from one of the beds. This confused Winnie, who knew nothing of its disposal. Police had found the blood spots on the walls near the bed and drawn the conclusion that the murders must have happened in the bedroom. Winnie tried to explain Jack's involvement in the clear-up, and that the blood must have come from his movement of the bodies, but she was not heard. Neither was the autopsy report which claimed that the dissection of Sammy's body was more than likely to have been performed by somebody who had been trained in anatomy. Revealed instead was a letter which

Sammy had happened to write to her sister on the very day of the crime in which she explained that she and Anne were both much happier since Winnie had moved out as Winnie and Anne were arguing on so many occasions, sometimes violently. But its words had been twisted and the original gave no indication of violent clashes at all.

Winnie described the struggle and her self-defence, showed the bullet wound she received, and told of Anne's attack on her with the ironing board. Physicians found multiple wounds on her and reported that she must have 'put up a tremendous fight for her life'. Yet these reports mysteriously never surfaced during the investigation. It was claimed she was lying and that she shot herself to support her self-defence claim.

It is believed that the persecution of Winnie and the court's refusal to acknowledge many of the facts which supported her case was in fact to protect Jack Halloran, Phoenix's 'Golden Boy'. Any incriminating evidence which pointed to him, such as numerous sightings of his car at both the scene of the crime and outside Winnie's home that weekend were never recorded in court reports. His name, despite appearing in media reports all over the United States, was never reported in a Phoenix newspaper. In any discussion of a possible second person he was named simply 'Mr X', but even this suggestion was quickly dismissed. A diary kept by Anne surfaced during the search of their home, and it contained the names of many of the Phoenix elite, including Jack Halloran, who frequented the girls' apartment and employed their 'services'. Yet again, this was never brought into the investigation.

The sham and farce of the investigation was matched, nay bettered, only by the trial itself. Vital evidence was ignored during the trial and even when it came to light afterwards, such as the fact that the dismemberment of Sammy's body looked to professional eyes as if it could only have been performed by a surgeon or somebody trained to do so. Also never taken further was the fact that a Dr Charles Brown, friend of Jack's and one whom Jack professed prior to the murders to be 'in his debt', turned up at the prison where Winnie was subsequently incarcerated, asking to speak to her and claiming that he was the only one who knew the truth about Winnie Ruth Judd, and then fled before further questioning to be found dead three days later in apparent suicide. Evidence regarding the crime scene, the location of the murders, the lack of any obvious premeditation, and the disappearance of one of the mattresses was never adequately explored and to many suggested a clear cover-up, or political interference. Winnie was never even called to speak during the trial. Surprisingly, given how often his name came up, neither was Jack Halloran.

Winnie was tried for Anne's murder only and, found guilty, she was sentenced to death by hanging and sent to death row. But suspicion around the botched trial, and public support for Winnie, was growing. Appeals were launched, sabotaged by Jack Halloran in court. Winnie's execution date was put back. Realising that they were not going to beat the courts in a fair trial, Winnie's defence told her to claim insanity. Although far from insane, Winnie and her family pleaded so, recounting tales of madness through the generations, with their testimonials interrupted on occasion by staged, crazed outbursts from the defendant. It worked. Winnie was declared insane and transported to the state hospital. Here she lived as a model prisoner (in spite of her seven successful escape attempts, including one which actually gave her freedom for seven years) and she was looked on more as a member of staff than a patient. Jack would come to the hospital on occasions to taunt her, but he was eventually banned from the grounds.

Her placement in the hospital had always been on the grounds that should she ever recover her sanity, her death sentence would still stand. In 1952, a final appeal was made to overturn this ruling. It was successful, and Winnie Ruth Judd became free from the threat of the noose. She returned to the asylum, safe in the knowledge that future appeals (which would maybe reveal her sanity) could never lead to her death. Of these future appeals, there were two. One in 1969 which was denied, and another in 1971 which finally, and with the backing of the nation, was successful.

She lived for twenty years, under an alias name, in California but returned to Phoenix for the last decade of her life. She died quietly in her sleep at the age of 93.

Halloran's true involvement in the crime and attempted cover-up was never established.

I Don't Like
Mondays

On Monday January 29, 1979, as the teachers and children of Cleveland Elementary School in San Diego were arriving for the start of a new week, sixteen-year-old Brenda Spencer, who lived just across the street from the school, was taking aim with a rifle which she had been given for Christmas by her father just a month previously. She opened fire, killing Principal Burton Wragg who was attempting to save the children in his care, and custodian Mike Suchar who came to Wragg's aid. Eight children and a police officer sustained bullet wounds; that these injuries did not prove fatal was the result purely of luck rather than intention. One of the children who survived the attack had been hit by a bullet which struck him just one inch away from his heart.

Spencer resisted arrest for six hours. When it was finally over, she told the police that were questioning her that quite simply, she didn't like Mondays and that this livened up the day. She admitted that there was no motivation whatsoever for the shooting spree and compared the morning's activity to 'shooting ducks in a pond' and the children to 'a herd of cows standing around'. She told officers that it had been really easy pickings.

In a fairly straightforward trial, she pleaded guilty to two counts of murder and assault with a deadly weapon. The court sentenced her to twenty-five years to life, in prison, which she was sent to serve in the California Institution for Women. Each of the four parole boards she has since appeared in front of have turned down her appeal.

Her indifference and lack of remorse was waning by the third parole appeal in which she expressed some guilt. She further went on to claim that she had been sexually abused and beaten by her father as a child, an accusation which she had hitherto not made, and one which he denies. She claims that she actually asked her father for a radio for Christmas but received the rifle instead, which was to become the murder weapon. His reasons for this, she believes, were to encourage her to kill herself. She even cites suicide as the reason for her shooting spree that morning, hoping that the police may have shot her dead by the end of the six-hour stand-off. With a history of depression, Spencer had attempted suicide before but each attempt had failed.

She also expressed some remorse over the responsibility which she feels for every 'school shooting' which has occurred since, and regret that her actions may have in part inspired the perpetrators' actions.

Her account has changed on a number of occasions. She has claimed that not only was she drunk at the time of the shootings, but that she was also under the influence of hallucinogenic drugs. When tests were produced at the time of the shootings, there was no evidence of such substances in her system. She argued that these results were fabricated and that the real results had been hidden by the prosecution. She then asserted that there was no proof that any of the victims had been shot with bullets from her rifle and instead that they could have been killed by the police. Spencer also told the board that she was given mind-altering drugs after her arrest, and was made to sign, say and do things during her confession and trial which she didn't mean. She made a statement saying that roughly fifty other women whom she had met in prison had been treated the same way and that she intended to file a federal civil rights suit.

She will no doubt attempt to go up again for parole. But Brenda Spencer's anger and ability to handle stress is still questionable. After the break-up of a relationship with another inmate, Brenda carved the words 'courage' and 'pride' into her chest with a heated paperclip. Also against her is the fact that California rarely grants parole in cases of murder.

PART FIVE

FIENDISH DOCTORS

DOCTOR WILLIAM PALMER

Over 30,000 people crammed the streets of Stafford to witness the grisly spectacle, some of them having spent the entire night in the pouring rain just to make sure they had a prime viewing position. The case of Doctor William Palmer had become so notorious that no one wanted to miss the occasion of him being hanged on June 14, 1856. Although he had allegedly been responsible for around fourteen deaths, including members of his family, he was only tried for one murder, that of John Parsons Cook.

William Palmer was born in Rugely, Staffordshire, in 1824. As a young adult he gained a reputation as being a bit of a rogue who loved gambling and had an eye for the ladies. Even as a boy at school his former schoolfriends said that he was 'always up to his tricks'. He would trick men that were employed by his father into lending him money.

His medical training was constantly interrupted by allegations of stealing money, probably due to the large debts he had accrued from his bad habits. While working at Stafford Infirmary, he was accused of poisoning a friend during a drinking competition. Although nothing was ever proved, the hospital decided to put their dispensary under lock and key just to be on the safe side. Palmer was even dismissed from his first job in Liverpool for stealing money sent in a letter that was addressed to his employers.

In 1845, Ann Brookes, who had only just left finishing school, met the charming young Doctor William Palmer. Ann was the wealthy heiress to the Noah's Ark hostelry in Stafford, and having been warned by her guardian about Palmer's reputation, she decided to turn down his first offer of marriage. However, Palmer was persistent, seeing a prosperous future with the not only pretty, but wealthy, nineteen-year-old young woman. Eventually, Ann gave in and agreed to marry him. The wedding took place in 1847 at St Nicholas Abbey in Abbotts Bromley.

Within a year of being married, Palmer was borrowing money from his mother-in-law, Mary Thornton. Mary had hated her new son-in-law right from the outset, and had done everything in her power to convince Ann not to go ahead with the wedding. Their first child was born in 1848 and shortly afterwards, Mary Thornton came to live with the Palmers to help look after the baby. Within two weeks Mary had been taken seriously ill and died.

Mary's life had been insured for a hefty £12,000, but Palmer was disappointed when the insurance company refused to pay out the full sum. He constantly complained to his wife about the meagre allowance that was paid to her by her trustees four times a year. With his debts mounting any money coming into the Palmer household was soon swallowed up. By the end of the year Palmer was strongly implicated in the murder of Leonard Bladen, to whom he owed £600.

Over the next four years, Ann gave birth to four more babies, but each one died within weeks of being born. They all died suddenly, with the same symptoms, as did two of his illegitimate children, the result of his many affairs.

By 1854 Palmer was deeply in debt and couldn't see any way of ever getting clear, so he decided to insure his wife's life for £13,000. After just one payment, Ann Palmer mysteriously died, the death certificate gave the cause as 'cholera'. His housemaid bore Palmer an illegitimate child just a few months later, but this baby also died after being attended by the kindly doctor.

JOHN PARSONS COOK

By 1855 William Palmer was seriously in debt and

several of the moneylenders were starting to make threats. Palmer had insured his brother, Walter's, life, but the insurance company had refused to pay out due to the suspicious circumstances of his death. Adding to his worries, was the fact that a former lover, Jane, the daughter of a Staffordshire policeman, was blackmailing him. Palmer had no scruples, and had even forged his own mother's signature on several loan agreements, for which he knew he could face fraud charges.

Palmer knew the only way out of this mess was to turn to gambling to try and win enough money to pay off all his debts. On November 13, 1855, Palmer went to Shrewsbury Races accompanied by his close friends, John Parsons Cook and a man called Cheshire, who was the Rugely postmaster. Cook, who was a weak, pale-looking young man, got exceptionally excited when his horse, Polestar, came first, potting him a tidy sum of £3,000. An hour later, a despondent Palmer, who had won nothing, decided to return to Rugely and leave his friends at the racecourse.

Cook, on the contrary, decided to celebrate and held a celebratory dinner for some of his friends at the Raven Hotel, treating his guests to glasses of sparkling champagne.

The following day, November 14, Palmer received yet another threatening letter, this time from a solicitor called Pratt, demanding his money. Palmer decided to go back and try his luck at the Shrewsbury races, this time in the company of a saddler by the name of George Myatt. That evening after a small win, Palmer dined at the Raven Inn in Shrewsbury with Cook, Cheshire, Ishmael Fisher, a wine merchant, George Herring, George Myatt and George Read. At some point in the evening, Palmer went out to the housemaid's pantry where he was seen by a lady from Manchester, who has been described as 'a lady who loves to attend races'. She noticed that Palmer was pouring some liquid from a small, brown bottle into a tumbler, which he then shook before putting it up to the gaslight. Palmer didn't seem at all distressed when he realised the lady had seen what he was doing.

Palmer returned to his friends at the dining table, after which a tray of brandy was brought in and handed round to each of the men. After Cook had taken several sips of his brandy, he stood up and complained that the liquid was burning his throat. Palmer then picked up his glass, drank from the tumbler, and then passed it on to George Read to taste, saying, 'Taste it. There's nothing in it. Cook says it's drugged.'

Read replied, 'What's the use in giving it to me, when you have drunk the very dregs!'

Cook was feeling unwell and retired to his

bedroom accompanied by Herring and Fisher. To be on the safe side he handed Fisher his money belt. His friends sent for a doctor, and had to ask for help again in the middle of the night. By the morning Cook was feeling a little better and managed to get up and eat some breakfast.

That day Palmer returned to the races, but lost heavily when his horse, Nettle, failed to finish its race. Had his horse come in first, he would have won £5,000 which would have gone a long way to ending his troubles. In the evening Cook and Palmer booked into a room at the Talbot Arms, a hotel which was directly opposite Palmer's house in Rugeley. Cook, who still wasn't feeling 100 per cent decided to go straight to bed.

On Friday, November 16, Palmer invited Cook to dinner. The following morning when Palmer went to take his friend some coffee, he found Cook had been violent sick all night and he spent the rest of the day in and out of his room.

By Sunday, November 18, Cook was no better, and Palmer decided to call an old family friend, Dr Bamford, to get a second opinion. The chamber-maid, Elizabeth Mills, told Bamford that she had also been sick after she tasted some of the broth that Palmer had sent up to his sick friend.

On Monday morning, Palmer went to London, taking Cook's betting slips with him and managed to obtain the majority of his winnings before returning to Rugeley. On arriving back home he found that his friend was feeling a little better.

In the early hours of Tuesday morning, Cook took a turn for the worse. Cook's long-time friend and doctor, Jones, was called and arrived at about 2.00 p.m. Cook was in a terrible state, shrieking wildly and tossing about in fearful convulsions. All his limbs went rigid and within minutes his heart had stopped beating and he was dead.

Suspicions of foul play were heightened when Palmer attempted to bribe several people who were involved with the coroner's inquest. Mary Keeley, who had been asked to 'lay out the body' said she had seen many corpses, but none that were as stiff as Cook's. There was also a witness to say that Palmer had bought strychnine from a pharmacy, the night of Cook's death.

ARREST AND TRIAL

Palmer was arrested for the murder of John Parsons Cook. The bodies of his wife and his brother were exhumed and re-examined, although their bodies did not show enough evidence to charge Palmer for their deaths. Because the police felt that a Staffordshire jury could be biased, they sought an Act of Parliament, which allowed the case to be heard at the Old Bailey in London.

Despite the evidence only being circumstantial, the similarity between Cook's death and that of strychnine poisoning was such that the jury found Palmer guilty of his murder. Although there is no proof, many people believe that Palmer could have killed as many as eleven people, others say that he was just convicted because of his bad reputation. Whatever the case, Palmer became famous and was christened by the newspapers as 'The Rugely Poisoner' and 'The Prince of Poisoners'. Such was his notoriety that broadsheets and ballads were sold on the streets and souvenirs and even the rope-maker sold sections of his noose for a guinea a piece. His life and death gave rise to an entire genre of artefacts, known as Palmeriana, which ranged from reports of his trial to Staffordshire china figurines and reproductions of his death mask. It was customary in the nineteenth century to make a death mask after someone has been executed, and Palmer's can still be viewed today in the County Museum at Shugborough.

DOCTOR THOMAS NEILL CREAM

According to an article in the *British Medical Journal*, medicine has produced more serial killers than all the other professions put together. Dr Thomas Neill Cream was a physician with a homicidal hatred of women, especially those who worked under the cover of night. Cream was known to have killed at least seven women in Canada, Chicago and London, which is where Scotland Yard finally caught up with him in 1891.

THE FORMATIVE YEARS

Thomas Neill Cream was born in Scotland in May 1850, the oldest of a family of eight children. Four years later the family moved to Canada, where Cream undertook medical studies at McGill College in Montreal. A handsome, suave young gentleman, Cream graduated with honours on March 31, 1876, and immediately set his sights on London. England had a shortage of doctors at the time, due to poverty that had manifested itself during the Industrial Revolution. However, his exodus from Canada was hampered when he ran into an angry mob led by the father of a young woman by the name of Flora Brooks. Flora had been seduced by Cream and as a result had become pregnant. In his panic to get rid of the child, Cream performed an abortion, nearly killing Flora in the process. Mr Brooks was understandably angry and held Cream at gunpoint, forcing him to marry his daughter. The wedding took place on September 11, 1876, but when Flora woke the following morning, she found her new husband had fled to London, leaving a brief note promising to stay in touch.

THE TEMPTATIONS OF LONDON

Cream loved London and studied at St Thomas' Hospital, where both Thomas Lister and Florence Nightingale had once worked. He took advantage of everything that London had to offer, including all of its illicit temptations. He went dancing, drinking, frequented music halls and theatres and had liaisons with both society women and prostitutes alike.

Cream was reinstated to his bachelor status when Flora mysteriously died in 1877. Freed from his marriage, Cream opened a medical practice in the centre of Edinburgh. Things were going well for the promising new, young doctor – that is until another mysterious death occurred in 1879. The body of a young, pregnant woman was found dead in a shed directly behind Cream's surgery. Lying beside the body of chambermaid Kate Gardener was a bottle of chloroform. Despite all the evidence pointing to Cream, he was acquitted of murder, but his reputation had gone down the pan.

Cream decided to move his business to Chicago, which is where his murderous predisposition really revealed itself. He had set up his practice close to the city's red-light district, and he soon made his trade by performing illegal abortions. Although it was strictly against the moral code in the nineteenth century, it wasn't unusual for doctors to make some quick money in this way. Unfortunately, many of the women fell victims to these abortionists, who really could be classed as 'butchers' rather than doctors. Many bled to death or contracted diseases from unsterilized instruments. When two prostitutes died after receiving abortions from Cream, the police started to take an interest in the new physician on their patch. One of the women had bled to death, while the second had been prescribed 'anti-pregnancy' pills, which were later discovered to be the poison strychnine. The latter was Cream's preferred method of killing his victims, convincing the prostitutes that the pills would help to prevent sexually transmitted diseases. Little did they realise that they would die in the most excruciating way. Cream, who was thought to be addicted to cocaine and morphine at the time, was arrested, but once again narrowly escaped murder charges.

Cream continued his practice in Chicago, but expanded his repertoire by inventing what he called an 'elixir for epilepsy'. It wasn't long before he acquired quite a considerable following of patients who swore by his miracle potion. One of his patients, a railway agent by the name of Daniel Stott, made the terrible mistake of sending his wife, Julia, to the good doctor to fetch regular doses of his elixir. However, Cream provided her with more than a dose of medicine, and Stott eventually became suspicious that the couple were having an affair. When things got a little too close for comfort, Cream added a new ingredient to Stott's medication – strychnine. Stott died on June 14, 1881, and if it hadn't been for an act of sheer stupidity, Cream would have got away with the perfect crime.

Stott's death had been attributed to his epilepsy, but for some unknown reason Cream wrote a letter to the coroner saying that the pharmacist was responsible for his death and requested that the body be exhumed. Although the coroner dismissed

the letter, the District Attorney was not so disdain-
ful and ordered that Stott's body be exhumed. When
the coroner found that his stomach contained an
unusually large amount of strychnine, Cream's luck
had finally run out. He was found guilty of murder
and imprisoned for life in the Illinois State Penitentiary at Joliet.

GIVEN A SECOND CHANCE

Due to good behaviour, or possibly a bribe, Cream
was granted early release on July 31, 1891. After a
quick detour to Canada to pick up an inheritance of
$16,000, Cream set sail for England. Back on home
ground, Cream started to frequent many of his
previous haunts, such as the prostitutes who
worked by Waterloo Bridge. He had taken lodgings
near St Thomas' Hospital, where he posed as a
resident doctor, signing his name 'Thomas Neill,
MD'. Back to his old habit of ingesting large
amounts of morphine, Cream returned to his other,
even nastier habit of murder.

Just two days after his return to England, two
young prostitutes fell victim to his promises of good
health. Matilda Clover and Ellen Donworth were
both found to have lethal levels of strychnine in
their stomachs when the coroner carried out his
postmortem. However, because the women were

'working girls', a trade that thrived in Victorian England, neither the Metropolitan police nor Scotland Yard pursued the matter and Cream was left alone to kill again.

After a brief romance with a woman named Laura Sabbatini, Cream resumed his murderous activities, but one prostitute managed to get the upper hand over him. Cream met a young working girl by the name of Lou Harvey in Piccadilly and convinced her to meet him later that evening so that he could take her to the theatre and dinner. Just before the couple parted, Cream handed Harvey some pills, saying they would help her with her pale complexion which he diagnosed as being caused by the contaminated London air. However, Harvey was suspicious of 'Dr Neill' and waited until he was out of sight before throwing the pills into the Thames. Prepared to confront him, Harvey turned up for the proposed assignation, but of course Cream didn't arrive, presuming that she was already dead.

TOO COCKY FOR HIS OWN GOOD

Scotland Yard eventually started to pay attention when two more prostitutes were found dead from strychnine poisoning. It is possible that Cream would never have been discovered if it hadn't been for his own arrogance. Cream had made friends with a former New York City detective by the name of John Haynes. Haynes was now living in London and was desperately trying to get a position in Scotland Yard. The murder of the prostitutes had become big news and Haynes was fascinated, reading every piece of information he could find about the case. Cream, foolishly started to brag to his friend about his vast knowledge on the murders, and even went as far as taking Haynes on a tour of the murder scenes. At supper one evening the men were talking extensively about the case, when Cream gave details of one of the victims, Lou Harvey. When Haynes asked his friend how he knew so much about the murders, Cream simply replied that he had been following the cases closely in the newspapers. Haynes, who had also been avidly reading the news stories, didn't remember any mention of a victim by the name of Lou Harvey.

Haynes took his suspicions to Scotland Yard and told a friend working there, Patrick McIntyre, what Cream had relayed to him. McIntyre decided to put the doctor under surveillance and soon found out that Cream had a forged passport in the name of 'Doctor Thomas Neill'. Cream was watched twenty-four hours a day and it wasn't long before prostitutes gave police details of being approached by a man matching Cream's description.

As evidence mounted against Cream, the police moved in and he was arrested on June 3, 1892. He continued to maintain his innocence and remained composed throughout his incarceration and forthcoming trial. In fact Cream showed no real emotion until the bailiff introduced Miss Lou Harvey into the witness box to give evidence. Cream's mouth fell open at the shock of seeing Miss Harvey alive, and that must have been the first time he really knew that his time was up.

The crowds gathered on November 16, 1892, to watch Cream get his comeuppance. According to legend, just before the trapdoor released Cream to his death, he is said to have uttered 'I am Jack . . .' but his sentence was cut short as the noose tightened around his neck. As the Ripper murder case was still being investigated at the time, the immediate assumption was that Doctor Thomas Neill Cream had confessed to being Jack the Ripper.

However, yet another good Ripper theory ended there, because Cream was incarcerated in Joliet, Illinois, in 1888 when the Ripper murders took place.

DOCTOR CRIPPEN

The bizarre case of Doctor Hawley Harvey Crippen began in 1910 in London and became famous for being the first British murder case in which Marconi telegraph signals were used to track down the suspects. During the Victorian era there were quite a number of high-profile murder cases involving poisoning, due to the fact that the purchase of toxic substances such as strychnine and arsenic was relatively easy. This was compounded by the rise in the number of life insurance companies doling out policies, which meant that any greedy relative could get their hands on the money if only they could get away with murder. Doctor Crippen, a homeopathic doctor, was just one of those people who felt they had committed the perfect crime.

Crippen was born in Michigan, USA, in 1862. His dream was to become a doctor, so when he was twenty-one years of age, Crippen went to England to improve his medical knowledge. He gained several diplomas, but these qualifications were not sufficient for him to practise as a doctor in the

United Kingdom. On his return to the USA, Crippen started practising homeopathic medicine in a number of cities, during which time his first wife died. They had a three-year-old-son, who Crippen sent to live with his mother-in-law in California.

During one of his stays in New York, Crippen met and married a seventeen-year-old girl by the name of Kunigunde Mackamotski, but who the doctor knew as Cora Turner. Cora, who was a very mediocre singer, preferred to use her stage name of 'Belle Elmore'. She was deluded into believing that she had a superb singing voice, and spent several months training as an opera singer. Cora was described as being an exceptionally overbearing woman with a love of frilly clothes, diamonds and alcohol, with a reputation for constantly flirting with men at parties. Crippen, by contrast, was a quiet-spoken man, short in stature and who was persistently nagged and henpecked by his wife.

In 1900 Crippen moved back to England, where he became manager in the Munyon Company's offices in Shafesbury Avenue in London. Although Cora pursued her career for a while in the theatres of New York, she eventually joined her husband in rented rooms in South Crescent, just off Tottenham Court Road.

Cora constantly moaned about her husband's inability to earn a good wage, and although he put up with her meanness for a while, he eventually found solace in the arms of twenty-eight-year-old Ethel le Neve. Ethel had worked as a typist for Crippen for over seven years and by 1910, the couple had been lovers for three years.

39 HILLDROP CRESCENT

Late in 1909, the Crippens moved to a much larger premises at 39 Hilldrop Crescent, in Camden Town. Due to an annual rent of £58 10s, they were forced to take in lodgers to compensate for Crippen's meagre income of around £3 a week. Cora continued her 'career' under the assumed name of Belle Elmore, which kept her in the lifestyle she loved, enabling her to buy furs and jewellery and to still put some money aside. Crippen, who was becoming overdrawn at the bank, was well aware that Cora had over £600 squirreled away in her name.

Cora by this time was getting bored with her husband and was well aware of his affair with Ethel. She threatened to leave him, which should have been excellent news for Crippen, but she was also planning to take their savings with her, which meant he would be left penniless. On December 15, 1909, Cora Crippen gave notice of withdrawal to their bank to remove her savings.

One month later, on January 17, Crippen visited a

chemist shop in New Oxford Street, Lewis and Burrows, and ordered five grains of the poison hyoscine hydrobromide, also known as 'nightshade'. Because it was such a large order – a quarter-grain would be sufficient to kill – the chemist had to place a special order. The chemist was not suspicious, as Crippen was a regular client of theirs and the drug was commonly used, in exceptionally small doses, to sedate insane or alcoholic patients. Crippen went and collected his order two days later.

On the evening of January 31, 1910, the Crippens held a dinner party for a retired music-hall performer, Mr Martinetti and his wife. After the meal the four of them played several games of whist until 1.30 a.m. when the Martinettis left.

Before retiring to bed, Crippen mixed his wife a drink, adding several grains of hyoscine hydrobromide. Neighbour's later reported hearing shouts followed by a loud noise, similar to that of a gunshot. Crippen then apparently dragged his wife's lifeless body to the cellar, where he disembowelled, decapitated and cut off her arms and legs before burying the body under the cellar floor.

The next day Crippen carried on as if nothing had happened. He pawned some of Cora's jewellery for £80 and that night Ethel le Neve slept at 39 Hilldrop Crescent. When neighbours asked what had happened to Cora, Crippen simply told them that she had been called suddenly to the USA to look after a sick relative. Crippen also told them that Ethel was his niece and that she had come to stay for a while. Crippen also forged a letter to the Secretary of the Music Hall Ladies Guild, saying that Cora was resigning her position as their Honorary Treasurer. When Mrs Martinetti called at the house later that day, Crippen told her the same story about the sick relative, but she reproached him for not telling her sooner about her friend's departure.

Crippen continued to pawn Cora's jewellery, but the pair made a silly mistake when they attended a ball later that year. They bumped into two good friends of Cora's, Mr and Mrs John Nash. Lil Nash happened to notice that Ethel was wearing an expensive brooch that she knew had belonged to her friend. When Mrs Martinetti called on Crippen and said she had heard nothing from Cora, he fabricated another story that his wife had been taken seriously ill in America and had died. When the Nash's heard the news, they asked Crippen exactly where her death had taken place, but he said he couldn't recall the name, 'some little town near San Francisco, with a Spanish name I think'. The Nash's were not convinced by his strange response and began to wonder if something had happened to their friend.

Crippen was starting to get nervous and decided to give three month's notice of his intention to vacate the property at Hilldrop Crescent.

SUSPICIONS MOUNT

Mrs Martinetti received a telegram on March 24, 1910, saying 'Belle died yesterday at 6.00 p.m.' It had been sent from London's Victoria Station just before Crippen and Ethel set off together for Dieppe. During their absence, many of Cora's friends were getting suspicious about what had happened to her. When Crippen and Ethel arrived back in England, he explained that his wife had died in Los Angeles and that her ashes were being flown back to England.

Crippen now thought that the heat was off and he started to go about his daily business. Ethel, on the other hand, stupidly continued to wear some of Cora's jewellery, something which her friends considered to be in very bad taste. The Nash's, who had not believed Crippen's story, decided to visit the USA and made some enquiries of their own. When their search proved to be fruitless, they returned to England and decided to take the matter further.

On June 30, 1910, at 2.00 p.m., John Edward Nash and his wife Lil walked into the Criminal Investigation Department at New Scotland Yard and asked to speak with their old friend Chief

Inspector Walter Dew. Nash told Dew that he wanted to report the disappearance of a close friend, Cora Crippen, also known as Belle Elmore, who had not been seen since February of that year. He explained that he had seen Doctor Crippen, accompanied by Miss Le Neve, who had been wearing a brooch that had belonged to Cora. He also explained to the inspector that Crippen's explanation as to the whereabouts of his wife's death was less than satisfactory.

Inspector Dew decided to start an investigation, as he also felt that Cora Crippen's disappearance was mysterious, and said in his report:

> *It will be gathered from the foregoing that there are most extraordinary contradictions in the story told by Crippen, who is an American citizen, as is Mrs Crippen, otherwise known as Belle Elmore . . . without adopting the suggestion made by her friends as to foul play, I do think that the time has now arrived when 'doctor' Crippen should be seen by us and asked to give an explanation as to when, and how, Mrs Crippen left this country, and the circumstances under which she died . . .*

Inspector Dew decided to pay Crippen a visit on

July 8, where he met Ethel le Neve for the first time. When Crippen was confronted by the police, he panicked and started to change his story, saying, 'I suppose I had better tell the truth, all my stories about her illness and death are untrue, so far as I know she is not dead at all'.

He explained in earnest that his wife had run off with her lover, a prize fighter by the name of Bruce Miller. He told Dew that he felt so humiliated, he had decided to invent a story about her death. The officers carried out a search of his property but found nothing suspicious and told the doctor that they were happy with his explanation. Dew told Crippen that he would like to come back the next day to clear up a few final points, but when the police returned Crippen and Ethel le Neve had disappeared.

CRIPPEN ON THE RUN

Not aware that the police were no longer suspicious, Crippen panicked and left for Antwerp with Ethel, disguised as a young boy. When Dew returned to the house and found it empty, he raised the alarm and obtained a warrant for their arrest. In the meantime, he had the house searched once again and, while in the coal cellar, Dew dug into the brick floor and uncovered the few gruesome remains of a human body.

There was no head, all the limbs were missing, as were all the bones, with the exception of one piece of thigh. The pathologist assigned to the case, Sir Bernard Spilsbury, established from an old operation scar and a single piece of hair, that the remains of the buried woman really were those of Cora Crippen. This was to be Spilsbury's first murder case and it was the one that eventually established his reputation. Dew ordered a massive manhunt and quickly distributed the descriptions of Crippen and le Neve.

The story soon made the headlines in the London tabloids and, getting nervous, Crippen decided to escape by boarding a ship heading for Canada. They hid for a while in a hotel in Brussels while they waited for the Canadian Pacific steamer *Montrose*, which was scheduled to sail from Antwerp to Quebec. Crippen attempted to disguise himself by shaving off his moustache, growing a beard and discarding his spectacles. He made Ethel have her hair cut short and put on boys' clothes, and she had to pull a hat down over her eyes whenever she was in public. Posing as father and son, Crippen signed the passenger list of the *Montrose* as Mr John and Master Robinson.

However, the captain on board the *Montrose*, Henry Kendall, considered himself to be a bit of an amateur detective and liked to keep a close eye on what was happening on board his ship. He thought it strange that a father and son should walk about the ship holding hands and occasionally disappear behind the lifeboats.

Wanting to investigate further, Kendall decided to invite the Robinsons to dine at his table. He told Crippen that he had a form that needed filling in before they reached North America. It was while they were eating dinner that Kendall noticed a number of safety pins on Master Robinson's clothes that were designed to disguise her feminine curves. When he compared their features to those in a newspaper article he became convinced that he had the fugitives on board his ship.

He sent a message via the Marconi telegraph on July 22 which read:

> *Have strong suspicion that Crippen London Cellar murderer and accomplice are amongst saloon passengers. Moustache shaved off, growing a beard. Accomplice dressed as a boy, voice, manner and build undoubtedly a girl.*

The *Montrose* was one of the few ships that was fitted with a Marconi telegraph and when Dew received the information he quickly boarded the White Star liner, *Laurentic*, in hot pursuit. Although the *Montrose* had a three-day lead, it was still eleven days out of Quebec. The *Laurentic* was a more powerful boat and easily overtook the *Montrose,* so when they reached the St Lawrence River, Dew, disguised as a tug pilot, boarded the *Montrose.* He walked up to Crippen, shook his hand and as he removed his pilot's cap said, 'Good afternoon, Dr Crippen, remember me? I am Inspector Dew of Scotland Yard'. Crippen stared in disbelief and then sighed, held out his wrists for the handcuffs and replied, 'Thank God it's over'.

THE TRIAL

Doctor Hawley Crippen and Ethel le Neve were taken back to London on board the White Star liner *Megantic* to face charges of murder. It was decided that they would be tried separately, and Crippen's trial opened before Lord Chief Justice Lord Alverstone on October 18, 1910, at London's Old Bailey. The trial lasted for five days, throughout which Crippen maintained his innocence. However, the prosecution gave incriminating evidence during the trial, which included the purchase of the poison and the identification of the old surgical scar on the torso of Cora Crippen by the pathologist, Spilsbury. The trial also revealed the meticulous manner with which Crippen had disposed of his wife's body. After killing her, he professionally removed her bones and limbs and burned them in his kitchen stove. He then dissolved her organs in a bath of acid and placed her head in a handbag, which he threw overboard on a day visit to Dieppe.

Crippen showed no remorse whatsoever during his trial and after just twenty-seven minutes, the jury returned a verdict of guilty. He was hanged at Pentonville prison on November 28, 1910, by hangman John Ellis.

Ethel le Neve, who hired herself a high-powered attorney, was acquitted as an accessory after the fact. She changed her last name to Allen and, on the morning of Crippen's execution, she set sail for New York. When she arrived at her final destination of Toronto, she changed her name again to Ethel Harvey. Although it is uncertain as to the date, Ethel eventually returned to England and married a clerk called Stanley Smith. They lived in Croydon and are believed to have had several children and grandchildren. Ethel eventually died in hospital in 1967, at the ripe old age of eighty-four.

The once-famous house, 39 Hilldrop Crescent, was destroyed, together with surrounding houses, by German air raids during World War II, leaving no grim reminder of the fiendish doctor Crippen.

DOCTOR JOHN BODKIN ADAMS

The town of Eastbourne in East Sussex nestles under the shadow of the South Downs, and has for many decades been a favourite place for retirement. Its genteel reputation and healing sea air made it ideal for people to spend the last years of their life, especially if they had money. Doctor John Bodkin Adams, a general practitioner who resided in Eastbourne, preyed on his elderly patients, including a large number of extremely well-to-do widows.

Adams graduated from medical school in 1921 and arrived in Eastbourne the following year, where he set up practice. Intially he lived with his mother, but in 1929, he borrowed a sum of money from an old friend and patient named William Mawhood to buy a house in the select area of Trinity Trees. However, Adams had not taken into account Mrs Edith Mawhood, who became suspicious when the doctor asked to be left alone with her husband. She decided to listen at the door, and it was just as well that she did, because she heard Adams asking the elderly man to leave his estate to him and that he would make sure that Edith was well looked after. Mrs Mawhood was fuming and stormed into her husband's bedroom wielding a walking stick. She struck out at Adams, forcing him to run out of the room and down the stairs.

Adams was certainly a most popular doctor, who seemed to have a certain bedside manner, especially with the elderly widows under his care. He charmed them by stroking their hands and combing their hair, but what he also did was make sure they weren't in any pain. In his little, brown doctor's bag, Adams not only carried large amounts of painkilling injections such as morphine, but allegedly blank will forms as well.

However, one fact that should be taken into account is that Adams trained in the 1920s, when there were very few trusted and tried remedies. Much of a patient's wellbeing came from a good bedside manner, and the ability to make the person as comfortable as possible in their final years. Many patients probably pleaded with their doctor not to let them suffer and this is probably the way Adams worked, but with an extra bonus at the end. It is obvious that the good doctor certainly eased his patients' passing into the next world, but whether he did it with malicious intent will always be a matter of contention.

The case of a Mrs Emily Mortimer is similar to the one regarding the Mawhoods. When a member of the Mortimer family passed away, the estate was always divided up between the remaining relatives, in that way the money always stayed within the family. However, when Emily Mortimer was being treated by Adams, he managed to convince her to break with tradition. Shortly before she died she signed a will which transferred £3,000 of the family money to her doctor. Several days before her death, she signed a second document leaving Adams £5,000, which meant that the Mortimer family were totally cut out of the will.

The first rumours regarding Adams' method of treating his patients started in 1935, when he received the first of many unsigned postcards. It was just after he had inherited the sum of £9,385 from a patient by the name of Mrs Matilda Whitton, whose whole estate only amounted to £11,465. Although Mrs Whitton's relatives contested the will, it was upheld in court.

SUSPICIONS MOUNT

On July 23, 1956, the Eastbourne police received an anonymous phone call from a popular music hall comedian by the name of Leslie Henson. He was concerned because his friend Gertrude Hullett, had died unexpectedly while being treated by Adams. During the ten months prior to her death, Hullett had been prescribed 165 grains of morphine and 140 grains of heroin, not as one would have imagined for pain, but merely because she was unable to sleep. A strange prescription for such a minor ailment.

Mrs Edith Alice Morrell was exceedingly wealthy and during the months Adams treated her, he received many gifts. She left him a canteen of silver cutlery and an antique Elizabethan cupboard. In March 1950, Adams called on Morrell's solicitor, saying that his patient wished to bequeath him her 1929 Rolls Royce as well. In September, Adams decided to go on holiday, which was something that made Morrell very angry and she cut him out of her will. Adams immediately rushed back to Eastbourne and managed to placate his patient, reinstating himself back in her favour and in her will.

During the last few days of Hullett's life, her doses of opiates were greatly increased. These were given by injections, either by Adams himself or the attending nurses and his eventual murder case was to hinge on these administrations.

When Morrell died on November 13, Adams deliberately lied on the cremation certificate, stating that he had no pecuniary interest in the deceased's estate. Also, when questioned about the administered drugs, he replied, 'Easing the passing of a dying person is not wicked. She wanted to die. That cannot be murder.'

At the time of Morrell's death no action was taken, but six years later rumours started to escalate and eventually the police were forced to launch an investigation. It was felt that the death of Edith Morrell was a strong enough case and Adams was brought to trial for her murder on March 18, 1957.

The investigation was led by Detective Superintendent Herbert Hannam of Scotland Yard, who had made a name for himself during the infamous Teddington Towpath murders in 1953. Adams fully cooperated with the investigations and seemed to be at complete ease answering Hannam's questions. As the evidence mounted, it was discovered that the kindly doctor had not only amassed numerous trinkets, cars, antiques and Old Masters, but over his twenty-five years of administering to his elderly patients, he had also become the beneficiary in no less than 132 wills.

Hannam managed to collect enough evidence on four cases and of these Adams was charged with the murders of Edith Morrell and Gertrude Hullett.

THE TRIAL

The prosecution was led by the Attorney-General himself, Sir Reginald Manningham, who was famous for his bullying tactics. Adams' defence was led by Geoffrey Lawrence, QC, who was little known at the time of the trial, but soon became a hero as the case got underway. On the first day, the prosecution pointed out the excessive amounts of drugs that had been ordered from the dispensing chemist. This evidence was followed by that of the four nurses who had looked after Mrs Morrell at her home. They confirmed in exact detail, even though it was six years later, that large quantities of opiates had been administered to Mrs Morrell and that they had all been recorded in log books. When asked the whereabouts of these records, the nurses replied that they had long since disappeared.

Lawrence faced the judge and said, 'If only we had those old books, we could see the truth of exactly what happened.' To the astonishment of the court, he ordered that a large suitcase be brought in as evidence. When Lawrence opened the case, to everyone's surprise it contained all the record books of the last eighteen months of Mrs Morrell's life. It turns out that Adams had actually filed them away, but they had been forgotten about until a couple of days before the trial. This all happened on the second day of the hearing and Lawrence methodically went through the books year by year and soon found glaring inconsistencies in the nurses' stories.

On day three, Lawrence pulled off his *coup de*

grâce. The QC had established that all four of the nurses had travelled from Eastbourne to the Old Bailey in London in the same railway carriage and, no doubt, discussed the case in detail, even though two of the nurses had not yet taken the witness stand. What they didn't know, however, was that the man sitting in the corner of the carriage reading his newspaper, was a senior civil servant who was fully aware of the legal implications that this conferring would have on the outcome of the case. This information, plus the evidence in the books showing far lower doses of opiates than stated by the nurses, cast considerable doubt on the case put forward by the prosecution.

Then the prosecution brought in the heavy artillery, in the name of Doctor A. H. Douthwaite. He was a senior physician at Guy's Hospital in London and was also President-Elect at the Royal College of Physicians. He was a man at the top of his profession and he told the court that, in his opinion, the doses given to Mrs Morrell were such that were intended to kill. The evidence in the books, however, disproved this, showing that the amounts given were not high enough to cause addiction, let alone death. When Lawrence cross-examined the doctor, he said, 'Would not another doctor reviewing the matter be forced to a different conclusion?' Douthwaite, regrettably, had to admit that this was the case, and his confusion added to the element of doubt already put in the minds of the jury.

As the trial entered its third week, Dr John Bodkin Adams had not been called to the witness box. However, despite normal procedure, Lawrence had another trick up his sleeve and decided not to call the accused to the stand. Although this was un-precedented, Lawrence felt by keeping Adams out of the witness box, it also kept him away from the bullying tactics of Manningham. Lawrence was well aware that the bumbling, now ageing Adams, could well have hanged himself if he had had to face such a fierce prosecution.

By the end of the trial the jury were so confused as to what was a lethal dose of morphine and what was not, Lawrence felt he had handled his defence perfectly. After three weeks of high drama, on April 15, 1957, the jury only took forty-five minutes to re-turn a verdict of Not Guilty, to the astonishment of the legal and medical professions and all the good folk of Eastbourne.

Doctor Bodkin Adams, with a grin all over his face walked from the courtroom straight into the waiting arms of the *Daily Express*, selling his remarkable story for £10,000.

REPUTATION INTACT

Doctor Bodkin Adams left the Old Bailey with his reputation intact, and it wasn't long before he was back patting the hands of his wealthy, silver-haired old ladies, who seemed only too willing to part with a little bit of their antique silver in return for some TLC. Adams died in 1983 at the age of eighty-four, leaving behind him an estate worth £403,000. As he had never married and had no family, the money was divided equally among the forty-seven friends who had supported him throughout his ordeal back in the 1950s.

The case of Doctor Bodkin Adams has gone down in the annals of history because of the sensational aspects of the trial. The defence cleverly manipulated the jury over the issue of whether palliative care, which hastens death, is a bad thing. One thing is for certain though, Adams seems to have got one over on the legal fraternity, which not only failed to convict him for numerous murders, but allowed him to go free and resume his medical career, only to kill again. The final conclusion will have to be in the hands of the reader as to whether Adams was in fact a fiendish killer, or just a kindly old doctor trying to appease the suffering of his infirm, but wealthy, patients.

DOCTOR JOSEF MENGELE

Most people have seen gruelling images of truck-loads of people arriving at the Auschwitz concentration camp, but how many know what went on behind closed doors. Amid all the despair stood a solitary figure wearing an immaculate SS uniform and white gloves, inspecting the new arrivals and dividing them up into two separate groups merely by the wave of a riding crop. The group on the left were heading straight for the gas chambers, while the ones on the right were heading for a fate far worse than death. The man making this decision was Josef Mengele, dubbed the 'Angel of Death', one of the many doctors assigned to Auschwitz, where medicine was used as a tool for genocide.

EARLY LIFE

Mengele was born on March 16, 1911, in Gunzburg,

in Germany's Bavarian region, and was the eldest of three sons. His father Karl Mengele had a successful company producing farm machinery, Karl Mengele & Sons, and Josef was expected to following in his father's footsteps. However, the young Mengele had far greater aspirations.

In October 1930, a confident and ambitious young man left his family home and headed for the Bavarian capital of Munich. The city was fast becoming impregnated with the racist doctrines of Adolf Hitler's National Socialist German Workers Party. Mengele, who had had a strict Catholic upbringing, found it difficult at first, but soon discovered that the Nazi movement had a strong attraction for him. It was in Munich that Hitler first gave birth to his idea for a new German super-race that Mengele was eventually to get involved with.

Mengele enrolled at the University of Munich and studied philosophy and medicine. He also went on to study anthropology and paleontology and showed intense interest in the evolution of man. Precisely what corrupted the young Mengele's mind is hard to ascertain, but it is obvious that at this stage in his life he was driven by a searing ambition to succeed.

Mengele passed his state medical examination in Munich in 1936, and for four months was a resident junior doctor, a compulsory period of work that was required for his full medical practitioner's degree. During this period of long hours and exhausting ward rounds, Mengele met Irene Schoenbein, his first and only real love. Irene was just nineteen, blonde and beautiful, and together they cut a dashing pair.

Mengele was desperate to return to his studies in genetics and with the help of one of his professors, T. Mollinson, he was appointed as a research assistant at the Third Reich Institute for Heredity, Biology and Racial Purity at the University of Frankfurt. It was this appointment that changed Mengele's life. Working under one of Europe's foremost geneticists, Professor Otmar Freiherr von Verschuer, he devoted much of his time to studying the genetics of twins. Verschuer was quite open with his new student about his admiration of Adolf Hitler and his dream of a perfect race.

Mengele soon became Verschuer's favourite student, and they developed a mutual respect for each other. Mengele became indoctrinated into the Nazi theories of race 'purification' and was just one short step away from the act of genocide. By the time his education had finished, Mengele was a member of both the National Socialist Party and the SS, and had developed a deep hatred of the Jewish race.

ACTIVE SERVICE

By July 1938, Mengele had finished his medical training and had received his degree. In July 1939, he married Irene, who was just twenty-one years old, after an initial hitch when her family had to be tested to make sure it carried no Jewish genes.

With war clouds gathering over Europe, Mengele was keen not to be left out of the action and at the beginning of World War II, was enlisted for service with the Waffen-SS. Mengele served as a medical officer and was stationed with various units in the Ukraine, receiving four medals for his bravery. However his career in the Army was cut short when he was wounded and declared unfit for active service.

AUSCHWITZ

In 1942, Mengele was posted to the Race and Resettlement Office in Berlin, which meant he was involved in the medical supervision of the concentration camps. It is pretty certain that this position was secured with the helping hand of his old tutor and friend, Professor Verschuer. At the time Verschuer was the director of the Kaiser Wilhelm Institute in Berlin, which was responsible for overseeing research programmes into racial purity. There is evidence that Verschuer convinced Mengele to take the next major step in his career – to go and work at Auschwitz.

Mengele's posting came in May 1943, and by the end of the month the young captain arrived at the vast barbed-wire enclosure in a swampy valley just a short drive from Krakow in southern Poland. In just twenty-one months at Auschwitz, Mengele was to commit untold atrocities 'all in the name of science'!

Anyone who survived the concentration camp, remembered vividly the slightly built man, with the immaculate uniform, the tilted SS cap, the well-scrubbed face and neatly combed hair. Unlike the other physicians stationed at Auschwitz, Mengele seemed to glory in the power and was in total agreement with the brutal treatment of the inmates. He liked to be present to supervise the selections of incoming transports and it is believed that as many as 400,000 babies, children, mothers, fathers and grandparents were given their fate by just the flick of his riding crop. He wasn't opposed to actually using this riding crop on any insubordinate prisoners and there are even reports that he used his pistol under extreme circumstances.

Mengele, although not the chief physician at Auschwitz, was appointed his own laboratory block with independent financing. At thirty-two years of age, he was in charge of his staff of inmate physicians, who were well aware of his feelings towards the prisoners. In his mind they were not fit to be humans and his behaviour reflected this attitude. This became apparent from the moment Mengele arrived at Auschwitz, when he ordered 600 sick women that he found in the camp hospital to be taken directly to the gas chambers. However, it was not just his harsh administration that Mengele will be remembered for, it was also the perverse experiments he carried out on his hapless victims.

The main reason Mengele wanted to be present at the arrival ramps was his obsession with twins. He gave strict orders that any twins were to be housed in separate quarters, pampered and treated like priceless objects. Mengele felt that by studying the identical features of the twins he could somehow unlock the secret to creating a genetically engineered perfect human being. Each twin was carefully measured and his findings were carefully recorded, with the dissection report always coming last. However well the twins were treated, Mengele never saw them as people – to him they were just his subjects of research. He carried out twin-to-twin transfusions, stitched twins together, sex change operations and the removal of organs and limbs, all under the guise of experimental surgery. He injected them with viral and bacterial agents to see how long it took each twin to succumb to the infections. He tried swapping body parts from one twin to another to see if it would continue to thrive. There was no end to Mengele's research, and he had no compunction whatsoever about personally killing the twins as the final step.

His research didn't stop at twins, however, he also had a 'collection' of dwarves and people (especially Jews) with any genetic abnormality. He became interested in a condition called 'noma', which was gangrene of the face and mouth caused by extreme debilitation. Although the condition was caused by the conditions at Auschwitz, Mengele was still obsessed in finding the genetic causes for the disease.

Another horrifying type of experiment carried out by Mengele were his attempts to change the colour of a person's eyes. He began by injecting various chemicals into the eyes, but, of course, the end results were pain and infections which usually led to blindness.

He was known to have conducted some of the most abominable experiments ever carried out during World War II. He would strap children to slabs of marble and then, without medication or any form of anaesthesia he would perform macabre surgical procedures, which nearly always ended in death. His behaviour certainly defies rational explanation, and his reputation became equal to that of a demon. In addition to his own experiments at Auschwitz, Mengele also sent specimens such as eyes to his old associate Professor Verschuer, to carry out his own research.

Not many children survived Auschwitz, but those who did recall the smiling Uncle Mengele bringing them sweets and clothes before being taken to his laboratory, where the nightmare would begin.

LAST DAYS IN EXILE

Mengele's days as a 'doctor' at Auschwitz came to an end on January 17, 1945, when the Soviet Army marched into Poland. The only option Mengele had was to flee the country. Using a false identity, he managed to reach Argentina on an Italian ocean liner, where he was harboured by a number of South American families.

By the time the Brazilian police tracked down his whereabouts, all that was left was a grave marked 'Wolfgang Gerhard' and a few skeletal remains. Mengele was eventually broken by more than thirty years of being on the run. Although he died in 1979 from a stroke while swimming near Sao Paulo in Brazil, news of his death did not reach the rest of the world until 1985.

There is no doubt that Mengele was a fiendish killer, a direct result of Adolf Hitler's seduction and perversion of the German people. Although there is some consolation in the fact that the once frightening figure died a lonely and embittered old man, there is no justice, however, in knowing that Mengele remained unrepentant and untried to the very end.

DOCTOR JEFFREY MACDONALD

Jeffrey MacDonald and Colette Stevenson had been high school sweethearts and their relationship continued when they went off to college. They had both grown up in New York and within two years of starting college, the pair decided to marry in 1963. Their first child, Kimberly, was born in April 1964 and Colette became a full-time mother while Jeffrey continued his education.

When MacDonald left Princeton University, he attended Northwestern University Medical School in Chicago. Times were difficult for the young couple, and they found it even harder when the second child, Kristen Jean, was born in May 1967. After qualifying, MacDonald joined the Army and the family were relocated to Fort Bragg, North Carolina, the home of the Paratroopers and Special Operations.

Life started looking up and MacDonald was soon promoted to a surgeon with the Green Berets. Colette was expecting their third child and she wrote excitedly to all her friends back home about their new life. However, her new-found joy was to be short-lived.

A VERY BAD DAY

It was a cold, rainy morning on Tuesday, February 17, 1970, and for the MacDonald family it turned out to be a very bad day. At about 3.30 a.m. a telephone operator took an emergency call from a desperate sounding man. He said he was Captain MacDonald and that he needed her to call the military police and an ambulance to 544 Castle Drive. Then, just before he passed out, he managed to whisper the words 'stabbing – help!'

A number of military policemen (MPs) were despatched to the house, but they did not call the base hospital to send an ambulance until they found out whether it was absolutely necessary. When they arrived at Castle Drive they found the house in darkness and entered through the back door. Inside the master bedroom lay the body of twenty-six-year-old Colette, laying on her back and covered in blood. Her face and head had been badly beaten, her legs were splayed apart and her pyjamas had been ripped to reveal her chest.

Lying next to Colette was her husband, Jeffrey, with his arm draped across his wife's body. As one of the MP's, Kenneth Mica, bent down to see if he was still breathing, Jeffrey managed to whisper, 'How are my kids? I heard them crying?'

Mica immediately stood up and ran into the other bedroom. To his relief he found five-year-old Kimberly asleep under the covers, but as he shone his flashlight on the child the sight sickened him to his stomach. Her head had been smashed in and there were several stab wounds around her neck.

In the third bedroom, two-year-old Kristen lay dead with multiple stab wounds to her chest and back. Then Mica rushed back to MacDonald, who was having problems breathing, so he gave him mouth-to-mouth resuscitation. When MacDonald started to regain consciousness, he tried to push Mica away and shouted at him to attend to his wife and children.

Mica tried to get out of MacDonald who had carried out such a vicious attack and he managed to tell him, 'Three men – a woman – one man was coloured, he wore a field jacket, sergeant's stripes. The woman, blonde hair, floppy hair, short skirt, muddy boots – she carried a light, I think a candle.'

Mica remembered seeing a woman wearing a floppy hat standing out in the rain as he was on his way to Castle Drive, and at the time he thought how strange it was. However, as he was on his way to an emergency call he didn't stop to speak to her.

Eventually the ambulance arrived and they wheeled the semi-conscious MacDonald out on a stretcher, still calling to see his wife and kids.

MACDONALD'S SIDE OF THE STORY

Jeffrey MacDonald had to stay in hospital for seven days and was treated for wounds to his head, various cuts and brushes on his shoulders, chest, hands and fingers, plus several puncture wounds around his heart. One of the knife wounds had punctured his lung, causing it to collapse, and he wasn't considered well enough to interview until February 25.

MacDonald told the military police that his wife had gone to bed before him, because he wanted to stay up and watch something on television. A little while later he heard Kristen crying and made her a bottle. He said he checked that the windows were only open a little way and then returned to watch television. When he did eventually go up to bed he found that Kristen had climbed into his side but had wet the covers, so he moved her back to her own bed and went to sleep on the living room sofa.

He found it very hard to talk about his family and kept breaking down during questioning. He managed to compose himself enough to give them his side of the story. He told the police that he had been woken by the sound of his wife screaming but before he could get off the sofa he was attacked by a black man with a baseball bat, while two white men held him down. His pyjama top had been pulled up over his head, which prevented him from fighting back, because his arms were trapped in the sleeves. He remembered being stabbed several times with a sharp object and a blonde woman standing close by with a candle yelling, 'kill the pigs' and 'acid is groovy'. He said he was continually hit round the head until he lost consciousness. When he came round the intruders had gone and he tried to revive Colette with mouth-to-mouth resuscitation. When he knew it was hopeless he ran to try and help his children, but when he realised it was useless he phoned for the emergency services.

The Army investigator at Fort Bragg was young and inexperienced and didn't believe MacDonald's story. He told the CID that he felt he had fabricated the whole thing and injured himself to prove his innocence. The CID took notice of the investigator and then focussed all their efforts on trying to prove MacDonald's guilt, ignoring all the evidence back at the house.

In fact the whole investigation turned into a complete fiasco because the MPs made no effort to make sure the evidence at the house was left untouched. The telephone receiver, which had been left dangling after MacDonald made his call, was picked up and used by one of the MPs to let headquarters know they had arrived at the scene. After MacDonald described his four assailants to Mica, he made no effort to set up roadblocks on the exits leaving the Army barracks, despite several suggestions from his men. Added to this, at least a dozen MPs had been running about the house after the call-out, and as it was a wet night, it would have been impossible to know who brought in the wet grass that had been tracked in from outside, the police or the intruders. No fingerprints or hair samples were taken from the victims, with the exception of a sample taken from MacDonald, which actually turned out to be hair from a pony he had bought for his daughters.

MacDonald was officially charged with murder on May 1, 1970 and his outraged father-in-law, Freddy Kassab, started his own publicity campaign to show that the charges against his son-in-law were completely false.

In the meantime, Bernie Segal, MacDonald's attorney, was given a tip-off regarding the identification of the woman in the floppy hat. Her name was Helena Stoeckley, the daughter of a retired Army officer. Not only was she involved with drugs and the world of witchcraft, but she was also an informant for the local police. Unfortunately, by the time the police were given this information, Helena Stoeckley was nowhere to be found.

THE TRIAL

During the trial Segal called a number of MacDonald's friends and family to stand as character witnesses. The most important of these, was his father-in-law, who gave an exceptionally emotional testimony on behalf of himself and his wife, Mildred:

> *We know full well that Jeffrey MacDonald is innocent beyond any shadow of doubt, as does everyone who knew him. I charge that the Army has never made any effort to look for the real murderers and that they know Captain MacDonald is innocent of any crime.*

The same sentiment was echoed time and time again, confirming that MacDonald was a devoted husband and father and an outstanding young soldier. The only blemish to his otherwise squeaky-clean record, was a number of illicit liaisons while he had been away on business trips.

After a gruelling six-week trial, the case against MacDonald was reluctantly dropped on the basis of insufficient evidence. The Army, who were still smarting from the humiliation of their indiscretions during the investigation, vowed to carry on their campaign to get the captain convicted.

THE INVESTIGATION GOES ON

MacDonald, not surprisingly after the way he had been treated, applied for a discharge from the Army. He desperately needed to find a job to pay his mother back for the legal bills that had mounted up during his trial. While he struggled to return to civilian life, MacDonald made the mistake of still publicising the Army's incompetence, even going as far as appearing on public television. However, the lighthearted way in which he talked about the death of his family lost him credibility with a lot of people, including his in-laws.

The CID and the Army carried on with their investigations into the MacDonald case, desperate to try and clear their names. They managed to locate Helena Stoeckley, who told the police that she believed she had been a witness to the murders, but asked for immunity from prosecution. Forensic officers were unable to match her fingerprints with the few remaining prints that had not already been obliterated from the crime scene, and she was subsequently cleared as being a suspect. MacDonald, on the other hand, again became the prime suspect.

Unaware of the latest revelations, MacDonald was busy rebuilding his own life. He had taken a job in the emergency department of the St Mary Medical Center in Long Beach, California. With the help of his close friend Jerry Hughes, MacDonald transformed the department into one of the best in the state.

In August 1974, prosecutors contacted MacDonald's attorney, Segal, and told him that they wanted access to MacDonald's psychiatric files. Segal agreed as long as the doctor who read the report, Robert Sadoff, was prepared to give his evaluation to the grand jury. However, the doctor did not keep his part of the bargain. Then one of the grand jurors asked if MacDonald would take a sodium amytal test, a form of behavioural testing by injecting anaesthetic into part of the brain. MacDonald agreed quite willingly to the test, so long as Sadoff was present to supervise the procedure. However, despite the fact that a room was prepared for the test, the chief prosecutor never had any intention of letting it go ahead, nor indeed letting Sadoff testify, so it was called off. The grand jury, falsely believing that MacDonald had refused to take the sodium amytal test, had the doctor indicted for the second time for the murder of his family. His new trial was set for the middle of 1979.

THE SECOND TRIAL

Little did MacDonald and Segal realise, but the odds were severely stacked against them. Dr John

Thornton, a forensic scientist, who had been hired by Segal during the first trial, had never been given permission to see the original evidence or laboratory notes taken by the Army and the FBI. When Segal eventually managed to get permission, Thornton was only allowed to view the evidence once, which did not give him sufficient time to check the validity of what he saw.

One vital piece of evidence that was concealed from Segal, was a strand of long, blonde, synthetic fibre, which was found clutched in Colette's hand. It was the type of fibre used in making wigs, something which Helena Stoeckley openly admitted to wearing. She said she had worn a blonde wig on the night of the murder, but had disposed of it a little while later. There were also samples of skin and hair found underneath the fingernails of Colette and the children, neither of which matched MacDonald's. However the original laboratory notes had deliberately been held back, as this would have immediately indicated that MacDonald was innocent.

Ironically, Helena Stoeckley had confessed to Murtagh before the trial that she had been present on the night of the murders, but didn't remember much because she had been taking drugs. She said she was there with her boyfriend Greg Mitchell and several soldiers from Fort Bragg. She remembered seeing the MacDonald family being attacked, but became hysterical at the sight of all the blood and had to run from the house. However, like the other evidence, this was never made available to the defence. Fortunately, her confessions were recorded on video because Stoeckley died at the age of thirty from liver complications in 1982.

Apparently Fort Bragg had serious problems with drugs in the late 1960s and early 1970s, and MacDonald was one of the physicians who was very concerned about the situation. He had threatened to try and resolve the situation and report on any soldiers who he knew regularly used drugs. So once again the evidence pointed to the fact that the attacks had been drug-related.

Despite hundreds of items placed in evidence and the testimonies of over sixty witnesses, after six-and-a-half weeks of another gruelling trial, Jeffrey MacDonald was found guilty. The federal government were happy, satisfied that this time justice had been served.

The final piece of evidence that made the jury sit up and take notice was the pyjama top worn by MacDonald on the night of the murders. He had told investigators that during the struggle with his attackers, his top had got pulled over his head and that his hands had become entangled in the sleeves. For this reason, he said, he was unable to fend off the blows from an ice pick. However, the prosecution said that the pyjama top told a completely different story. They claimed if MacDonald was telling the truth, then he wouldn't be alive today. They claimed that he had folded the top and placed it on top of Colette's body and then repeatedly stabbed her through it with the ice pick.

TWENTY-FIVE YEARS LATER

Twenty-five years after MacDonald was convicted of murder, Bernie Segal is still frustrated with the outcome of the case. He is convinced the trial was corrupt and that vital evidence was either lost or withheld from the defence. The courts chose not to believe the evidence of Helena Stoeckley even though the details she gave to the police could be corroborated. For example, she said she had tried to ride a rocking horse at the MacDonald house on the night of the murders, but the spring was broken. The only people who knew about that spring was the MacDonald family so it was not something she could have fabricated.

Forty-four-year-old Kathryn married Jeffrey MacDonald on August 30, 2002, after reading his story and writing to him in prison. Three times a week she makes the long drive to visit her husband at the Cumberland Federal Prison in Maryland. With a new life waiting for him outside, MacDonald applied for parole. With the help of his loyal wife, MacDonald continues to fight and he still says that he knows one day he will be free. MacDonald will be eligible to reapply for parole in 2020 when he will be seventy-six years old.

Whether or not MacDonald was a fiendish killer or not will always be a matter of contention, but regardless of that his story still makes very interesting reading.

DOCTOR MICHAEL SWANGO

Michael Joseph Swango, could be described as the 'Doctor of Death', because he was suspected of administering lethal injections to as many as thirty-five of his patients between 1983 and 1997. Swango was well aware of his good looks, popularity and charisma, all of which he used to his advantage to cover a web of lies and suspicious operations.

EARLY SIGNS

Michael Swango studied medicine at Southern Illinois University, and it was here that the early signs of his macabre nature started to show. Many of his fellow students described him as being 'nuts' as the demanding workload forced them to work in close proximity with each other. Despite being a bright pupil, Swango was lazy and lacked the enthusiasm of the other students. He found the written part of his course a breeze, but when it came to the practical side he struggled even to identify the position of a human heart. On one occasion, when he was required to dissect a cadaver, he made such a mess of it that he became the laughing stock of the class. Swango seemed to be unaffected by this ridicule and let it ride over him.

Two other traits manifested themselves during his training. One was a complete lack of bedside manner and the other was a morbid interest in death. He seemed to show an abnormal curiosity in any terminally ill patients and, as soon as they passed away, he used to scratch 'DIED' across their charts in large red letters. While attending university, Swango worked for the Ambulance Service and, even though it meant he missed out on valuable study time, it gave him a chance to see the blood and gore the job afforded. The sight of blood seemed to excite him and he loved nothing better than to try and prise loose unfortunate victims of road accidents.

During his last year at university, Swango's father died and, although he was never close to the man he decided to do the honourable thing and attend his funeral. At the graveside his mother handed Swango a scrapbook, which his father had kept showing the world's worst disasters. Swango was fascinated and thumbed through the pages in delight, exclaiming, 'Hell, I guess Dad wasn't such a bad guy after all.'

Inspired by what his father had done, Swango continued to scour the papers for any interesting articles that went into gory details and added more pages to the scrapbook.

Swango failed to graduate with the rest of his class in 1982, and was forced to retake some of his course work. Despite a poor recommendation from Southern Illinois University, Swango managed to get a surgical internship at Ohio State University. The university had a reputation for its professionalism and it soon became obvious to Swango's superiors that he wasn't really competent to practise medicine. He had a brusque bedside manner and seemed to be indifferent to his patient's feelings. His fellow interns described him as strange and wondered whether he was ever really paying attention to what was being taught.

UNETHICAL PRACTISES

On January 31, 1984, Swango walked into the room of a neurosurgery patient by the name of Ruth Barrick. He was supposed to check her intravenous drip, but the attending nurse wondered why an intern was making the check so late in the morning, something which was normally carried out by a doctor. Against her better judgement, the nurse left Swango on his own as he had requested. She returned to the room about twenty minutes later to find Swango gone and the patient turning blue and gasping for breath. The nurse called the emergency team, who were able to resuscitate her and she made a full recovery. The hospital physicians, however, were puzzled as to what had caused such an unexpected respiratory failure.

The following week, another nurse noticed an unsual reading on the gauge of an intravenous tube. She called a doctor to check it and Swango answered the call. He asked the nurse to leave him with the patient, but when she was concerned about the amount of time he was taking, she went back inside the room to see if there was a problem. Swango told her abruptly that there was no problem and seemed to be angry at the interruption. When Swango finally left the room, the nurse went back in to check the dressing that she had applied earlier. The patient was gasping for breath and, despite emergency treatment, did not recover. While the team tried to resuscitate the patient, Swango merely stood at the base of the bed doing nothing, seemingly totally unaffected by the whole thing.

Twenty-four hours later, nurse Beery was doing her rounds and went into a room to check one of her elderly patients who was recovering from an operation. When she opened the door, she saw an intern injecting something into the patient's intravenous tube with a syringe. At first Beery assumed that he was attending to a blockage in the tube, which wasn't abnormal and when Swango realised he was being watched he quickly left the room. Within minutes the patient was shaking uncontrollably and turning blue. The emergency team were able to save her life and as soon as she was strong enough she motioned for a notebook and pencil. She wrote: 'Someone gave me some med in my IV and paralyzed all of me, lungs, heart, speech.' When she was able to speak she was able to describe the intern as being tall and blond, a perfect description of Swango. Swango denied having been anywhere near the room, but there were nurses on the floor who were convinced that they had seen him darting out of a lavatory just down the corridor. When one of the nurses went to check the lavatory, she found a syringe that had recently been washed out and wrapped in a piece of tissue.

With the recent rise in the number of deaths, and the suspicions of several nurses, the staff decided it was time to present their misgivings to the Neurosurgery Professor, Joseph Goodman. However, Goodman wanted to maintain the reputation of the university and only a superficial investigation was carried out. Although he read the reports, the professor never interviewed any of the nurses or the emergency teams who carried out the resuscitations. Swango was considered to be a victim of the staff's paranoia, and he was taken off probation with full intern privileges.

The gossip had barely died down, when Swango was transferred to Doan Hall to work surgery rotation. It wasn't long before another series of mysterious deaths occurred. One patient bled profusely from all her body orifices following an examination by Swango. A twenty-two-year-old woman who was recovering from a simple operation, died after Swango gave her injection as he so politely put it 'to increase her blood pressure'.

Putting the suspicious deaths aside, the medical review committee ruled Swango's performance as 'poor' and they failed to offer him a position as a resident physician. Swango was angry when he left the university at the conclusion of his internship in June, and decided to return to Quincy, Illinois. He told his family that he had been the victim of a personality clash with his superiors and he set about seeking another position.

A SECOND CHANCE

Back on old territory, Swango managed to get a job with the Adams County Ambulance Corps. Unaware of his background, his new employers felt they had gained a real asset to their team, especially with all his medical knowledge. Working twenty-four hour shifts the ambulance teams spent a lot of time in each other's company and soon formed close friendships bonded by dedication to their job. All, that is, with the exception of the new recruit, who simply didn't fit in with the rest of the team. Swango quite openly admitted that he was turned on by violence and he started telling stories about his fantasies. Everyone thought he was just a talented 'crank' who made up stories to get attention – that is until the incident with the doughnuts.

The members of the ambulance team used to take it in turns to bring in treats such as biscuits or cakes to have with their coffee. On this particular morning in September, it was Swango's turn and he brought in an assortment of freshly baked doughnuts. The other four paramedics on duty were delighted and ate them straight away, but within an hour they were to regret being so greedy. One after another they started to complain of stomach cramps, nausea and dizziness, and then they started to vomit and each one had to go home. No one had noticed that Swango was the only one who hadn't eaten any of the treats.

The following evening Swango was on duty with a fellow medic when he said he was thirsty and said he was going to buy himself a cola. His co-worker asked if he would get him one as well but after drinking about half the bottle, the medic had to return home complaining of a headache, nausea and dizziness, which lasted for three days.

Swango immediately became a suspect, and none of his fellow workmates would eat or drink anything that he had touched. Except for one relatively new paramedic who made the mistake of accepting a can of soda from Swango.

TRAPPED IN HIS OWN WEB

After the latest episode, Swango's workmates decided to check out the bag that he always carried to work. As soon as Swango was called out on duty, they forced his locker open and rifled through his bag. Inside they found a box of ant poison, which, according to the label, was comprised mainly of arsenic. Aware that they had all been the subjects of poisoning, his colleagues set a trap. The men left a freshly brewed pot of iced tea on the counter when they knew Swango would be on his own.

When they returned, Swango was no longer around and the men took a sample of the liquid to the local coroner, who arranged for it to be tested. Sure enough it contained traces of arsenic.

When the sheriff searched Swango's apartment, amid all the mess he found vials, bottles, syringes and other medical equipment, alongside numerous bottles of chemicals which they suspected to be poison or poisonous compounds. There were several recipes for poisons and the police also found a stash of handguns and a range of knives.

Swango was arrested and his trial opened on April 22, 1985. It didn't take too much investigative work for the prosecution to uncover Swango's dodgy medical past, and at the end of the trial the jury came back with a unanimous guilty verdict. As the judge read out his sentence he turned to the prisoner and said:

> *It's clearly obvious to me that every man, woman and child in this community or anywhere else that you might go is in jeopardy as long as you are a free man . . . You deserve the maximum under the law because there is no excuse for what you have done.*

Despite the severity of Swango's crimes he was only given a five-year sentence to be served at the Centralia Correctional Center in Illinois and his licence to practise medicine in Illinois was revoked.

NOT THE END OF THE STORY

Swango was released from prison for good behaviour on August 21, 1987, after having only served two years of his sentence. His name had long since left the headlines, but to be on the safe side he decided to put miles between himself and Illinois. Swango moved to Newport News in Virginia, but when he applied for a medical licence, his past caught up with him and he was turned down. His first job at a Career Development Center was brief, as his employers felt he spent far too much time on his peculiar habit of adding pages to his weird scrapbook. From there he obtained a position as a laboratory technician at Aticoal Services, a company responsible for exporting coal. He seemed to fare better in this position and, although his co-workers thought he was a little strange, they were quite prepared to sit and have lunch with him. A big mistake, however, when several of his colleagues fell ill and almost died from severe 'food poisoning'.

KRISTIN KINNEY

Swango was desperate to get back into the medical profession, but his past record was holding him back. When he first met the attractive, red-haired, twenty-

six-year-old, Kristin Kinney, she was engaged to a
doctor at Newport News' Riverside Hospital.
Swango was taking a refresher course at the hospital
and at first their relationship was purely on a platonic
level. Many of Kristin's friends tried to dissuade her
from having a friendship with Swango, as it was
common knowledge he had been turned down by
the hospital because of some past scandal. Kristin just
laughed it off and said they were being unfair.

Swango continued to apply for medical posts
around the country and his diligence paid off when
he received a letter in September 1991 from the
University of South Dakota. When Swango phoned
Dr Anthony Salem, he was congratulated on his
excellent CV but asked him to clarify certain episodes
he had mentioned in his covering letter. Swango lied
and said he had become involved in an unsightly
brawl in a bar and had been arrested for battery.
Salem said he was impressed with his honesty and
invited Swango to come for an interview. Kristin
kissed Swango goodbye and wished him luck as he
waited for the plane on October 3.

The interview was held in front of a number of
resident internists, who centred their questions on
his medical background, but ironically no one
bought up the matter of his criminal record.
Although many of the interviewers felt there was

something not quite right about Swango, his name remained on their shortlist and by June 1992 he was offered a residency.

To celebrate, Swango proposed to Kristin, who had long since broken off her previous engagement. She accepted his proposal and they planned to move in together in Sioux Falls. Kristin was hired as a nurse at a memorial hospital and she was looking forward to a bright future, despite the continued warnings of her friends and family.

At first it appears as though their misapprehensions were unfounded, as Swango soon proved himself to be one of the best emergency-situation doctors the hospital had ever had. Kristin made a difference with her bright, attentive personality and very soon the couple were popular and envied by many in their field. However, by October 1992, Swango became far too cocksure and applied for membership in the American Medical Association (AMA), despite the fact that he had obtained his internship under false pretences. For some reason Swango must have assumed that they wouldn't check his credentials, but this is where he was wrong.

While the hospital were learning that their talented doctor was not what he appeared, Kristin and some of her colleagues watched a television programme about a doctor who had intentionally infected his workmates with poisoned doughnuts. Kristin was devastated and Swango, who by this time had been dismissed from his post, was in no frame of mind to pacify his girlfriend. Swango ranted and raved that he had been the subject of a set-up, but never once comforted Kristin, leaving her feeling rejected.

Some of Kristin's friends at the hospital tried to show their support by inviting her and Swango to a party. However, Kristin noticed that the host followed Swango from room to room and watched him closely whenever he went near the food.

Kristin started suffering from debilitating headaches. At first she put them down to tension, but as they continued she couldn't put the niggling thought of her mind that Swango might be putting poison in her food. Using her intuition as a nurse, she decided to get away from Swango and returned to live with her mother in Illinois, where miraculously the headaches stopped. In her heart she wanted to believe that Swango was innocent because she continued to love him despite her suspicions. In the end her emotions got the better of her and Kristin took her own life, leaving a note for Swango saying:

I love you more! You're the most precious man I've ever known. Love KK

MOVING ON

With Kristin gone, Swango concentrated on himself and successfully acquired yet another medical post in the State University of New York. When the matter of his past conviction was raised yet again, Swango used the old guise of a bar room fight and then produced a forged pardon. Once again no one bothered to check whether Swango actually had a practising licence – had they done so they would have realised they were hiring a fraud. Instead, they offered him a position with the Veterans Administration complex on Northport, Long Island.

Swango was back to his old tricks on the very first evening, when a man who had come into the hospital with a mild dose of pneumonia, mysteriously died after being attended by the new doctor. One by one elderly patients started dying of heart failure when they had appeared relatively healthy just hours before.

Suspicions reached a height when the wife of an elderly patient, Barron Harris, found Swango in his room with the light off, injecting something into her husband's neck. When she asked Swango what he was giving her husband, he replied dismissively, 'vitamins' and hurried out of the room. When Mrs Harris asked one of the nurses about the injection, the nurse looked shocked and replied, 'Doctors don't give shots. That's what we're supposed to do.'

Within days Harris's condition had deteriorated and he slipped into a deep coma. When Swango wrote 'DO NOT RESUSCITATE' on his chart, Mrs Harris demanded to know why, and Swango told her unemotionally, 'his brain is virtually dead'.

Mrs Harris attempted to sue the hospital for negligence, but the case was dismissed for lack of evidence. However, things were soon to change for the over-confident Dr Swango.

WANTING ANSWERS

Kristin's parents were not prepared to lay back and accept their daughter's suicide – they wanted some answers. They were convinced her death was due to the influence of Swango, someone who they had always considered to be an exceptionally evil man. They decided to contact some of Kristin's nursing friends back in South Dakota. Her friends were horrified when they learned that Swango had been given another medical post and immediately went to the Dean of their hospital with their suspicions.

The Dean immediately contacted the hospital where Swango was working and he was summoned to a meeting with Dr Miller. Miller pushed Swango about the real reason for his prison sentence, and eventually he admitted that it had not been for a fight but for suspicion of poisoning his fellow paramedics. Swango was immediately dismissed and the media had a heyday. Two doctors responsible for hiring Swango at the University of New York resigned and later told a reporter that 'Swango was a charming, pathological liar'. However, before resigning Dr Cohen sent a letter to every medical school in the USA, warning them about the bogus doctor.

Swango fled and, despite constant searching, the FBI were unable to track their suspect down. They assumed Swango had either taken his own life or, more likely, fled the country.

LIFE OVERSEAS

Now that most of the hospitals in his own country had been warned about him, Swango had to take his skills overseas. In November 1994 he resurfaced in Zimbabwe, South Africa, working at the Mnene Hospital. This mission hospital thought they had an excellent catch, as American doctors were hard to come by. He had come armed with pages of forged papers, attesting to his outstanding work in the USA. However, his attitude of disdain and the onset of several mysterious deaths, caused the nuns at the hospital to raise the alarm. Swango's cottage was searched and they found numerous syringes filled with liquid and bottles of substances that were unknown to the Zimbabwe doctors.

Swango was arrested and accused of poisoning his patients, but he managed to escape before his trial date and fled from South Africa. A year-and-a-half later, Swango was heading for Saudi Arabia using false papers, with a stopover at O'Hare Airport in Chicago, Illinois. On June 27, 1997, Swango was finally apprehended by FBI officers and then escorted back to New York for trial.

Three years later, on July 22, 2000, Michael Swango pleaded guilty to killing three patients and also to fraud. He was sentenced to life imprisonment, with no chance of ever receiving parole.

Michael Swango openly admitted to inmates that he killed 'for the pleasure of it' and no one can be sure as to how many people died as a result of his medical 'administerings'.

DOCTOR HAROLD SHIPMAN

Like his predecessor Bodkin Adams, Dr Harold Shipman preyed on his elderly, vulnerable patients, who were mostly women who lived alone. Despite the fact that his patients were dying in unusually high numbers, Shipman was seen as an 'angel of mercy', for as long as he eased their suffering, his patients remained loyal to the end. Amazingly, Shipman was allowed to practice for over twenty-four years in which time it is estimated that he could have been responsible for as many as 236 deaths.

THE YOUNG FREDDY

Known to his family as Freddy, the young Shipman was the middle one of three children and definitely his mother's favourite. Born on June 14, 1946, Harold Frederick Shipman had a far from normal childhood, due to the overpowering nature of his mother, Vera. She had high hopes for her son and decided to take control of his life from an early age. She vetted his friends, what he wore and where he went. He was reasonably bright as a young student, but his real love was athletics, at which he excelled. His mother had instilled in him a sense of superiority, something which stopped him from forming any close relationships in his formative years.

Shipman idolized his mother and was devastated when she was diagnosed with lung cancer. As soon as school was over he would rush home and make her a cup of tea, tears rolling down his cheeks as he watched her suffer. He would watch in fascination as their family doctor injected morphine into his mother's veins, amazed as the pain quickly subsided from her body. The calming bedside manner of the doctor and the relief obtained from the 'miracle morphine' left an indelible image on the young teenager, and it was a scene he would recreate time and time again in his future years.

Vera died in June 1963 when Shipman was only seventeen, leaving him with a tremendous sense of loss and for a while he struggled to find his way.

MEDICAL SCHOOL

Two years after his mother's death, Shipman was admitted to Leeds University medical school, after struggling first time round with the entrance exam. He found the academic life hard, but his grades were sufficient to earn him a degree and a hospital internship. His fellow students found him distant and many described him as 'strange', as he found it hard to form any deep relationships.

Shipman finally found his soulmate in a girl called Primrose, who was three years his junior. He found her company comforting, sympathising with an upbringing similar to his own. Primrose, who described herself as no oil painting, was delighted to have finally found herself a boyfriend, and before long she found herself pregnant. The couple married when Primrose was just seventeen and by 1974, Shipman was a devoted father of two and a medical practitioner in the town of Todmorten, Yorkshire.

Shipman seemed to blossom in his new post and became a respected member of the community. He was popular with his fellow doctors and patients, although occasionally the staff would see a different side of the young man when he would appear unnecessarily rude. Gradually Shipman became a control freak and seemed to have the knack of getting things done in his own way. Everything seemed set for the Shipman family to have a prosperous future, but then disaster struck in 1975.

PROBLEMS WITH DRUGS

The once hardworking, enthusiastic young doctor suddenly slowed down when he started having blackouts. As a cover-up, he told his partners that he was suffering with epilepsy, but the truth came out when their receptionist, Marjorie Walker, noticed some unusual entries in the narcotics ledger. The records showed that Shipman had ordered an excessively large amount of pethidine in the names of several of his patients. When his partners started to investigate the patients on Shipman's list, they soon discovered that they neither needed nor received the prescribed drug.

When Dr John Dacre confronted his young partner, Shipman confessed to using the drug for his own purposes, but pleaded for a second chance. When his request was denied, Shipman lost his temper and flung his medical bag to the floor, threatening to resign. His partners were horrified at the change in Shipman – it was a side they had never seen before.

When Shipman arrived home and told Primrose what had happened, she went to the surgery and stormed into the room where his partners were discussing the best way of getting rid of him. She yelled at the top of her voice that her husband would never resign, shouting 'You'll have to force him out!' That is precisely what they did and Shipman was forced to go into a drug rehabilitation centre in 1975.

Shipman was ultimately fined £600 for forging prescriptions but, amazingly, was not struck off the medical register. Two years later, apparently cured of his addiction to pethidine, Shipman was back in business as a family doctor.

LICENCE TO KILL

Shipman accepted a position at the Donneybrook Medical Centre in Hyde, in the north of England. He was quite open about his previous abuse of pethidine, and asked his superiors to keep an eye on him. It is obvious from what happened over the next twenty years, that people did not watch him close enough. By allowing Shipman to continue as a medical practitioner, the authorities had plain and simply given him a licence to kill.

It still seems incredible that one doctor could have so many patients dying under his care, without arousing any suspicion among his colleagues. Between the years 1974 and 1998 he was literally free to kill at random, and probably would have continued in this way had it not been for a woman called Angela Woodruff.

A BIG MISTAKE

The sudden death of eighty-one-year-old Kathleen Grundy on June 24, 1998, came as a shock to anyone who knew the previously spritely old woman. A wealthy, former mayor of Hyde, Grundy was energetic and a tireless worker for local charities right up until the day she died. When she failed to turn up at the Age Concern club, where she used to help serve the meals, her friends suspected there was something wrong. They immediately called round to her home and found her lying, fully dressed on her sofa. When they realised she was dead they phoned her family doctor, Shipman.

In fact, it turned out that Shipman had been the last person to see her alive. He had visited Grundy just a few hours earlier, allegedly to take routine blood samples. Shipman confirmed that Grundy was dead, and he phoned her daughter, Angela Woodruff, to break the sad news. Shipman told Woodruff that there was no need for a post-mortem because he had seen her shortly before she died.

Mrs Woodruff was understandly upset at the death of her mother, but accepted the kind words of the doctor, and Kathleen Grundy's body was laid to rest. Shipman was rubbing his hands together, realising he was about to profit from another death, unaware that he had made his first big mistake.

A QUESTION OF THE WILL

After the funeral, Woodruff received a worrying phone call from a firm of solicitors who claimed to have a copy of her mother's will. Mrs Woodruff was a solicitor herself and as far as she was aware the original will made in 1986, was still lodged with her own law firm. She immediately became suspicious and made an appointment with the solicitors. The moment she set eyes on the badly-typed document, Angela Woodruff knew it was a fake. Knowing her mother so well, Woodruff knew she would never have signed a document that was so badly worded and on top of that the signature looked strange, somehow too big. Then she continued reading the document which stated that the sum of £386,000 had been left to none other than Dr Harold Shipman. She had always liked her mother's doctor, but reluctantly she had to admit that it appeared as though Shipman had murdered her mother for profit.

Mrs Woodruff took her suspicions and the will to Detective Superintendent Bernard Postles. His own investigation convinced him that Woodruff was right, saying that you only had to look at the document to know it was something 'off a John Bull printing press'. As the police delved deeper into the life of Shipman, they uncovered numerous complaints about his callous attitude towards some of his patients. Postles decided to obtain an order to exhume the body of Kathleen Grundy. Although the body was exhumed during the night, the media were still alerted to a good story, and very soon the town of Hyde was swarming with members of the press.

While the body of Grundy was being examined, the police searched Shipman's house and discovered he owned an old Brother typewriter that matched the type used on the counterfeit will. When questioned about it, Shipman came up with the story that he had lent the typewriter to Mrs Grundy because she wanted to change her will.

As news of the investigation leaked out, various doctors and undertakers came forward with their suspicions about the number of deaths among Shipman's patients. Postles studied Shipman's book of death certificates carefully and made a list of fifteen deaths that he felt should be further investigated. On the list nine had been buried and the other six cremated, something which Shipman tried to encourage the relatives to do, obviously to destroy any incriminating evidence.

When the toxicology report was handed to Postles, he was quite shocked to find that the level of morphine in Grundy's body was the cause of death. He was shocked because he felt that a doctor would surely have realised that morphine was one of the few poisons that could remain in the body tissue for many years. He had expected the results to show a high level of insulin, something which the body produces naturally, and which would be much harder to prove was a result of foul play.

Postles soon realised that the case of Harold Shipman went far beyond one death, and the investigation was broadened immediately, with the nine other bodies being exhumed.

When Shipman was questioned about the level of morphine found in Grundy's body, he tried to imply that his patient was addicted to the drug, which he had tried to back-up by forging back entries in his drug records. Some people believed that Shipman saw himself as invincible, perhaps feeling that no one would ever doubt the word of a doctor, but his own arrogance and ignorance eventually turned out to be his downfall.

THE TRIAL

The trial began in October 1999 at Preston Crown Court. The Crown was represented by Richard Henriques QC, a prestigious barrister who had handled many sensitive and difficult trials. When he outlined the case to the jury he advised them to dismiss the theory of mercy killing as none of the victims had actually been suffering from a terminal illness. He claimed that Shipman had killed his patients simply because he enjoyed doing it and that sometimes there was an added bonus at the end. As the case continued, witness after witness, many of them relatives of Shipman's victims, painted the picture of a callous and deceitful man, who didn't know how to tell the truth.

When the defence got their chance, they tried to portray Shipman as a kind and caring family doctor, pointing out that he was not some fiendish killer but a happily married man with four children. No matter how hard the defence tried, they just couldn't make any headway due to the constantly mounting pile of evidence put forward by the prosecution.

After an intense and gruelling trial, the jury returned their verdict on January 31, 2000, with a unanimous decision. Shipman was found guilty of all fifteen counts of murder and several cases of forgery. Mr Justice Forbes closed the case by saying:

> *You murdered each and every one of your victims by a calculated and cold-blooded perversion of your medical skills, for your own evil and wicked purposes.*

The judge handed out fifteen life sentences with the recommendation that Harold Shipman should never be released.

FOUND DEAD IN HIS CELL

Harold Shipman took his own life on Tuesday, January 13, 2004, by hanging himself with his own bed sheet at Wakefield Prison. He died with the reputation of being one of the world's most prolific serial killers with an estimated 236 deaths, using lethal injections of diamorphine. Although Shipman never publicly confessed – in fact he emphatically denied the allegations – a fellow inmate at Preston Prison said that the doctor had confessed to him that he had killed as many as 508 patients. Although many believed that he killed his wealthy patients for monetary gain, further investigations have shown that his motive seems to have been more to exercise control, similar to Dr Swango, who killed his patients because it gave him a thrill and a feeling of power. Shipman never showed any remorse or guilt for his crimes, which left many people angry that he had been allowed to take his own life. One thing that will always come to mind in the case of Harold Shipman, is how on earth a man in the public eye could be allowed to have such a free rein over such a long period of time, with such devastating results.

PART SIX

VAMPIRES

GILLES DE RAIS

Although the fictional image of a vampire is someone who drinks the blood of another, a vampire can also be described as a person who appears to gain energy and life-force out of killing and extracting blood, as in the case of Gilles de Rais and Elizabeth Bathory.

Gilles de Rais, born in 1404, was a French noble, a brave young soldier and also a patron of the arts. Although he painted a fine figure, underneath was a far more sombre character, someone with a macabre fascination with children. He was convicted with the torture and rape of children between the ages of six and eighteen years, and it is thought that he lured as many as 200 innocent victims into his bedroom.

A TROUBLED CHILDHOOD

To try and understand a little more about Gilles de Rais it is important to know about his troubled childhood years. The marriage between Guy de

Rais and Marie d'Craon was not a match made in heaven, but a union solely for financial and political gain. Gilles de Rais was born nine months after the wedding, and his brother, Rene, two years later. Having been born into one of the wealthiest families in France, Gilles was raised by a nursemaid and rarely got to see either of his parents. When he did, he was expected to behave more like an adult than a child, so many of the normal antics of a young boy were suppressed.

In France, a boy reaches the 'age of reason' when he is seven, and the young Gilles was trained not only in the classic arts, but had to undergo military training as well.

The death of three members of his family before he was eleven years old had a major effect on Gilles de Rais. The first was the death of his uncle Amaury d'Craon, who was the sole male heir to his grandfather Jean d'Craon. The second was the death of his mother in 1415 and finally his father, who died a short while later during a hunting trip.

The two de Rais brothers were sent to live with their grandfather, Jean d'Craon, at Champtoce, despite the fact that their father had left strict instructions before he died that he was to have no part in their upbringing. Jean d'Craon was well known for his violent temper and was a bad role model for the two de Rais children. It is believed that it was Gilles's years with d'Craon that embedded the bad seed that blossomed as he grew into adulthood. The only real lesson of importance that Gilles learned from his grandfather was the art of fighting.

Jean d'Craon never made any secret of the fact that he intended to use his grandson to increase his own wealth, and when Gilles was just thirteen years old he negotiated a marriage with the daughter of Lord de Hambye of Normandy, Jeanne Peynel. Because Peynel was an exceptionally wealthy woman, the Parliament of Paris did not allow the marriage to go ahead, purely because their combined wealth would have made the house of d'Craon the most powerful in the whole of France.

Ten months later, d'Craon announced the engagement of Gilles to Beatrice de Rohan, who was the niece of the Duke of Burgundy. However, for some unknown reason, this marriage never took place either.

Eventually, under the advice of his grandfather, Gilles married his own cousin, Catherine de Thouars of Brittany, who was the heiress of La Vendee and Poitou, but he had to kidnap her first. The marriage took place in 1420, and his union to the extremely wealthy heiress meant that Gilles de Rais was now one of the richest noblemen in Europe.

For the next eight years Gilles de Rais served as a commander in the royal army, fighting alongside Joan of Arc in the wars against the English and their

Burgundian allies. It wasn't until Gilles retired from the army in 1435, that the murders began.

FROM HERO TO VILLAIN

When the fighting subsided, the nobles were expected to disband their armies and return to their estates to try and rebuild the wealth lost during the years of war. Gilles returned to Champtoce, but the sedentary lifestyle after all the glory of the battlefield left him depressed and needing excitement. He yearned for the excitement of spilling blood and when his uncle, Jean d'Craon, died in either 1432 or 1433, Gilles had a totally free rein. He moved to his castle at Machécoul, where his bloodlust began in earnest.

An accomplice to many of Gilles's crimes was a young boy by the name of Etienne Corrillaut, better known as Poitou. He was taken to the castle one day and raped, after which Gilles prepared to cut his throat. However, one of Gilles's servants pointed out that he was such a handsome young boy that he would make a perfect page and so his life was spared. From then on he became Gilles's most trusted servant.

The more Gilles craved blood, the more manic he became. He was fascinated with the beauty of young boys and the pain they seemed capable of enduring. He would lure them to his castle on some pretext or other and then once inside, Gilles satisfied his appetite. The victim would normally be hung from the ceiling on a rope or chain until he lost consciousness. Then, as part of his sick perversion, Gilles would take the boy down and comfort him, telling him that no further harm would come to him. This of course was a pack of lies, as he tore the clothes off the victim's body and raped him, after which one of his servants would decapitate him. Often Gilles was not satisfied and would continue to abuse the dead body, playing grotesquely with the head as if it were some kind of trophy. In the height of his frenzy he would cut open the stomach, crouch among the entrails and then relieve himself by masterbating over the bloody mess. It was very rare that Gilles left a child alive for more than one evening and after he had finished with his victim, he would retire to his bed where he would remain comatose for many hours. His servants, in the meantime, disposed of the evidence by cremating it in a room called the chamber of horrors. The fire was designed to burn slowly so that it would not create too much smoke and alert the villagers to his evil ways. Afterwards the ashes would be removed and dumped in the moat surrounding the castle.

The village on the outskirts of the castle at Machécoul became a place to avoid. Rumours started to spread as they heard of the castle's fearful reputation, 'They eat little children there ...'

However, even with all these rumours and many enquiries by the parents of the missing children, no investigation was ever carried out.

BLACK MAGIC

Added to his depravity, Gilles loved to spend money and surrounded himself with riches. He had a retinue of over 200 knights, and was known to hold lavish banquets where he lorded over the festivities like a Roman god. In a period of three years it is estimated he spent the equivalent of millions of dollars, leaving him in a penniless state. He was forced to sell off some of his more valuable estates, something which alarmed his brother, who approached the king asking him to forbid Gilles to sell any further land. Gilles, without any money to spend, went into a deep depression and he decided to turn to his other love, black magic, to try and help him out of his predicament.

In fact, mysticism, spirituality and religion played major roles in the life of Gilles de Rais. In direct contrast to his debauchery, Gilles was a generous supporter of the Church, and even went as far as building several chapels and one cathedral for his people. However, when he became desperate for money he was not opposed to pawning the gold from these churches. Having witnessed first-hand the miracles of Joan of Arc, Gilles was convinced that alchemy was the way forward, but unfortunately it had been outlawed by the Church and the king in the fifteenth century, so he had to carry out his black magic in secret.

In his greed for riches, Gilles became easy prey for fraudulent alchemists, and for some strange reason he never seemed to be aware that he was being conned. Records show that he was tricked, quite humorously, on two separate occasions. The first alchemist was introduced to Gilles by his favourite priest, Blanchet. The conman was a goldsmith, who told Gilles that he had discovered how to turn silver into gold. Gilles arranged to meet the man at a local tavern, where he was asked to produce a silver coin. The blacksmith asked Gilles to leave him alone to practise his craft, but when he returned he found the man intoxicated and in a state of unconsciousness. It appeared the only magic that man could do was to turn a silver florin into a flagon of wine.

Gilles's second involvement with a magician cost him a lot more money than a mere silver florin. It was once again his priest, Blanchet, who introduced the magician to Gilles, who said he was able to conjure up the devil. They met up one evening, the magician, Jean de la Riviere, wearing white armour and carrying a sword. Riviere led Gilles and his men to a clearing in the woods, and told them to wait while he went to summon Satan. They stood and waited and then they heard the sound of clanging, as if Riviere was beating on his own armour. Seconds later, he arrived, ashen-faced and shaking, swearing that he had seen the devil in the form of a leopard.

Gilles was impressed and was totally convinced that Riviere was genuine and took him back to his castle where he held a feast in his honour. Knowing that he had got Gilles hook, line and sinker, Riviere asked Gilles for some money to buy the supplies he needed to continue his evocations. He gave the man 20 ecus and asked him to come back to the castle as soon as possible. Needless to say, Riviere disappeared, along with the money, and was never seen again.

THE BIG MISTAKE

During his years of murder and lust, Gilles came close to being discovered on several occasions. The first real scare was in 1437 when he decided to sell off the family's estate at Champtoce, despite a royal interdict to stop him. When the crown moved to seize the property, Gilles panicked because he knew he had left the mutilated bodies of numerous children there. Scared that they would also try and seize Machécoul, Gilles quickly removed the remains of about forty children with the help of his trusted servants. The bodies at Champtoce had, remarkably, gone unnoticed, but the Duke of Brittany imposed a huge fine on Gilles, aware that he would be unable to pay. At the same time he started an investigation into the disappearance of hundreds of children.

Gilles made a major mistake when he decided to break into a church and kidnap the priest. Shortly after mass at the church of St Etienne de Mer Morte, Gilles had the priest dragged outside and beaten. The priest had a brother, Geoffroy de Ferron, who was the Treasurer to the Duke of Brittany, to whom Gilles had been forced to sell some of his property. The priest had been entrusted by his brother to watch over this property and Gilles decided to take control of the situation in his own way. Having violated ecclesiastical privilege, which was a capital offence, and also stepped on the toes of the Duke of Brittany, Gilles was in big trouble. Added to this, the duke's investigations into the missing children was starting to pay rewards and Gilles was indicted for 'the murder of children and sodomy, the invocations of demons, the offending of Divine Majesty and heresy'.

Gilles was denied the privileges of Communion and Confession, so when he entered the court he was contrite and admitted to his perverse habits, but denied attempting to summon the devil. However, the court was not satisfied with his denial of black magic, and decided to try and extract a full confession by using torture. Ironically, there was a chance he could be pardoned for the murder and sodomy, but summoning a demon was heresy with a punishment of death.

After severe torture sessions – although they were not nearly as evil as those he carried out on the children – Gilles confessed to it all. Bravely he tried to take the total blame in an effort to allow his accomplices to go free. But the court was not convinced, especially after hearing the testimonies of over 110 witnesses. Gilles gave such lurid details of his perverse activities that the judges ordered the worst sections to be stricken from the record.

On October 25, 1440, the ecclesiastical court handed down a sentence of excommunication against Gilles, followed by forty-seven charges including conjuration of demons, abuse of clerical privileges and sexual perversions against children. Charged and condemned with him were his faithful mignon Henri Griard and his page, Poitou. They were hanged on October 26, 1440, after which their bodies were placed on a funeral pyre.

Before Gilles died he sang the *De Profundis* in a loud voice while standing underneath the gibbet. Then he got down on his knees and prayed along with hundreds of spectators who joined him. In his agonies of guilt, he said to the families of the murdered children:

You who are present – you, above all, whose children I have slain – I am your brother in Christ. By Our Lord's Passion, I implore you, pray for me. Forgive me with all your hearts the evil I have done you, as you yourselves hope for God's mercy and pardon.

Perhaps in deference to his status as a nobleman, Gilles's relatives were allowed to remove his body before the flames took hold, and he was buried in the nearby Carmelite church. His two companions were not so lucky however, their bodies were burned to ashes.

There is no doubt that Gilles de Rais was a fearsome, fiendish killer, who is considered by some to be the precursor of the modern serial killer. Rene, now the Baron de Rais, took over Champtoce until his death, but the de Rais line, which Jean d'Craon had fought so hard to preserve, faded into obscurity with the death of Rene's daughter in 1473, who never bore any children to carry on the line.

ELIZABETH BATHORY

Erzsébet Báthory or Elizabeth Bathory was born into one of the wealthiest families in Transylvania in 1560. She came from good stock as her relatives consisted of a cardinal, princes, a cousin who was the prime minister of Hungary and, most importantly, Istvan Bathory who was prince of Transylvania and king of Poland from 1575 to 1586. However, among these prestigious relatives were a few strange ones as well. One uncle was known to be a devil-worshipper, while other family members were pronounced mentally insane. Quite what happened to Elizabeth to turn her into such a blood-thirsty killer, can only be conjectured, but she is alleged to have killed over 600 women and young virgins, quite literally to bathe in their blood. Her love of blood helped to inspire, in part, a young Irishman by the name of Bram Stoker to write about the legendary Dracula, the prince among vampires.

It has been reported that at around the age of four or five, Elizabeth was subject to violent seizures. Although it is uncertain as to what caused them, it is possible that these were contributory to her psychotic behaviour later in her life.

In spring 1575, when Elizabeth was fifteen, she married twenty-six-year-old Count Ferenz Nadasdy. Wishing to keep her family name, her husband adopted the name of Bathory. After the wedding the couple moved to Castle Cséjthe, which was situated high above the village of Cséjthe, in the north-west of Hungary.

Elizabeth's husband was a brave warrior, but this meant he was away from their home for much of the time. Elizabeth became lonely and depressed and spent endless hours admiring her own beauty. To pass away the time she took many young men as lovers, even going as far as eloping with one of them. But the affair fizzled out and she returned to her forgiving husband. Back at the castle she struggled because she hated her domineering mother-in-law, and she spent more and more time visiting her favourite aunt, Countess Klara Bathory, an open bisexual. It was also around this time that Elizabeth's maid, Dorothea Sventes, also known as Dorka, introduced her to the joys of the occult.

For the first ten years of her marriage, Elizabeth bore the count no children, purely because they spent so little time together because of his military career. She had her first daughter, Anna, in 1585, and over the next nine years gave birth to two more girls, Ursula and Katherina and finally, in 1598, her only son, Paul. She proved to be a loving and protective mother, but there was another, far more sinister side to her character.

Influenced by Dorka, Elizabeth found pleasure in inflicting pain on her young servant girls. She liked to strip them naked, hang them up and then whip them, watching in delight as their faces contorted in pain. She also used to stick pins under their finger-nails and other sensitive parts of their body. The other people who joined her in these sadistic pleasures were her old nurse Illona Joo, her manservant Johannes Ujvary and a maid named Anna Darvula, who many believed to be Elizabeth's lover. With the help of this evil crew, Elizabeth turned Castle Cséjthe into a truly sinister place.

THE REAL TERROR BEGINS

Although Elizabeth's behaviour had been far from saintly, it wasn't until Count Ferenz died in 1600 that her real reign of terror began. As soon as she was in control, Elizabeth sent her detested mother-in-law away from the castle. Having borne four children and now forty years of age, Elizabeth became paranoid that she was losing her youth and good looks. Then one day a small incident was to change the course of her life. Her chambermaid was busy brushing Elizabeth's hair when she accidentally pulled it. Elizabeth was fuming and slapped the girl's head with such force that blood spurted from her nose. The blood splashed onto Elizabeth's own skin and she was immediately convinced that where it had touched, her skin had taken on the youthfulness and vitality of the young chambermaid's. She told Ujvary and Dorka to strip the girl naked and while they held her over a large vat, Elizabeth cut her arteries. When the body had completely drained of blood, they disposed of it and Elizabeth stepped into the vat and bathed in her young victim's blood. She truly believed that at last she had found the answer to eternal youth.

For the next ten years, her trusted, yet evil band of servants kept her supplied with beautiful young girls from the neighbouring villages. Each one was taken to the castle, bled dry, just so the countess could retain her beauty. Sometimes, as an added bonus, she would drink their blood in an effort to retain inner beauty as well.

For some unexplainable reason Elizabeth decided that all her victims should have Christian burials and approached the local Protestant pastor. This worked well until he became concerned about the large number of young women who had died of what he was told were 'unknown and mysterious causes'. When he refused to carry out any further burials and threatened to go to the authorities, Elizabeth intimidated him into keeping silent.

MOVING UP A CLASS

When Elizabeth realised that her blood baths were not having the desired effect on her appearance, she decided she needed a better quality of blood. Instead of the peasant girls she had been killing, Elizabeth ordered her servants to bring her young virgins of nobility. These were destroyed in exactly the same beastly fashion as the peasant girls who preceded them, but Elizabeth was now becoming very careless and indiscreet. She started running out of burial sites and many of the bodies were disposed of in a haphazard manner. They were left in conspicuous places such as nearby fields, the kitchen garden and in the stream running behind the castle. Added to this, members of the nobility were not so prepared to let the matter rest when their daughters went missing, and rumours had started to reach the Hungarian Emperor.

The final straw came when one of her young victims managed to escape and tell the authorities exactly what was happening at Castle Cséjthe. Elizabeth's own cousin, Count György, was sent to search the estate. He sent his soldiers on the night of December 30, 1610, to raid the castle, but they weren't expecting the horrific sights that met them. In the main hall of the castle lay the body of a young girl, drained of blood. Another girl was still alive, despite the fact that she had had her veins pierced. When they went down to the dungeons they found several girls waiting in prison cells, some of whom had been brutally tortured. When they dug up the floor beneath the castle, they found the bodies of over fifty other young women. They were sickened to their stomachs, realising that they had literally uncovered a factory of death.

ELIZABETH ON TRIAL

In 1611 a trial was held at Bitcse, but Elizabeth never actually appeared at the proceedings, refusing to plead either guilty or not guilty to the charges. Johannes Ujvary was cross-examined and said that about thirty-seven virgin girls had been killed, six of whom he had recruited personally to work at the castle. The truth of the matter was that Elizabeth Bathory had killed 612 women, proof of which was in a diary kept by her, which was retrieved from the castle by the authorities. A complete transcript was made of the trial and survives to this very day in Hungary, although all records were sealed for more than a century and her name was forbidden to be spoken in Hungarian society for many years.

Because of her social standing, Elizabeth Bathory was not allowed to be executed and believe it or not the court never convicted her of any crime. She was merely placed under house arrest in her very own torture chamber. Stonemasons were brought to Castle Cséjthe, to wall up the windows and doors, leaving only a small gap in the wall for food to be passed through to her.

Elizabeth dictated her last will and testament on July 31, 1614, at the age of fifty-four. She left her entire wealth to be divided up between her four children. Towards the end of August, four years after she had been incarcerated in a prison of her own making, Elizabeth Bathory was found lying face down by one of her jailers. The villagers refused to allow the body of the infamous 'Blood Countess' to be buried in their town on hallowed ground, and eventually her body was placed in Ecsed, which was the original Bathory family seat.

Elizabeth Bathory will always be remembered for her seemingly inconceivable disregard for human life. Although it would be nice to think that she was mentally deranged, there is evidence to disprove this theory and it appears that she was in total control of her faculties and just got immense pleasure from pain, killing and the taste of blood – a fiendish killer indeed.

ARNOLD PAOLE

Our modern concept of a vampire is an animated corpse rising up from the dead, preying on human victims at night, and drinking blood in their quest for immortality. Arnold Paole fits perfectly into this description.

Paole returned from active service in Greece in the spring of 1727 to his native village of Meduegna, near Belgrade. Having claimed to have had enough adventures to last him a lifetime, Paole decided to settle down and purchased a cottage and two acres of ground. He soon established himself into the village community, although many wondered why such a young man would want to retire from active service in the prime of his life. He appeared to be an honest man, and yet the locals sensed a certain strangeness in his manner, even though they weren't able to put their finger on it.

Several months after arriving back at the village, Paole started dating the daughter of one of his neighbours, a young girl called Nina. Her father was a wealthy farmer and within a very short time the couple were married. Nina, like the other villagers, felt there was something not quite right about her new husband and decided to ask him what it was that troubled him so much. He told her that he was constantly haunted by the fear of an early death. He went on to tell Nina that where he had been stationed, the dead frequently came back to torment the living and that he, himself, had experienced a visitation from an undead being. Paole was told that the only way to rid himself of a troublesome vampire was to eat some of the earth from its grave and smear the creature's blood onto his own skin. Paole did exactly that, and for a long time it seemed to work as an effective deterrent.

Shortly after his marriage to Nina, Paole had a serious accident while working on the farm. He fell from the top of a loaded hay wagon and was carried, unconscious, back to his house. His injuries were so severe that Paole only survived a couple of days. His body was laid to rest in the village churchyard but it appears his soul was far from being at peace.

REPORTS OF A VAMPIRE

About one month after Paole died, rumours started spreading round the village that people had seen him wandering around the neighbourhood after dark. Several people reported that he was haunting them and seemed to appear when they were feeling particularly weak or vulnerable. Those who claimed to have seen Paole, fell into a state of debility a few days later and, when several of them died, panic spread throughout the neighbourhood. As the dark, winter nights approached, no one dared to venture outdoors. However, this was quite ironic as the spectre was able to penetrate the walls and it seemed no lock or bars at the windows could keep it out. The whole village remained in a state of terror throughout the harsh winter and eventually, in a state of desperation, the villagers decided that the body of Paole must be disinterred.

The party chosen to carry out the grisly task consisted of two military officers, two army surgeons, a drummer boy who carried their cases of instruments, authorities from the village, the old sexton and his assistants. They set out for the graveyard in the early hours of the morning while a thin grey mist still hung over the tops of the gravestones. For the most part the graves were well kept and it was easy to find the grave of Arnold Paole. They started to dig away the earth from around the wooden coffin, and when it was uncovered the men managed to drag it out onto the ground. The young drummer boy stood apparently frozen by horror. As the men knocked off the lid they saw that the corpse inside had moved to one side. The jaws were wide open, the lips were blue, but trickling from the corners of his mouth were thin streams of fresh blood. Even the soldiers and the surgeon, who were accustomed to the atrocities of the battlefield, gasped in horror. As they stared at Paole's corpse, despite being exceptionally pale, it had the appearance of a body that had only been dead for a day, not the several months since his funeral. The drummer boy fainted as the doctor said it was obvious that they were looking at the body of a vampire. On closer inspection, underneath the old, flaking external skin, they found new, clear skin and fingernails clearly growing on the body.

The men decided to waste no time in taking appropriate action to rid themselves of the monster. They scattered garlic over the corpse and then drove a stake through his heart. As the stake pierced his body, it is alleged that he let out a piercing scream and warm, fresh blood spurted out of the wound. Not prepared to take any risks, the men decided to exhume the bodies of the four people who had died as a result of Paole's visitations, fearing that they would also have taken on the form of vampires. They dealt with them in the same way as they had with Paole's corpse and then burned all five bodies, placing their ashes on consecrated ground.

The men were now happy that they had dealt

with the matter satisfactorily and that the village of Meduegna would have no more unwelcome night visitors.

NEW VICTIMS

Indeed, everything was quiet in Meduegna until 1732, when there was a second spate of inexplicable deaths. The victims all appeared to have died from loss of blood, their bodies being in a terrible state of anaemia. Apparently, even though they had destroyed Arnold Paole, humans were not his only victims. He had also drunk the blood of cattle which had subsequently been eaten by some of the villagers. In a period of three months, seventeen people died both young and old, all with no previous history of illness.

The officials wasted no time in visiting the graveyard for a second time, examining all the graves. Several eminent surgeons were invited to Meduegna and their investigations yielded some quite extraordinary results. Three distinguished army surgeons – Johannes Flickinger, Isaac Siedel and Johann Friedrich Baumgärtner – wrote detailed reports on what they found, the most remarkable of which were:

A woman by the name of Stana, twenty years of age, who had died three months before, after an illness which only lasted three days and which followed directly after her confinement. Upon her deathbed she confessed that she had anointed herself with the blood of a vampire to liberate herself from his persecutions. The body of the child, owing to a hasty and careless interment, had been half scraped up and devoured by wolves. The body of the woman, Stana, was untouched by decomposition. When it was opened the chest was found to be full of fresh blood, the viscera had all the appearance of soundest health. The skin and nails of both hands and feet were loose and came off, but underneath was a clean new skin and nails.

One Joachim, a boy of seventeen, who was the son of a heyduk. He had died after a short illness of three days, and had lain buried for eight weeks and four days. His complexion was fresh, and the body unmistakably in the vampire condition.

A SCIENTIFIC REASON

All of the phenomena described above can be explained scientifically, because they are all characteristic at certain stages of decomposition. It is not uncommon for the body to appear ruddy in complexion, and non-coagulated blood is often present and may be seen escaping from the orifices. Whatever your belief, let's hope that the tormented soul of Arnold Paole has now found its resting place.

PETER
PLOGOJOWITZ

Peter Plogojowitz was a farmer who lived in the
early eighteenth century in the village of Kisolova in
what was then Austrian Serbia (modern-day
Hungary). The previous hale and hearty sixty-two-
year-old died suddenly in 1725 and was buried in
the churchyard of his village. His family mourned
his death, but little did they realise that that was not
to be the last time they would see him. Just three
days after his death, Plogojowitz appeared at midnight at his own front door and asked his son for
some food. The following night was peaceful and
passed without incident. The next night the vision
of Plogojowitz appeared again to his son, but this
time the younger man refused his father any food.
Having been turned down, the ghostly corpse cast
his son a threatening look and then disappeared.
The following morning the younger Plogojowitz
was dead.

Two months later, nine other villagers of differing ages died within a single week, all from a mysterious twenty-four-hour illness. On their deathbeds, each one of them claimed to have been visited by the corpse of Plogojowitz. They said that he had bent over them while they lay in their beds and had sunk his teeth into their necks. It appears that instead of resting peacefully in his grave, Peter Plogojowitz had become a vampire. The widow of Plogojowitz further frightened the villagers when she told them that her husband had visited her and demanded his old shoes. Fearing for her own life, Plogojowitz's wife fled Kisolova.

At the time of these mysterious deaths, Kisolova and the surrounding district was under the imperial rule of Austria. Many Austrian officials had come to live in the region to serve in the government, and it was one such official that was approached by the Kisolova villagers. They asked the Imperial Provisor to oversee the opening of Plogojowitz's grave and make an official report. Although the Provisor wished to seek advice from his superiors in Belgrade, the villagers were too terrified to let the matter rest and went ahead with the exhumation of the remains of Peter Plogojowitz.

The reluctant Provisor and the local priest accompanied the crowd and watched as they dug up the coffin. Everyone was shocked when they slid back the lid. Despite the period of time that Plogojowitz had been in the ground, his corpse did not emit the usual foul odour and the body was amazingly intact, except for the nose which had decayed away. The old skin was white, but most of it had peeled away to reveal a new one growing underneath. Also, Plogojowitz's hair and beard had grown, he had new nails on his hands and feet, and there were traces of fresh blood around his mouth.

The Provisor had to admit that the corpse showed every sign of having become a vampire and ordered the men to drive a sharpened stake through its heart. As the stake entered the body, fresh blood poured from his nose and mouth and the corpse showed signs of visibly struggling. The body was burned to ashes and then scattered on consecrated ground.

Remembering the stories surrounding the death of Arnold Paole, the official decided to inspect the graves of the people who were said to have been visited by Plogojowitz. There were no signs of vampirism and the men simply treated their graves with the traditional method of placing garlic and whitethorn next to their bodies.

Both Plogojowitz and Paole lived in a part of the world where it was widely believed that the dead could be transformed into undead souls who preyed on the living. They also believed that they could only be dealt with by the traditional methods.

These thoughts have haunted people for centuries and have been romanticised in literature and film.

Even as late as 1912, a story appeared in *The Daily Telegraph* on February 15, reporting that a Hungarian farmer was convinced that he had been visited by a vampire.

> *A Buda-Pesth telegram to the Messagerro*
> *reports a terrible instance of superstition.*
> *A boy of fourteen died some days ago in a*
> *small village. A farmer, in whose employment*
> *the boy had been, thought that the ghost of the*
> *latter appeared to him every night. In order to*
> *put a stop to these supposed visitations, the*
> *farmer, accompanied by some friends, went to*
> *the cemetery one night, stuffed three pieces of*
> *garlic and three stones in the mouth, and*
> *thrust a stake through the corpse, fixing it to*
> *the ground. This was to deliver themselves*
> *from the evil spirit, as the credulous farmer*
> *and his friends stated when they were*
> *arrested.*

PETER KURTEN

Peter Kurten was a mild-mannered, soft-spoken man who, to all intents and purposes, appeared to be totally harmless. Yet this middle-class man concealed a very sick, sadistic nature which would eventually come to the fore in the form of vampirism. He struck terror among the inhabitants of Düsseldorf as the man they had dubbed 'The Vampire of Düsseldorf' demonstrated his full range of bestiality.

ROTTEN CHILDHOOD

Kurten was born on May 26, 1883, the eldest of thirteen children. The Kurten family lived in abject poverty in a one-bedroom apartment in Cologne. Peter's father was a moulder by trade but spent most of his leisure hours in a state of inebriation which left him with an uncontrollable temper. The family lived in fear of him coming home from work and the young Peter often felt the brunt of his anger. He was also forced to watch as his father repeatedly raped his mother and sisters and, subjected to this daily form of brutality, Peter Kurten grew up a bitter and twisted young man.

When Peter was only nine years old he pushed a friend off a raft as they played on the river. When another boy jumped into the water and tried to save his drowning friend, Peter held the boy's head under the water until he suffocated. The boys' deaths were treated as an accident and the young Kurten was cleared of any blame.

When he was sixteen, Kurten ran away from home and had to beg and steal to survive. For the next twenty-four years, Kurten was in and out of jail and it is alleged that his brutal treatment during this time left him wanting to take revenge on the society that had treated him so cruelly.

CRUEL REVENGE

When Kurten was released from prison in May 1913, he was a handsome young man who had no problems attracting the opposite sex. However, his past left him incapable of forming any lasting relationships and with a lack of normal human emotions he went in search of revenge. Kurten was prowling the streets of Cologne looking for a house to break in to, when he came across a young girl asleep in her bed. He cut her throat and then sexually abused the child, leaving a trademark on his way out – a handkerchief bearing his initials. The body of ten-year-old Christine Klein was found the next morning and suspicion immediately fell on her uncle, Otto. He was charged with Christine's murder, but was cleared by a jury and the real killer would not be apprehended for another eighteen years.

With the rumblings of war growing over Europe, Kurten was called to fight for Germany. However, Kurten did not fit comfortably into the military lifestyle and he deserted. He was captured and arrested and spent the remainder of the war incarcerated. Due to his insubordinance, Kurten spent much of his time in solitary confinement, dreaming up wild and abhorrent fantasies that he hoped one day to fulfil.

When he was eventually released in 1921, Kurten went to live with his sister in a small town by the name of Altenburg. It was here that he met a former prostitute who had spent a few years in jail for shooting a man who had jilted her at the altar. They started to date and within a few months Kurten asked her to be his wife.

After they were married they lived in Altenburg until 1925, with Kurten earning an honest living as a moulder in a local factory. However, his 'normal' existence didn't last for very long and he abused a couple of servant girls. With the finger of suspicion pointing at Kurten, the couple moved to Düsseldorf in 1925, and it was here that his reign of terror began in earnest.

THE VAMPIRE OF DÜSSELDORF

Throughout 1929 and 1930 the streets of Düsseldorf were eerily empty as soon as the night closed in. Everyone rushed to the safety of their houses, bolting their doors and drawing their curtains, living in constant fear of the 'beast' who had no face, no name and no definite form. It had already committed forty-six violent crimes, showing virtually every type of perversion. The citizens of Düsseldorf grew more frightened and angry with each new murder and the German newspapers carried headlines of 'monsters' and 'vampires' stalking the streets. However, the full atrocities of the creature now dubbed 'The Vampire of Düsseldorf' revealed themselves on the night of August 23, 1929.

The people who lived in the suburb of Flehe had gathered to celebrate an annual fair. Everyone was starting to relax, feeling comfort in the closely packed crowd. There were old-fashioned merry-go-rounds and stalls selling food and beer, all to the sound of German marching songs.

At about 10.30 p.m., two foster sisters, fourteen-year-old Louise Lenzen and five-year-old Gurtrude Hamacher, left the safety of the fairground and started to walk home. As they made their way across some allotments they didn't notice the shadowy figure following them along the footpath.

Louise stopped and turned round when she heard a gentle-sounding voice speaking to them.

'Oh dear, I've forgotten to buy some cigarettes. Look, would you be very kind and go to one of the booths and get some for me? I will look after the little girl while you are gone,' the man said.

Louise trusted the stranger, took his money and ran back towards the fairground. As soon as Louise was out of sight, the man carried Gurtrude behind some beanpoles, strangled her and then proceeded to cut her throat. When Louise returned with the packet of cigarettes, she asked where her sister was, but the man didn't answer and simply dragged her off the footpath and she met the same fate.

The attacks continued unabated throughout the summer and autumn of 1929. Some of the victims were lucky enough to survive the man's attacks and were able to give a rough description of a tall white man. However, this description could have applied to half the male residents of Düsseldorf.

MARIA BUDLICK

Back in the city of Cologne, a twenty-one-year-old housemaid by the name of Maria Budlick was reading the ghastly details of the deaths that had taken place in Düsseldorf. She commented to her friends that she was glad she was miles away, but a few weeks later Budlick lost her job and was forced to move elsewhere to look for work. She decided to head for Düsseldorf, not realising that her encounter with the 'vampire' was so close. As soon as she stepped down from the train, a man walked over to her and offered to show her to the local girls' hostel in the town. She felt comfortable with the man all the time they were walking along the brightly lit streets, but as soon as he started heading towards the dark area of Volksgarten Park, Budlick halted in her tracks. She remembered all the stories she had read in the newspapers about a monster prowling the streets of Düsseldorf and refused to go any further. An argument broke out and as they raised their voices a second man approached the pair to see if the girl was alright. The man who had approached her at the railway station backed off straight away and walked off, leaving Budlick with the second man to show her the way.

Foolishly, feeling safer with her new companion, Budlick agreed to accompany him to his apartment in Mettmannerstrasse. He asked her if she was hungry, and gave her a ham sandwich and a glass of milk. After feeling refreshed the man offered to take her to the hostel and they rode a tram to the north-eastern edge of the town. As they started to walk away from the tram, Budlick was aware that the man was leading her deeper into a secluded, wooded area and she could feel the hairs rise on the back of her neck. Her companion turned to her and said, 'You are alone with me in the middle of the woods. Now you can scream as much as you like, and nobody will hear you!'

The man lurched forward and grabbed Budlick by the neck and tried to force her to have sexual intercourse. Budlick struggled as hard as she could but the hand was tightening on her throat and she could feel herself slipping into unconsciousness. As she was about to pass out, Budlick felt the man release his hold on her neck and then asked her if she could remember the address of his apartment. Budlick replied, 'No', which was the one word that apparently saved her life. To her surprise the man let her go and even showed her the way out of the woods and back onto the road.

Of course, Budlick had lied, she vividly remembered the street name, despite the fact that she was traumatised from the attack. Ashamed of the stigma of having been raped, Budlick did not go straight to the police but wrote a letter to a close friend telling her of her narrow escape from death. As luck would have it, the letter never reached her friend and ended up at the house of Frau Brugman, who immediately took it to the police. Detectives managed to trace Budlick and persuaded her to give them the full details of her attack. Twenty-four hours later she led some plain clothes detectives back to Mettmanner-strässe and studied each door carefully to see if she recognised the apartment. She eventually stopped at number seventy-one and asked the landlady if there was a 'fair-haired, rather sedate man' living in the house. The woman led Budlick up to a room on the fourth floor which she immediately recognised as the place where she had eaten her snack two nights earlier. As she headed back down the stairs to tell the detectives waiting outside, she saw her attacker coming towards her. The man looked shocked to see her, but simply walked past her and into his room, closing the door behind him. Several minutes later he left the house again, this time wearing a hat which he had pulled down over his face and carrying a bag containing some clothes. He passed the two detectives standing in the street, but by the time Budlick had reached them the man had disappeared round the corner.

Kurten moved to another apartment, aware that the only crime he was suspected of was that of rape, and doubting that they could link him with the other murders. However, the following morning he met his wife at the restaurant where she had been working late and confessed to her, 'I am the Vampire of Düsseldorf.' His wife panicked, saying that he would be sent to jail and that she would be left destitute. Kurten said he had a plan. He told her to go to the police with information about the murderer so that she could claim the large reward being offered.

Frau Kurten told her story to the police on May 24, 1930, adding that she had arranged to meet her husband outside St. Rochus Church at 3.00 p.m. Although Kurten had planned one last grisly murder before he was finally locked away, his plans were foiled when he was surrounded by armed police as he walked to meet his wife. Kurten simply smiled in the face of the revolvers pointed at him and said, 'There is no need to be afraid!', holding his hands out in front of him ready to be handcuffed.

THE TRIAL

The trial of Peter Kurten opened on April 13, 1931, after intense questioning. He openly admitted to sixty-eight crimes and told the police that he had already spent twenty years of his life behind bars. The converted drill-hall at the Düsseldorf police headquarters was packed with people wanting to get their first glimpse of the 'monster'. A special cage had been built inside the courtroom to prevent his escape, behind which was an array of gruesome exhibits. There were skulls from several of his victims, along with pieces of equipment he had used, articles of clothing and a spade he had dug one of the graves with. When Kurten was eventually led into his cage, a gasp went round the courtroom. Far from being an ugly, misshapen monster, with blood trickling from his mouth, the man in front of them was a handsome, quiet, ordinary-looking human being. He was not the image of the vampire they had imagined, in his immaculate suit, his neatly combed hair and the hint of eau de Cologne. The people sitting in the courtroom immediately jumped to the conclusion that they had arrested the wrong man. However, when Kurten started talking in his quiet, methodical voice about his life of perversion and bloodlust in such minute detail, even the hardened court officials found it hard to stomach.

Far from being a deranged, crazed monster, the court doctor pronounced that Kurten was totally sane and aware of his actions at all times. Kurten explained to the court that his sadistic impulses were aroused by the violence that he had suffered at the hands of his father as a child. He said that these urges took over his whole body and that it had started to form a terrible pattern during his adult life.

The jury took one and a half hours to reach a verdict – GUILTY ON ALL COUNTS – and Peter Kurten was sentenced to death nine times.

On the night before his execution, Kurten was offered the traditional last meal and he asked for Wienerschnitzel, fried potatoes and a bottle of wine. He told the prison guard that he enjoyed the meal so much that he could eat it all over again.

At 6.00 a.m. on July 2, 1931, Kurten was led to the guillotine with a priest on either side. As he faced the blade in the yard of Klingelputz Prison, the Attorney-General asked, 'Have you any last wish to express?'

Kurten replied without showing any emotion, 'No'. He had already told his prison psychiatrist that the thought of the blood gushing from his severed neck would be the 'pleasure to end all pleasures'.

Peter Kurten has to go down in history as one of the most fiendish killers to walk the face of this earth. Not only did he get extreme pleasure out of killing, torturing, maiming and sexually abusing his victims but he openly admitted that the sight of his victim's blood was enough to bring on an orgasm. He even disclosed with a smile on his face that he had drunk the blood of his victims on several occasions as it pumped out of their bodies.

VAMPIRE KILLER OF SACRAMENTO

Richard Trenton Chase was an exceptionally disturbed individual right from his early childhood. In January 1978, Chase went on a four-day blood binge in California, which claimed the lives of six people. He earned himself the nickname of 'Vampire Killer of Sacramento' due to his lust for drinking the blood of his victims, which he claimed stopped his own blood from turning into powder. Although he was institutionalised on two occasions, his doctors decided Chase was not certifiable and he was released to wreak havoc on the citizens of Sacramento.

Born on May 23, 1950, Chase was raised in a household full of anger and violence. He was frequently beaten by his father who was a strict disciplinarian, and by the time he was ten years old Chase was showing signs of abnormal behaviour. He loved to start fires, and had a morbid obsession with mutilating and killing small animals and drinking their blood. By the time he reached his late teens, Chase was not only a drug addict but a disturbed hypochondriac as well. He was always convinced there was something wrong with him, even going as far as visiting a hospital and claiming that someone had stolen his pulmonary artery. He spent two lengthy periods in a mental institution after a psychiatrist feared he was suffering from paranoid schizophrenia, but in 1978 his doctors felt the prescribed medication had his problem under control and he was released. He was allowed back into society and deemed no longer a danger to himself or anyone else – or so they believed!

On his release Chase decided to stop taking his medication and his old problems promptly reared their ugly heads once again. He was now convinced that his blood was turning into powder and that his own mother was being paid by the Nazis to poison him. The voices in his head returned to haunt him and kept telling him to do something about the condition of his blood. Chase took to killing rabbits and other small animals. He would either smear their blood all over his body, or drink their blood which he mixed with portions of their internal organs.

He soon moved from the neighbourhood dogs and cats to larger animals, and was once found in the back of his car smeared with the blood of a cow's liver. Gradually his sense of boundaries deserted him and he moved on to human sacrifices.

THE FIRST MURDER

The police department north of Sacramento received a phone call on the night of Monday, January 23, 1978, to say that a terrible murder had been committed. David Wallin, a twenty-four-year-old truck driver had returned to his suburban home at about 6.00 p.m. to find their dog, a German shepherd, waiting in the hall, but his wife didn't seem to be home. There was a rubbish bag lying on the floor with the contents spilled everywhere and what appeared to be some oil stains on the carpet. The stains led him all the way into the bedroom and when he looked inside the room David started to scream. He ran to a neighbour's house and asked them to call the police.

Wallin was so traumatised by what he saw that he was unable to talk to the authorities when they arrived at the house. When they saw the body, the police realised that they were dealing with some sort of monster killer, not just a regular murder as the result of a burglary. The body of twenty-two-year-old Terry Wallin was lying just inside the door on her back and the fact that she was three months pregnant made the crime even more abhorrent.

Terry's jumper had been pulled up over her breasts and her underwear was round her ankles. Her knees were apart and her legs were open as if she had been raped. Her left nipple had been cut off, her stomach had been cut open and her spleen and intestines had been removed. There was blood everywhere and it was later discovered that the killer had smeared Terry's blood all over his face, licking it off his fingers. Near the body was an old yoghurt carton which the police believed the killer had used to drink his victim's blood. But perhaps the most heinous part of his crime was the fact that he had stuffed animal faeces into her mouth.

The police were horrified, mystified and alarmed because it was obvious that this person had a deranged mind and would most likely kill again. They tried to build up a profile of the killer, and their worst fears were confirmed when news of more grisly murders reached their offices on Thursday, January 26. At about 12.30 p.m. a neighbour had found three bodies at a house that was within a mile radius of the Wallin home.

The victims were thirty-six-year-old Evelyn Miroth, her six-year-old son Jason and fifty-two-year-old Daniel Meredith, who was a friend of the family. Evelyn had been babysitting her twenty-month-old nephew when an intruder had broken into the house. Daniel Meredith lay in the hall in a pool of blood with a gunshot wound to his head. There was blood everywhere and the trail led into the bathroom, where the bath was full of bloody water. Evelyn was lying naked on her bed with her legs splayed open. Two bloodstained carving knives lay near the body, which the police assumed had been used to slice open her abdomen. As in the murder of Terry Wallin, the intestines had been pulled out and blood rings on the carpet suggested he had used some containers to collect his victim's blood. On the far side of the bed, the police officers found the body of a young boy who had been shot twice in the head at close range.

The police searched the house thoroughly but the body of the baby was not found. They felt from the amount of blood found in the playpen that he was probably not still alive. The intruder had left bloody footprints everywhere which resembled the shoe prints from the Wallin house.

Meredith's stolen red station wagon was found abandoned with the keys still inside not far from the murder scene. The police, using the new evidence, started a concentrated search within a half-mile radius of the abandoned station wagon, knocking on everyone's doors to see if anyone had seen anything suspicious in the area. The police search uncovered a dog that had been shot and disembowelled close to where the station wagon had been abandoned and they felt their suspect probably lived quite close to the scene of the crime.

Although two witnesses came forward to say they had seen a stranger driving the station wagon, they were unable to give any sort of description other than the fact that it was a white male. The most promising lead came from a woman in her late twenties who told the police she had bumped into a young man who used to attend the same high school as herself. She said what struck her as odd, was her old classmate's appearance. She described him as being stick thin, dishevelled, wearing a bloodstained T-shirt and with some sort of yellow foodstuff caked around his mouth. He had extremely sunken eyes and when he tried to open her car door to speak to her, she said she simply drove away. When she heard that the police were looking for someone wearing bloodstained clothing, she contacted the authorities and told them the man's name was Richard Trenton Chase.

By Saturday, the police had found out that Chase lived just one block way from the abandoned station wagon. They placed officers to watch his apartment and waited for him to come out. They had tried phoning and knocking on the front door but had obtained no answer, so when he didn't appear by late afternoon, the officers decided to try a ruse and lure him out. They knew they had to be careful because Chase owned a .22 revolver and he wouldn't be afraid to use it. One policeman went to the manager of the apartment blocks to pretend to use the telephone, while the other one quite openly walked away from the front of Chase's own apartment. Just minutes later, Chase had taken the bait and appeared at his front door carrying a box under his arm. He looked up and down the street and then made a run for his truck. As soon as he made a dash for it the police pounced and after a brief struggle managed to apprehend their suspect by grappling him to the ground. As they pushed him to the floor, a .22 revolver fell out of Chase's gun holster and in his back pocket was Daniel Meredith's wallet. The box that he had been carrying when he came out of the apartment, was full of bloody rags.

When they searched Chase's truck and apartment, both were messy and littered with old newspapers, beer cans, plates with dried food on them, milk cartons and a large number of dirty rags. A locked toolbox contained a bloodstained kitchen knife and his rubber boots appeared to have spots of blood all over them. In the kitchen were three food blenders which contained body parts and blood, and on the table was a newspaper cutting of the first murder. There were dirty clothes in every room, many of which were covered with bloodstains. Inside the refrigerator were dishes containing human body parts, and the kitchen drawers contained several knives taken from the Wallin house. The police had so much evidence they were in no doubt that they had found their sadistic killer.

Three months after Chase's arrest, the body of baby David Ferreira was found in a churchyard.

A LIFE FOR A LIFE

The trial opened on January 2, 1979. Chase originally told the FBI that he had killed in an effort to preserve his own life, but when the trial started he entered pleas of not guilty to all six murders due to his insanity. The trial had to be moved to San José because of the intense hatred shown towards Chase by the Sacramento residents. The trial lasted for four months and despite his constant pleas that he did not know what he was doing, the jury came back with a guilty verdict on all counts.

Chase was sentenced to death and incarcerated at San Quentin prison to await his turn in the electric chair. However, Chase managed to cheat the system, because on Boxing Day in 1980, his guard found him lying face down on his bunk. When they searched his cell they found a strange suicide note about taking some pills. Chase had been prescribed a daily dose of antidepressants which apparently he had been hoarding so that he could take his own life with an overdose.

Although Chase was a fiendish killer, he was also a classic example of a breakdown in the system. It is blatantly obvious that he should never have been allowed to live back in society on his own with his history of strange behaviour, and because of this society had to suffer.

VAMPIROIDS

Vampiroids are people who believe they are vampires. Despite the high proportion of relatively harmless vampiroids that exist, there are those that portray psychotic behaviour and will go to great extremes to carry out their beliefs. One such person was Rodrick Justin Ferrell, who was the leader of a gang of teenagers from Murray, Kentucky, known as the 'Vampire Clan'. In 1998 Ferrell pleaded guilty to the killing of a couple from Eustis, Florida, and became the youngest person in the USA on Death Row. Ferrell believed he was a 500-year-old vampire named 'Vesago', and was eventually diagnosed with Asperger's syndrome.

DANIEL AND MANUELA RUDA

Two other people who took their beliefs to the extreme were Daniel and Manuela Ruda. German-born Manuela claimed to have been drawn to Satanism when she visited Britain for the first time. She had already shocked her parents with her punk haircuts and outrageous clothes, and at the age of sixteen she ran away from home. Manuela got a part-time job working as a chambermaid in a hotel in the Scottish Highlands. She was fascinated by the cemetery close to the hotel and also the dark, gloomy weather which she said suited her moods. When the hotel shut during the winter, Manuela lived for a while with a sixty-two-year-old man called Tom Leppard in a cave-like dwelling on the Isle of Skye. Tom had had his entire body tattooed like a leopard.

Tired with her life in Scotland, Manuela headed for London and worked in a gothic club in Islington. It was here that she was introduced to Satanism for the first time. She worshipped the Devil, attended 'bite parties' where people would drink each other's blood, and slept on graves. On one occasion a few of her friends dug a grave and Manuela slept in it just to see what it felt like to be dead.

When Manuela returned to Germany she went to drastic measures to change her appearance. She had her two canine teeth removed and replaced with animal fangs. She had her head partly shaved and her scalp tattooed with an upside-down crucifix and a target. Manuela signed her soul over to Satan on the night of Halloween in 1999 and made contact with other vampiroids via the Internet. They would meet up in graveyards after dark and she said it was quite normal to 'have a chat and drink some blood'. Manuela's neck was full of scars where her vampire friends had reciprocated the favour and it is believed that the practice is being pursued by several thousand other young Germans.

Soon Manuela started to dream of offering up a real blood sacrifice to the Devil and this led her into deeper, more sinister vampire cults.

Manuela met Daniel Ruda through a heavy metal rock magazine, *Metal-Hammer*. He had placed a lonely hearts advertisement saying:

> *Raven-black vampire seeks Princess of*
> *Darkness who hates everybody and*
> *everything.*

Manuela was enchanted by Daniel as soon as they met and the couple had much in common. Daniel, another school dropout, had just lost his job as a used car salesman and they spent their nights digging up graves. Daniel had a dream featuring the satanic digits '666', which told him to carry out certain rituals including marrying Manuela. The couple were married on the sixth day of the sixth month, 2001, and just one month later, again on the sixth, they decided to look for a human sacrifice.

The victim they chose was a thirty-three-year-old friend of Daniel's by the name of Frank Hackert. The couple invited Hackert to a party and Daniel

picked him up from his home and took him back to
their flat. The place was dark and filled with candles,
skulls, handcuffs and pieces of stone ransacked from
old graves and former concentration camps. They
chatted and played music, and then Daniel's
expression changed and he turned and hit Hackert
on the head with a hammer. Manuela became
excited and shouted to her husband, 'Stab him in the
heart!' As they stabbed him in a frenzy, Manuela
later told the police that she saw the light in the flat
flicker as Hackert died. They were both in a state of
euphoria after the murder and finished off the
evening by drinking their victim's blood from a
bowl. Then the couple carved an occult star on
Hackert's stomach and had sex in an oak coffin
which Manuela often used as a bed.

The murder method appears to have been
modelled on the album cover of a band named
Cannibal Corpse. The album is called *Hammer-
Smashed Face* and features a heavily mutilated face.

After the murder Manuela and Daniel Ruda went
on the run. Manuela's mother became suspicious
when she had heard nothing from her daughter and
decided to contact the police. She accompanied
them to the Rudas' flat in Witten, in western
Germany. When they arrived, the shutters were
closed and the lights were not working. In the dim
light, however, the police could see that the walls

were spattered with blood. In the bathroom was a poster of hanged women, while skulls, scalpels stained with blood, vampire teeth and coloured contact lenses littered the other rooms. On the floor in the living room was a great deal of blood, and the body of Hackert was found lying next to the oak coffin. He had been stabbed sixty-six times and his face and arms had been viciously savaged with a machete. There was a scalpel lodged in his stomach, next to a pentagram that had been cut into his skin. Lying close to the body was a blood-stained list containing the names of fifteen people, whom the police believed were the couple's intended victims.

The police were appalled by the ferocity of the attack and started a major manhunt in the hope of stopping the couple before they killed again. The Rudas were eventually apprehended when they were spotted at a petrol station in the eastern town of Jena. They were taken in for questioning and were quite willing to confess to killing, but denied that either of them were murderers.

The trial was overseen by Judge Arno Kersting-Tombroke, who opened the case by saying that the couple had committed a 'terrible crime' by murdering their friend Frank Hackert. When Daniel took the stand he defended himself by saying that he was not a murderer because 'I got the order to sacrifice a human for Satan.'

Manuela gave the same story to the court: 'It was not murder. It was the execution of an order. Satan ordered us to. It simply had to be. We wanted to make sure that the victim suffered well.'

The case was sensationalised by the German media, with the couple playing up to the part of vampires. They appeared in court wearing black, posing for the photographers and constantly making rude gestures to the packed public gallery. Neither Daniel nor Manuela showed any sign of remorse for their crime and provoked hatred from the public by rolling their eyes when something controversial was being said.

As the sentence was passed at Bochum Court near Düsseldorf on January 31, 2002, the pair laughed audibly and cast mocking glances at the victim's distressed mother. Daniel, who was twenty-six years old, was sentenced to fifteen years and Manuela to thirteen years, both to be held in secure mental institutions.

They were both diagnosed as suffering from severe personality disorders and although the media portrayed them as 'monsters', in reality they were nothing but deeply disturbed individuals.

MATTHEW HARDMAN

Matthew Hardman was only seventeen years old,

but he was totally obsessed with immortality. The tiny community of Llanfairpwll, on the Isle of Anglesey, was sickened when they heard about the murder of ninety-year-old Mabel Leyshon on November 25, 2001. When the police arrived at Mabel's home they had to face one of the most callous and brutal murder scenes they had ever witnessed.

Mabel, who had been sitting in her favourite chair watching television, had died from multiple stab wounds. As if the sight of this frail, helpless old woman wasn't bad enough, what the killer had done following her death, made it even harder for the police to stomach. The assailant had then moved Mabel's body to another chair, placed two pokers in a cross formation at her feet, removed her heart and placed it in a saucepan, wrapped in newspaper. He then drained the blood from Mabel's leg into the saucepan and drank it.

After forensic scientists had studied the scene of the crime the police managed to retrace the killer's steps and discovered that he had removed a slate from the back garden and thrown it through a window on the ground floor. The intruder had left clear footprints on the broken glass and patio outside the window, and the forensic team were able to build up an impression of the shoes worn by the attacker. As they built up details of the crime it soon became apparent from the lip marks left on the saucepan, that they were dealing with vampirism.

Due to the severity of the crime the police put out an appeal on BBC's *Crimewatch* programme in December 2001. After the show, the phone lines were flooded with over 200 calls giving details of a suspect who had carried out an attack on a German student. This information led the police to the home of Matthew Hardman. Hardman was quite willing to give a swab of his saliva and, after searching the house, the police found a pair of Levi shoes which matched the footprints found at the scene of the crime. The police had expected the suspect to be much older, but on the basis of the evidence found, the young teenager was arrested in January 2002.

Hardman was officially charged with murder when the DNA samples matched those taken from Mabel's house. It soon became obvious that Hardman was obsessed with vampires and how to become one and frequently read magazines on the subject. Matthew Hardman was found guilty of murder at Mold Crown Court in August 2002 and sentenced to life imprisonment.

PART SEVEN

CHILD FIENDS

MARY BELL

Mary Bell, at eleven years old, was the youngest female killer in the United Kingdom. She was born in 1957 into the economically depressed area of Scotswood, Newcastle. Mary's mother, Betty, was single, which was unusual for the period, and she also displayed signs of mental depression. In fact Mary's brief childhood could be described as a nightmare of abandonment, sexual abuse and drug overdoses. Betty used prostitution as a way to earn money and was deeply distressed when she learned she was pregnant. As soon as Mary was born, Betty would leave her with friends and relatives, but despite her family's pleas to let them adopt Mary, Betty always returned to pick up her child and torment her even further. Possibly the greatest tragedy of Mary's childhood was her mother's use of her daughter during her prostitution. She would use her as a lure and ultimately a sexual victim of abuse. This bizarre and impressionable time in Mary's life would certainly help explain her irrational behaviour towards other children.

Mary was left to play unsupervised on an old industrial area littered with construction materials, old cars and pieces of dangerous debris. Mary had a close friend by the name of Norma Bell, who ironically shared the same surname, but was not related. In July 1968, the Scotswood estate went into panic as a three-year-old boy by the name of Brian Howe had gone missing. He usually stayed close to home, but when teatime arrived and Brian couldn't be found, his older sister, Pat, raised the alarm.

When the police started to search the area, Mary and Norma offered to help them and show the officers where they normally played. Knowing exactly where the tiny body lay, Mary was keen that the searchers shouldn't get too close and veered them away from the large concrete blocks. Pat was worried because a few weeks earlier another young boy, Martin Brown, had been found dead inside an abandoned house.

Later that night, at 11.10 p.m., when Mary and Norma were both back at home, the Newcastle police uncovered the body of Brian Howe. It was found sandwiched between large concrete blocks and the corpse was covered with grass and purple weeds. He had been strangled and close by lay a pair of broken scissors hidden by the long grass. On his thighs were puncture wounds, his genitals had been partially skinned and clumps of his hair had been cut away. The killer had left a trademark by carving the letter 'M' on his stomach with a razor blade.

The police had a nagging suspicion that Brian's murder had been carried out by an adolescent and they started interviewing all the children from the estate between the ages of three and fifteen. Gradually the police focused their attention on Mary and Norma, both of whom seemed vague about their movements on the day of Brian's death. Mary suddenly started remembering details that she had not reported earlier, such as seeing another boy playing with Brian on the afternoon he died. However, when the police checked this information, the boy Mary had named had been at the airport on that afternoon. Mary also revealed that she knew about the scissors, a piece of evidence that had been kept strictly confidential, and it soon became evident that either Mary, Norma, or indeed both the girls had been there when Brian died.

Adding to their already bizarre behaviour, the two girls broke into the local nursery school the day after Brian's murder. They trashed the place and then left handwritten notes saying:

I murder SO THAT I may come back.

Fuch off, we murder, watch out Fanny and Faggot.

*You are mice Y Becurse we murdered
Martain Go Brown you Bete Look out there
are Murders about by Fanny and auld Faggot
you Screws.*

*We did murder Martain Brown Fuckof you
Bastard.*

Mary and Norma, having first denied the break-in, eventually owned up. Norma also admitted, after days of questioning, that her friend had strangled Brian in her presence. She told the police that Mary had ignored her pleas to stop hurting the boy, so she ran away. The next time she saw Mary she was alone with Brian's dog.

ADULT COURT

Mary and Norma Bell stood trial in an adult court. There was no dock so that the children could stay close to their legal teams and their parents. Norma was acquitted of the murder of both boys, while Mary was found guilty of manslaughter on the grounds of diminished responsibility. As the verdict was read out, Mary broke down and cried, but Mr Justice Cusack described her as dangerous and that she was 'a very grave risk to other children if she is not closely watched'.

Because Britain was unaccustomed to putting girls as young as Mary under lock and key, it became a major issue where this eleven-year-old should be placed. The authorities knew that prison was out of the question and that mental hospitals were not really equipped to take someone of such a young age. She was considered to be far too dangerous to be placed in a regular institution for troubled children and Mary eventually ended up in an all-boys facility.

Mary served her time in Red Bank, an approved school in Newton-le-Willows in Lancashire. It was adapted to take Mary although there were fears that there would be a lot of disruption when she reached puberty. She stayed at Red Bank until November 1973 and formed a great respect for one member of staff named James Dixon, a former navy man who was known for his strong moral influence. For the first time in her life, it appears that Mary actually had someone she could look up to, giving her the father figure she never had.

Problems surfaced after Mary was moved to a less secure unit in 1977. She escaped and during her brief time on the run she met up with two young men. She lost her virginity and the man whom she had slept with later sold his story to the newspapers, claiming that she had only escaped from jail so that she could get pregnant.

Mary was released on licence in May 1980 and given a new identity so that she could start a new life away from the prying eyes of the press. For a while she moved back in with her mother, but met a young man and became pregnant. There was much concern over whether a woman who had already murdered two children should be allowed to become a mother herself, but she fought for the right to keep the baby which was born in 1984. The authorities felt that as she had not received adequate psychiatric treatment, Mary could not make the transition from a child killer to a loving mother. Mary herself claimed that she had found a new moral consciousness and felt deep regret for her crimes committed at a very troubled time in her life. Eventually Mary was allowed to keep the child, but it was technically made a ward of court until 1992.

Mary eventually learned to love and settled in a small town in a steady relationship. However, her probation officer had to inform the local authorities of her whereabouts and the villagers soon marched through the streets chanting 'Murderer Out!'

Mary's case raised fresh controversy when her book *Cries Unheard* was published in 1998. When the authorities learned that she was to be paid for her contribution to the book, they tried to block the payment as it is illegal in Britain to profit from crime. The publication also caused considerable grief to Mary's daughter, who discovered her mother's true identity on April 30, 1998, when her home on the South Coast was besieged by reporters. Up until that time she was totally unaware of her mother's previous life.

In 2003 the High Court made the decision that Mary and her daughter would be granted lifelong anonymity to try and protect them from vigilantes. After years of being hounded it appears that they will now be allowed to vanish and try to lead normal lives.

WILLIE BOSKET

By the age of fifteen, Willie Bosket claimed he had committed at least 2,000 crimes, including 200 armed robberies and twenty-five stabbings. Following two murders on the subways of New York City, Bosket was incarcerated for a term of five years, but because the violent boy grew into an even more violent young man, he gained the reputation of being one of New York's most dangerous inmates, and he seemed destined to spend the rest of his life behind bars. He was kept in virtual solitary confinement as he continually attacked the guards and staff, seemingly unable to control his inbred violence. What turned Bosket into this animal can only be a subject of conjecture, but his troubled childhood led to pent-up anger which he seemed unable to control.

Willie Bosket grew up in a tough area of New York City, rife with poverty and a constant background of street violence. He had no role model to turn to as his father was a convict who had been put away for murder. Bosket never really got to know his father but the similarities between the two are quite alarming. Each had a third-grade education, they were both sentenced to the same reform school when they were nine and they both went on to commit double murders. Although they both displayed a superior intelligence, this is where the two differ, as Bosket's father studied hard while he was in jail and became the first inmate to be inducted into the Phi Beta Kappa honour society. When Bosket Snr was released in 1983, he found work as a teaching assistant in a university, but his rehabilitation was short-lived. In 1985, he was re-arrested for molesting a six-year-old child and following a shoot-out with police, he shot his girlfriend and then turned the gun on himself.

Without the presence of a father figure, Bosket relied on his mother to guide him in his early years. However, she was a drug addict who had an addiction for violent men and was often prone to fly into a paranoid rage. She once accused Bosket of stealing money from her purse, but despite his pleading innocence, she grabbed a knife and attempted to stab him in the mouth. Too scared to live with his mother any longer, Bosket ran away to his grandmother's house. His grandmother immediately called child protection and took custody of the boy to try and protect him from any further violence.

However, life at his grandmother's house was little better and he had to fight for attention against the dominating characters of his aunt and uncle. Despite having an above-average IQ, Bosket dropped out of school and, before the age of eight, had mugged an old lady, terrorised his classmates and intimidated his teachers. He started playing on the streets and found solace with other children of neglect and abuse.

His behaviour was such that his grandmother was forced to have him placed in a juvenile correctional facility when he was just nine years of age. Being institutionalised seemed to bring out the worst in the young boy, and Bosket turned to arson, stealing a van and assaulting both inmates and staff with fists, teeth, chairs and a nail-spiked wooden club, in fact anything he could get his hands on. He also attempted to strangle a nurse with a telephone cord and eventually he left the facility a very angry twelve-year-old boy.

Shortly after his release, Bosket was arrested for playing with a loaded gun with some other street kids, leaning over an overpass and pointing it at cars, shouting 'Pow! Pow!' The police were alerted to the boys' behaviour and Bosket was sent away to another institute for several months. When he was released he was returned to the care of his grandmother, who died a little later that year. His aunt and uncle moved out of the house which meant that Bosket had to fend for himself. He took to stealing to survive and fought back against the sexual and physical abuse he had received not only from his family but from the detention facilities as well.

A STEP TOO FAR

Having been in and out of court on various charges since he was nine years of age, Bosket had little, if any, respect for the juvenile courts. Had he been able to control his lust for violence, Bosket would have been adopted by a couple who actually cared about what happened to him. However, the process of adoption was slow, and Bosket was left roaming the streets to fend for himself. On Sunday, March 19, 1978, Bosket decided to try his luck at robbery on the subways of New York City. He managed to steal $380 dollars out of the pocket of a sleeping commuter. He used the money to buy himself a gun from a man who was one of his mother's 'friends'. He told the fifteen-year-old boy that the gun would earn him respect on the streets, and Bosket strapped it to his leg and wore it with pride.

Later that same day, Bosket returned to the subway and found himself alone with a middle-aged man who was asleep in the corner of the carriage. He kicked the man in the leg, but failed to get any response so tried to extricate the gold watch from his wrist without waking him. Bosket noticed the man was wearing a ridiculous pair of pink sunglasses which made him feel angry, and when the man suddenly opened his eyes, Bosket shot him through the right side of his head, penetrating his brain. Bosket panicked, fearing that the man might still be alive, and shot him again. This time the man slumped to the floor with blood gushing from his head. Bosket removed the man's watch, found fifteen dollars in his back pocket and then slipped a gold ring off his finger. He stopped at a pawn shop on the way home and managed to get twenty dollars for the ring and he walked home elated. He had always wanted to know what it felt like to kill someone and now he could boast to all his friends that he was 'truly bad'.

His victim had been forty-four-year-old Noel Perez, who worked in a hospital and lived on his own. Bosket read about the killing the next day in the newspaper and he felt an overwhelming feeling of power and bragged to his sister 'I did that!'

THE URGE TO KILL

Just four days after killing Perez, Bosket had a renewed strength and he went out on the streets with his cousin, Herman Spates, feeling invincible. They headed towards the subway at Lexington Avenue and spotted a train engineer in a yard who was carrying a CB radio. They knew that they could easily convert the radio into cash and decided to follow the man. The engineer was a man named Anthony Lamorte, who was about to finish his shift when he noticed the two boys.

Lamorte shouted at the boys to 'Get the hell out', but this was a big mistake because Bosket did not like being told what to do. Bosket challenged the engineer to make them leave and, thinking the boys were too young to cause any real trouble, Lamorte started walking towards them. When he was within thirty feet, Bosket pulled out his gun and demanded that the engineer hand over the radio and any money he had in his pockets.

Lamorte realised that he had misjudged the boys and turned to run back towards the subway car. He could hear the boys running after him and then felt a pain in his back and right shoulder. He could hear the two boys running away and he managed to get to his manager's office and tell them that he thought he had been shot.

Over the course of the next few days, the two boys carried out three more violent robberies and shot another man in the leg when he resisted them. Bosket was feeling more powerful with each robbery, convinced that he would never get caught.

On Monday, March 27, Bosket and his cousin jumped over the turnstile and boarded the last carriage of a train heading uptown. There was only one passenger in the carriage and Bosket told his cousin to stand guard so that the man couldn't get off at the next station. He pulled out his gun and demanded money, but when the man told Bosket that he 'ain't got any', he pulled the trigger and the man slid off his seat and onto the floor of the train.

Bosket rifled through his pockets which only contained two dollars, and he flung the empty wallet in a rubbish bin as they walked back home. He was so excited now that he had killed again that he couldn't wait to read the newspapers the following day. When it made the front pages the next morning, he proudly showed the article to his sister. Ironically, that same day, the permission came through for him to be adopted as a foster child by a couple whom Bosket had hoped to be able to live with, but his life was not about to change for the better.

A MATTER OF DEDUCTION

Fearing that there was a serial killer on the loose, the police started an intense search of the area. Having found the discarded wallet, they thought the killer was probably from the local neighbour-hood and a computer search brought forward the names of Willie Bosket and Herman Spates. As they had both been arrested on numerous occasions, the police felt it was well worth pulling them in for questioning. The detective in charge of the investi-gation knew he had to tread carefully as Bosket, at fifteen, was still a juvenile. They managed to track down his cousin, Herman, who was with his probation officer, and lied that Bosket had already turned evidence against him. Herman immediately insisted that it was his cousin who had fired the shot and then gave them details of the previous murder and the whereabouts of the gun. They soon had enough evidence to take the foul-mouthed, un-restrained juvenile to court.

THE TRIAL

The trial of Willie Bosket was held in the Family Court building on Lafayette Street in Lower Manhattan and he was charged on two counts of murder and one attempted murder. The presiding judge had come across Bosket before, but this time she was shocked to see his complete lack of sensitivity. During the period he was confined waiting for his trial, Bosket had stabbed another boy with a fork, hit one of his counsellors in the face and attempted to strangle his psychiatrist. He bragged about the amount of crimes he had committed and flippantly told his lawyer to enter a plea of guilty. Due to the laws regarding the sentencing of juveniles, Bosket could only be put away for a maximum of five years, which meant that by the time he was twenty-one, this dangerous young man would be free to unleash his anger once again. However, little did the authorities realise that the system would do little to rehabilitate Bosket and he just became more and more violent as, in his own words, 'Violence earns me respect'.

LIFE IN PRISON

Willie Bosket seemed unprepared to change and even the restraints of prison did nothing to calm his rage against the system that he said had abused him all his life. Because he spent his time attacking guards, hurling faeces and food at them, Bosket has been placed in a special dungeon which has been lined with Plexiglas. There are video cameras that track his every move and because he causes so much trouble every time he receives a visitor, he has to be chained backwards to the inside of his cell door. Even these chains couldn't totally restrain the monster he had become, because he managed to break free on one occasion and attacked a guard leaving a six-inch wound. With each new attack Bosket's chances of ever being free become more remote and he now faces the rest of his life incarcerated, constantly fighting the prison system.

JESSE POMEROY

Jesse Harding Pomeroy became a fiendish killer at the tender age of fourteen. He was a cruel boy who took pleasure in inflicting pain and terror on those weaker than himself, gaining excitement as they writhed in agony. As in many other cases, his crimes started with beating and torture, but before long this was not enough and his acts soon took a far more sinister turn.

Pomeroy's appearance could be described as strange, if not a little inhuman, being larger than the majority of boys of his age. His head was oversized, with large ears that stuck out and a mouth that seemed too wide for his face. He was always sensitive about his appearance which was exacerbated by an almost pure white right eye, which gave him a somewhat eerie persona. He also suffered from epileptic-like shaking fits, leaving him a lone figure who was a prime target for the other kids in his neighbourhood.

Born in 1859, Pomeroy was raised in the suburbs of Boston, but his family life was far from happy.

His father, Charles, loved to drink which gave him a terrible temper. He took out this temper on his children, making them strip naked before they took a severe beating, often leaving them covered in bloody weals. It is possible that these beatings influenced Pomeroy to inflict pain on others, something which reared its ugly head when he was still a young boy. He seemed to have a strange passion for torturing animals, which came to his mother's notice when he killed the family's pet birds and a neighbour's kitten, sadistically twisting their heads off their bodies.

Pomeroy started to tire of his animal victims and decided to start looking for human targets. Possibly acting out his father's behaviour, he looked for victims who were weaker and smaller than himself.

UNTHINKABLE BEHAVIOUR

Pomeroy's first victim was a four-year-old boy named William Paine in December 1871. He had been lured to a small cabin in an area called Powder Horn Hill. Inside the cabin, Pomeroy hung the small child by the wrists from the central beam and then gave his semi-naked body a severe beating. His back was covered in welts, standing out open and bleeding against the paleness of his skin. William was too traumatised to give a description of his assailant and the police hoped and prayed that it was just an isolated incident. Unfortunately, just two months later, Pomeroy struck again.

This time, Pomeroy lured seven-year-old Tracy Hayden to Powder Horn Hill. Again he mimicked the actions of his father by stripping the boy naked then beating him with a switch. The boy's front teeth were knocked out, his eyes were blackened and his nose was broken as Pomeroy unleashed his fury. The only description the police could get from the young boy was that his assailant had been a teenage boy with brown hair, which didn't give them very much to go on. All they could do was wait, sure that their attacker would find another victim.

It was early spring when Pomeroy struck again. This time, using the circus as a lure, he convinced eight-year-old Robert Maier to follow him to his favourite lair. Pomeroy forced the young lad to remove all of his clothes and told him to repeat swear words as he beat him. Maier was freed but was threatened with death if he told anyone what had happened.

Anguished parents kept their children close by and warned them not to talk to anyone they didn't know. The police began a massive manhunt and questioned every teenage boy with brown hair in the area.

The attacks continued into July and eventually a

reward of $500 was posted for information leading to the arrest of what the papers described as the 'fiendish boy'. In July, Ruth Pomeroy decided to move her family to Chelsea Creek in South Boston. If his mother had been suspicious that her son was involved in the attacks, it must have confirmed her doubts when the attacks also moved to South Boston.

Pomeroy's next assault was on seven-year-old George Pratt, but this time his attack took on a new aspect. After the usual stripping and beating, Pomeroy bit a large chunk of flesh from the boy's cheek and tore at his flesh with his fingernails. After this he took a long sewing needle and started repeatedly stabbing George's ravaged body.

The police were joined by vigilantes as they started rounding up youths from all over the city. However, none of the young victims could pick their attacker from the line up and the police were no closer to making an arrest.

With each attack, Pomeroy became more frenzied and, when he abducted a six-year-old boy by the name of Harry Austin, he not only stripped him and beat him, but stabbed him under each arm and between the shoulder blades with a pocket knife. Pomeroy then attempted to cut off the boy's penis, but was disturbed by a noise nearby and fled before he could finish the job.

The attacks became more frequent and more

violent and eventually a five-year-old boy found tied to a post near a railway line was able to give the police their first real lead. He told them that his assailant had been a large boy with one eye that looked like a 'white marble'.

OUT OF HARM'S WAY

The Boston police conducted a search of all the schools in the area, convinced that this would turn up the boy with the marble eye. Eventually their perseverence paid off and they arrested Pomeroy and leaned heavily on him to try and force a confession. At first he adamantly stuck to his claim of innocence, but after a threat of a 100-year jail sentence, he caved in and confessed to his crimes.

At the hearing, Pomeroy hung his head in shame and told the magistrate that 'I couldn't help myself.' He was ordered to be placed in the House of Reformation in Westborough until he was eighteen years of age, out of harm's way.

Westborough House was a cruel place where the strong preyed on the weak, and it was somewhere that a character like Jesse Pomeroy could thrive. The discipline was harsh and the work was hard, but Pomeroy still felt he had a power over those smaller and weaker than himself. He learned quickly that if he were to be released before his eighteenth birthday he would need to show he was a reformed character, and indeed his records show that he was a model inmate.

The only incident that showed he still had a more perverse side to his nature was when one of the teachers asked his help to kill a snake. Eager to help her, Pomeroy followed the teacher down the garden, grabbing a stick on the way. After she showed him exactly where the snake was, Pomeroy seemed to work himself up into a kind of frenzy as he started to pulverise the writhing creature.

EARLY RELEASE

Ruth Pomeroy, who had always stood by her son and proclaimed his innocence, was staging a campaign for his early release. When his case came up for review, Ruth managed to convince the authorities that she could provide a caring environment for her son and that she could offer him work in the family's shop. Promising to keep a far more custodial eye on her son, Ruth managed to convince the courts and consequently, less than one and a half years after his arrest, Pomeroy was released from Westborough.

Just six weeks after being paroled from Westborough, Pomeroy was back to his old tricks, having been attracted by ten-year-old Katie Curran who came into the shop asking for a notebook. Pomeroy asked the other boy who worked in the shop to run to the butcher's to get some scraps to feed the cats, which left him alone with Katie. He told her that although he had no notebooks in the shop, they had a storeroom downstairs and that there might be some down there. He convinced the innocent young girl to follow him down into the cellar where he cruelly attacked her, severed her head and dumped her body behind the toilet.

After he had satisfied his lust, Pomeroy washed his hands and then ran upstairs, resuming his work as if nothing untoward had taken place.

When Katie's mother learned that Jesse Pomeroy had been released and was working close by, she almost fainted from shock. However, when she went to the police with her suspicions, she was told that the boy was no threat as he had been completely rehabilitated in the reform school. When Mrs Curran persisted, the police agreed to search the shop and were met by a very hostile Ruth Pomeroy who was well aware that there were rumours going round again about her son. The police search revealed nothing and eventually, following statements from witnesses saying that they had seen Katie lured into a car, the case was closed, concluding that she had been the victim of an unfortunate kidnap.

Having rediscovered the thrill of killing, Pomeroy was not satisfied to leave it there and went in search of his next victim. In April 1874, he lured four-year-old Horace Millen to the nearby harbour. In his frenzy Pomeroy inflicted an excruciating death on the toddler and killed him by eventually slicing through his windpipe. When the tiny body was discovered, the police were in no doubt that this was the work of the strange boy with the marble eye. Pomeroy was found at home and was taken into custody despite his mother's anguished protests. She promised her son that he would soon be home again, but that would be the last night that Jesse Pomeroy would ever spend in the family house.

When he eventually had to come face to face with what he had done, Pomeroy broke down and admitted to killing Horace Millen. He wept and pleaded with the police not to tell his mother, adding, 'Please put me somewhere, so I can't do such things.'

Some time after his arrest, the body of Katie Curran was discovered when the new tenant of the shop decided to do up the basement. Jesse Pomeroy now stood accused of two murders and it looked as though the fourteen-year-old boy would be the youngest person ever executed in the state of Massachusetts. The only way Pomeroy could escape the death penalty was if he was proved to be insane.

Although Pomeroy had freely admitted to the killings, just two months before he went to trial he changed his statement and denied having anything to do with either murder. A psychiatrist made a full report on the state of Pomeroy's mind and reported that although he could discriminate between right and wrong, he would always be a threat to society and needed to be permanently denied his freedom. He finished his report by saying that, in his opinion, Jesse Pomeroy was insane.

However, the prosecution placed their doctor on the stand, who contradicted the psychiatrist's report. He described Pomeroy as a deeply manipulative and cunning boy who was 'totally free of any mental defect'. On this evidence the jury found Pomeroy guilty of first-degree, premeditated murder, for which the mandatory sentence was death by hanging. A weeping Jesse Pomeroy was then led out of the court to await his execution.

A REPRIEVE

Although capital punishment was normally carried out fairly swiftly in nineteenth-century America, there was so much controversy about performing such a punishment on a teenager, that his execution was delayed. Eventually his death sentence was commuted to life imprisonment, on the condition that he served the remainder of his time in solitary confinement. He spent forty-one years locked away in his own concrete cell with only one visitor, his mother Ruth. Finally, in 1917, four decades later, Jesse Pomeroy was taken out of his solitary cell and allowed to move freely among the other inmates. Most of the men who had been there a long time knew of the infamous Jesse Pomeroy, but gradually, as the inmates changed, his notoriety dwindled. By 1929, the now seventy-one-year-old Pomeroy was starting to suffer from health problems and he was moved from Charlestown prison to Bridgewater prison farm where it was felt he could receive better medical care. Pomeroy's eyes stared out of the window of the car as they travelled to Bridgewater, showing no sign of emotion whatsoever, hardened over the years by solitude from a world he knew nothing about. Two years later, Pomeroy died, the once fiendish killer who ended up as one of the loneliest people in the entire world.

JESSICA HOLTMEYER

Kimberly Dotts was a rather shy teenager who attended Clearfield High in a small, rural Pennsylvanian town. She was a rather overweight fifteen-year-old with learning disabilities and was always eager to try and make friends. Kimberly's search for friends put her in touch with a group of kids who hung out together and called themselves the 'Runaway Gang'. Her introduction to the gang came from a fellow classmate, fourteen-year-old Dawn Lanager, who invited Kimberly to a sleep-over on the night of May 8, 1998. Kimberly's parents were pleased for their daughter when she told them excitedly about the invitation. The following day, Kimberly returned home briefly and just before leaving told her seven-year-old sister not to say anything because she was 'running away' with some friends.

Kimberly's nightmare began on Mother's Day, Sunday, May 10, 1998. Jessica Holtmeyer, a second-year student, was an exceptionally intimidating teenager, who loved to make fun of people and showed a particularly mean streak. She was a devil-worshipper who self-harmed with razors, and loved to frighten other kids by pulling out a knife. She was covered in tattoos, with the numbers '666' behind her left ear, being the sign of the devil. She also had a self-tattoo on her right forearm of a pentagram, one on the back of her neck saying 'Kurt Cobain 1967–1994' and her boyfriend's name on her shoulder. In fact it could be said that Jessica Holtmeyer had pure evil flowing in her blood and, like many other teenage killers, had started off by torturing animals. In her early teenage years she had placed six feral cats into a bin liner, set fire to it and then thrown it into a river. On another occasion, she strangled a poodle dog to death with its own lead.

PLANS TO RUN AWAY

When Jessica was sixteen, she started to hatch plans to run away from home with a group of six friends. The plan was to travel to Florida and Jessica gathered her friends at her grandparents' house on the morning of May 10, 1968. When they arrived at the house, Jessica was sitting in the lounge watching a videotape of the horror film *Scream*, in which a girl is found hanging from a tree. She turned to her friends and said, 'It'd be fun to hang someone,' to which remark she got a mixed reaction. What

Jessica didn't know at the time, was that the gang had invited Kimberly Dotts to join them.

When the doorbell rang, Jessica got up to open the door, but almost slammed it shut again when she saw who was standing there. Jessica turned to her boyfriend, Aaron Straw, and said, 'What is she doing here? You know I don't like her.'

Tracy Lynn Lewis, a distant cousin of Kimberly's, agreed with Jessica that she didn't want Kimberly around and it was left to Dawn to try and calm the situation as the tension started to mount. Eventually Kimberly was allowed in the house and the gang finished watching the rest of the film.

When the film had finished the gang hung around town for a few hours and then went to the house of twenty-two-year-old Mike Jarrett. Jarrett had a blue Dodge van and had agreed to drive them out of Clearfield, but before he was prepared to leave he told them he needed a rest before making the journey that night. To pass the time the gang hitched a lift into Shiloh, where they planned to break into some cabins owned by hunters to steal money and food for their journey. Among their booty were some bottles of whisky, a few sparklers and a length of nylon rope which Jessica decided would come in useful.

Jessica and Tracy were kindred spirits in their hatred towards Kimberly, especially when Tracy called her cousin a 'snitch' for getting her into trouble over drinking at a party. They talked of dumping her from their adventure, but decided instead to talk the rest of the gang into following them to a clearing in the woods known as Gallows Harbor. It had got its name from a nineteenth-century lynching and had become a popular place for Clearfield kids to gather, and so Kimberly happily followed her new-found friends deep into the woods.

THE INITIATION

Jessica led them to a clearing in the woods and announced to the group that she wanted to test Kimberly's loyalty to the gang. She proudly showed the nylon rope that she had stolen from one of the campers and then turned to fourteen-year-old Theresa Wolfe to make the rope into a noose. Jessica and Tracy grabbed the noose and looped it loosely around Kimberly's neck. Jessica started laughing and dragged Kimberly round for several minutes like a dog, until she lost her balance and fell into a patch of mud. Kimberly started to cry loudly, which seemed to make the situation worse as Jessica just dragged her face down through the dirt. The rest of the gang just stood by and watched, laughing as Jessica made a fool out of the unfortunate girl.

Eventually Jessica tired of the game and took the rope off Kimberly's neck. She passed the rope to her boyfriend, Aaron, and asked him to throw it over a branch of a tree which was about 14 ft off the ground.

Tracy announced that anyone who wanted to go to Florida had to put their head through the noose and so the initiation ceremony began. The first people to volunteer were Theresa and Dawn's boyfriend, sixteen-year-old Patrick Lucas. To show that he wasn't scared Patrick slipped his head through the noose, laughing nervously as he did it. Jessica and Aaron gripped the end of the rope, but were careful not to pull too tightly. Theresa did the same thing, followed by a Clearfield junior by the name of Clint Canaway. As the gang started to realise that nothing was going to happen, they relaxed and giggled, aware that Jessica was just playing an amusing game.

Tracy then turned to her cousin, Kimberly, and said, 'See Kimmie . . . there's nothing to be afraid of. Now it's your turn.' Kimberly had no reason not to trust her new friends and she stood while Jessica placed the noose round her neck. However, this time Jessica and Aaron used all their strength to pull on the rope, until Kimberly was lifted off the ground. Kimberly's hands immediately went to her throat to try and release the pressure, but all the colour drained from her face as she flailed erratically. The gang watched on in horror as Kimberly started to convulse, but not one person came to her aid. Tracy, Jessica and Aaron, on the other hand, were finding it all highly amusing and started to fall about with laughter. All of a sudden the gang heard the sound of a truck in the distance and dropped the end of the rope in panic. Kimberly fell to the ground with a thud and landed in a heap, crying and gasping for breath.

Most of the gang were relieved that Kimberly's torture was over, with the exception of Jessica, who informed her friends that she hadn't finished with her yet. Not wanting to be a part of what Jessica had in store, four of the gang – Clint, Dawn, Patrick and Tracy – left the clearing. With half the gang now walking off into the woods, Jessica resumed her torment on poor Kimberly, while the remainder of the gang looked on in amusement. Jessica and Aaron placed the noose around Kimberly's neck for a second time and pulled tightly on the rope. Again the poor girl thrashed around desperately trying to get air, but her face turned blue and she went into convulsions. As Kimberly's body went completely limp, Jessica and Aaron let go of the rope and let her fall to the ground.

Theresa walked over to Kimberly's lifeless body to see whether she was still alive. They kicked her and poked her with a stick but got no response. In the end Theresa, Jessica and Aaron started to cover Kimberly's body with some dry brush, believing her to be dead. Then, all of sudden, Kimberly's body twitched, making the three of them jump back in shock. Then she coughed and started to gasp for air, desperately trying to hang on to life.

Jessica was not happy that she had not managed to kill Kimberly, and picked up a large rock and dropped it onto her head. She continued to do this until Kimberly's head resembled a crushed watermelon. Theresa and Aaron just stood with their mouths agape, not quite believing what they had just witnessed. Theresa was crying and said, 'Why did you do that Jessie? You've killed her!'

Jessica just stared at her friend and, showing no emotion whatsoever, replied, 'That's what snitches get!'

They helped Jessica cover the body under a pile of twigs and leaves and just walked away swearing each other to silence. As they met up with the rest of the gang Theresa cried, 'I wouldn't go back there, you guys. They just killed Kim!'

OFF TO FLORIDA

An hour later the gang, with the exception of Jessica who had changed her mind at the last minute, were back in Mike Jarrett's van laughing and joking as they headed off towards Florida. They were accompanied by Mike's friend, John Appleton, and as they drove further away from Gallows Harbor they felt their spirits lift. Before leaving they had made a pact with Jessica that no one would ever breathe a word about what had happened to Kimberly, and agreed to tell the same fabricated story. They agreed to say that they had last seen Kimberly on the morning of Sunday, May 10, when they had dropped her off on their way down south.

On Monday, May 11, Jessica attended her classes at school as if nothing untoward had taken place. The rest of the gang – Tracy, Clint, Patrick, Aaron, Theresa, Mike and John were almost halfway to their destination.

In the meantime Kimberly's parents were beside themselves with worry and decided to post flyers around the town, asking if anyone had seen their daughter.

On May 13, the remainder of the gang arrived in Florida and Mike, John and Tracy dropped them off at one of their friends' houses and then headed back towards Clearfield. It was on the journey home that Tracy told the two boys about what had happened at Gallows Harbor. Just nine days after Kimberly Dotts went missing, John Appleton went to the police and told them the story of what had happened. After the police recovered the body of

Kimberly, Jessica and Tracy were taken in for questioning and the others were quickly expedited from Florida.

Because of the amount of publicity surrounding the case, Jessica's lawyers asked if the trial could be held in another town. The hearing eventually took place in Bloomsburg, which was 105 miles away from Clearfield. Back in Clearfield, all the locals had already made up their minds that Jessica was guilty, and there were cries that she should be hung up by the neck, to suffer the same way as her hapless victim had.

SENTENCING

In August 1998, Patrick Lucas was sentenced to six months in a juvenile detention centre for breaking into the hunting camp and for conspiracy. Dawn Lanager, fourteen, and Theresa Wolfe, fifteen, were both given separate trials. Dawn, the girl who actually enticed Kimberly into joining the gang, was given probation and was released on the day of the trial. Theresa, who helped make a noose out of the rope that Jessica had stolen, was sentenced to six months in prison.

Tracy Lewis, the oldest in the group at twenty-four, was already on parole for another minor offence, and was given a five- to twenty-year sentence for aggravated assault.

Clinton Canaway, eighteen, was placed in a juvenile detention camp and had to be put on suicide watch because he felt so guilty for not trying to stop the hanging.

As for Jessica Holtmeyer, seventeen, and Aaron Straw, nineteen, they were sentenced to life imprisonment with no chance of ever being paroled. Thanks to Kimberly's parents, Jessica did not receive the death penalty. Just after the jury found her guilty of first-degree murder, Kimberly's father said, 'I believe everybody deserves a second chance.' These were brave words from a man whose daughter had not been given a second chance.

JOSHUA PHILLIPS

On November 3, 1998, eight-year-old Madlyn 'Maddie' Clifton went missing after going outside to play in the quiet neighbourhood of the Lakewood section of Jacksonville, Florida. Her frantic mother phoned the police and, with the aid of hundreds of volunteers, they scoured the area. Joshua Phillips, who was fourteen at the time, grabbed his own torch and helped the police and neighbours search for the little girl.

As there were no leads and no clues to Maddie's whereabouts, her disappearance was featured on the *America's Most Wanted* television show on November 7, in the hope that someone would come forward with some information. The search went on for several days and a $100,000 reward was posted for any information leading to an arrest. Flyers bearing Maddie's photograph were handed out throughout the neighbourhood and also at the grounds of the local football club, the Jacksonville Jaguars. As each new enquiry led the police to yet another dead end, the FBI became involved in the search for Maddie. However, despite the rigorous investigation nothing turned up, that is until November 10, seven days after she disappeared.

THE UNTHINKABLE

Joshua's mother had decided to make a start on clearing her teenage son's bedroom because, despite constant nagging, he had made no effort to tidy it up. Shaking her head at the mess in front of her, Melissa didn't know where to start. She was about to pick up some clothes that were scattered on the carpet when she noticed a wet mark at the corner of her son's bed. Joshua slept on a waterbed and his mother wondered whether it had started to leak when she discovered the corner of the mattress was also wet. She lifted the mattress to try and determine how serious the leak was, and as she peered underneath noticed a white sock lying near the leg of the bed. She pulled on the sock but it was stuck fast and she also noticed some black tape holding the frame of the bed together. She wondered whether the bed had been leaking for some time, and if her son had made an attempt to repair it. As she pulled the tape from the leg, she felt something cold and wet touch her skin and it made the hairs stand up on the back of her neck. Unable to see what it was, Melissa went into another room to fetch a torch. Nothing could have prepared her for what she was about to find. Entombed under the waterbed was the body of a young girl.

Melissa's first reaction was to phone her husband at work, but when she failed to get an answer she knew she had to go and find a policeman to tell him what she had found. Very white and shaking like a leaf, she walked out of the house and down the road to where a policeman was still making house to house enquiries.

While the police went inside the house to investigate her grim discovery, Melissa sat hunched up in the back of a police car, dreading the thought of what was in store for her family.

Joshua was attending a geography class at school when the police called and took him down to the station for questioning. Joshua confessed to killing Maddie and told the police that he had been playing baseball in his back garden when he had accidentally hit her in the eye with a ball. When Maddie started screaming, Joshua told the detectives that he panicked and dragged her indoors to his bedroom, because he was frightened of being punished by his father. Maddie continued to scream and Joshua hit her over the head with a bat to try and stop her making a noise. Even after that, Maddie continued to moan and Joshua grabbed a knife and stabbed her in the neck until she became silent. Then he stuffed her under his waterbed and went to wash the blood off his hands. When he returned to his bedroom, he heard Maddie moaning from underneath the bed, so he dragged her out and repeatedly stabbed her until she stopped breathing.

The autopsy on the body of Maddie did indeed show that she had been beaten over the head and stabbed at least nine times in the chest and twice in the neck. Maddie's underpants and shorts had been removed, although there was no evidence that she had been sexually assaulted.

Joshua made his first court appearance the following day, on November 11, and he was ordered to be held in a secure unit at the Duval Regional Juvenile Detention Centre.

THE TRIAL

On November 16, prosecutors announced that they were going to try Joshua as an adult on charges of first-degree murder. Due to the intense amount of media coverage that the case attracted, the trial was moved 200 miles away from Jacksonville to the town of Bartow.

The trial was set to start on April 5, but was delayed when Joshua's defence attorney asked for extra time to obtain a medical report on their client. After a couple more delays the trial eventually took place on July 6, 1999, and lasted for only two days. Maddie's older sister told the court that they had been forbidden to play with Joshua by their mother, because he had previously talked to them about sex. Samples of blood and hair, and bloody ceiling fan blades, globe and cowling, which were taken from Joshua's room, were shown as evidence during the trail, and to all intents and purposes it was an open and shut case.

The jury deliberated for more than two hours before convicting the now fifteen-year-old Joshua Phillips of first-degree murder. Because Joshua was still under the age of sixteen he could not be given the death penalty, but was sentenced to spend the remainder of his life behind bars.

Many people feel that perhaps the verdict was a little too harsh and that there are still too many unanswered questions surrounding the death of Maddie. It was obvious that it was not a pre-meditated murder and that had he been convicted of second-degree murder, or even manslaughter, he would be eligible for release while still young.

As for Joshua, if he were to speak to Maddie's parents he would like to say: 'I'd beg for forgiveness. That's all I could say; there's nothing else I could say. I guess I'd say I'm sorry but that wouldn't be enough.'

THE MURDER OF JAMES BULGER

When the media published the story of the murder of two-year-old James Bulger in 1993, it sent a wave of shock and disgust throughout the nation. That the crime had been committed by two ten-year-old boys was bad enough, but what was even more nauseating was that what they did to the toddler was so horrendous that James's mother was forbidden from identifying the body.

Jon Venables and Robert Thompson were playing truant from school on February 12, 1993, something which was quite a regular occurrence for the two boys. They went to the Bootle Strand Shopping Centre in Merseyside to try their hand at shoplifting, but soon tired of the activity when they found it too easy. They decided to change their tactics and tried to kidnap a two-year-old boy while his mother was distracted, but failed when the woman turned round and called her son to her side.

James Bulger's mother only turned her back on her son for a matter of seconds, but this gave Jon and Robert enough time to take her son's hand and lead him out of the shopping precinct with the promise of giving him sweets. Denise Bulger had only been momentarily distracted and when she turned round her son had disappeared.

WALK OF DEATH

Jon and Robert led James Bulger out of the shopping centre at 3.42 p.m. and were captured by the surveillance camera as they left. They started walking away from the centre and up Stanley Road, carrying James as he was now crying loudly for his mother. They embarked on a two and half mile journey, during which time they tortured the toddler – dropping, kicking and hitting him. Unbelievably, no fewer than thirty-eight witnesses saw the two boys with James Bulger, but no one thought to stop them even though the toddler was showing signs of distress and injury.

The first time the boys inflicted any pain on James was when they walked underneath a bridge towards the canal. It was an isolated area and Jon and Robert joked with one another about pushing James into the water. It was here that they picked up the toddler and dropped him on his head, but for some unexplainable reason they were not prepared to kill James at this stage and left him alone crying by the canal. At this point a woman heard James's loud crying, but assumed he was with some older children who were playing nearby.

Instead of walking away at this point, Jon and Robert turned round and walked back to James, saying, 'Come on, baby'. In his complete innocence, the little toddler took the boys' hands and once again went with his tormentors on another journey. As a big bruise and cut were now visible on James's forehead, the two boys decided to pull the hood of his anorak up so that the wound would be less visible. Several people saw them walking down the road, sometimes dragging the crying toddler behind them. One witness even reported seeing one of the boys kicking James in the ribs, but despite this no one thought to stop them.

By now it was late afternoon and James was again crying for his mother. They reached a grassy spot by a reservoir and sat down with James in between them. While some people approached the boys to see what was going on, no one thought to intercede on James's behalf, believing Jon and Robert's stories about being his older brothers. This lack of action by so many people would later spark its own outrage, after the media published details of the missing toddler.

James Bulger's nightmare journey ended when the three boys arrived at an isolated spot on the railway tracks near Walton, Merseyside. Jon and Robert amused themselves by throwing blue modelling paint in James's face and then beating him with bricks, stones and a 22-lb iron bar. After this he was sexually assaulted and a battery was stuffed in his mouth. When they had finished their evil forms of torture, Jon and Robert laid James's body across the tracks and weighed him down with stones in the hope that a train would run him over and hide the evidence of what they had done.

James's body was not discovered for another two days and the search for his murderers began in earnest.

THE GRIM TRUTH

The video images from the security camera at the shopping centre were studied carefully to see if they could determine who had led James away to his death. Although the images were a little blurred, almost ghostlike, the police watched in disbelief as they realised they were not dealing with an adult paedophile, but two young boys who were nothing more than children themselves.

Jon's father became suspicious about his own son as he appeared to show a rather abnormal interest in the story of James's disappearance. When the news reported that blue paint had been found on the body, he questioned his son about the blue paint on his coat sleeve, which Jon replied had been thrown at him by Robert. Added to this was the fact that Jon was wearing a mustard-coloured jacket on the day of the murder, the same as that worn by one of the boys in the video recording.

The police received an anonymous phone call from a woman, saying that she had a friend called Susan Venables who had a son named Jon. She also added that Jon had been playing truant from school on the day of the murder and that he had blue paint all over his jacket sleeve. The caller went on to say that Jon had a friend called Robert Thompson, who had also skipped school that day, and the police decided to bring the two boys in for questioning.

When the police knocked at the Thompsons' door at 7.30 a.m. on February 18, Robert immediately started to cry and clung to his mother. They searched the house and found a pair of shoes that had splashes of blood on them.

Jon was just as distressed when the police called to pick him up and cried hysterically. However, despite their reactions when the police arrested the two boys, they did not immediately suspect them of being the killers as there were far more violent boys living in the area.

From fingerprints and samples of blood and hair taken from both the boys, the police were more than convinced that they had their suspects and Jon and Robert's case was held in Preston, close to where they were being held in secure units under assumed names.

When the verdicts were read out, Denise Bulger attended the court for the first time, sitting beside her husband Robert. When the defendants were found guilty, Jon sobbed loudly while Robert sat motionless with a blank expression. The judge turned to the boys and said: 'The killing of James Bulger was an act of unparalleled evil and barbarity . . . In my judgement your conduct was both cunning and very wicked . . . You will be securely detained for very, very many years, until the Home Secretary is satisfied that you have matured and are fully rehabilitated and until you are no longer a danger.'

BRIEF BACKGROUNDS

Robert Thompson was one of seven children and it is alleged that he came from a dysfunctional family that suffered from abuse, alcohol, poverty and a father who was very rarely around. It appears that Robert was the ringleader and the one who lied to anyone who stopped to question them while they were with James Bulger. When the verdicts were read out in court, Robert showed no emotion and he has been described as having a 'chilling glare' in his eyes.

During his time in the juvenile centre, Robert has been said to have made exceptional progress and accepts responsibility for the grave acts carried out on James. Since being sentenced, Robert has achieved five GCSEs and A levels and has shown an interest in textile and fashion design.

Jon Venables was described as the weaker of the two boys and somewhat of a follower. He was one of three children, but his parents were separated and he was in the care of his mother who was severely depressed and suicidal. While in custody Jon achieved six GCSEs with good grades and some A levels and has reportedly made exceptional progress in his personal development.

RELEASE AND NEW IDENTITY

When the announcement was made in June 2001 that Jon and Robert were shortly to be released from detention, the news was greeted by a hysterical campaign. Now eighteen years old, the two boys were to be released but, because of the threat to their lives, they would be granted lifetime immunity from any exposure by the media.

Having been carefully assessed as to whether they still posed as a danger to the public, both young men were declared as 'extremely mature and caring young men who are filled with deep regret and remorse'.

Although many people see it as an outrage that these two young men should ever be released after the unspeakable evil they inflicted on James Bulger, in reality they will probably spend the rest of their lives having to look over their shoulders just in case someone discovers their true identity.

James's mother, Denise, who has since remarried, set up a website called 'Justice for James', and has constantly campaigned to try and block the release of Jon and Robert. She has pleaded with people to take every opportunity to try and ensure that their identities are revealed so that they might suffer the way her young son did in his last few hours.

MENENDEZ
BROTHERS

When the trial of brothers Joseph Lyle (Lyle) and Erik Galen (Erik) Menendez was broadcast on television in 1993, it became a national sensation. The defence portrayed the brothers as victims of abuse who were driven to ridiculous lengths by their tyrannical father. José Menendez, a Cuban immigrant, was a self-made millionaire with an obsession for success. Their mother, Kitty, was described as a troubled woman who abused her body with alcohol and drugs, possibly trying to hide from the sexual abuse dished out by José to his two sons. The two brothers were gradually drawn to one another for companionship and solace in the face of their father's control and Erik grew up worshipping his older brother. They often talked about their life and discussed ways of killing their father to release themselves from the constant abuse and domination. Lyle was born in January 1968 and Erik in

November 1971, and over the years they developed very different personalities. While Lyle was described as being aloof and witty with a strong character, Erik was quite the opposite, being very sensitive and quiet.

The first sign that there were flaws in their characters came in 1982 when their cousin Diane came to stay at the Menendez house for the summer. One night when the three cousins were having a playful wrestle in Diane's bedroom, Lyle and Erik suddenly decided to tie her up and take her clothes off. Without warning, the brothers climbed on top of their cousin and started to fondle her breasts and, had she not been able to free herself, she felt it would have gone much further.

THE MURDERS

It was a balmy evening in Beverly Hills on August 20, 1989. José and Kitty Menendez had fallen asleep while watching a James Bond movie and the rest of the house was quiet as the maid had the night off and their two sons had gone out for the evening. At about 10.00 p.m. a small car pulled up outside the Menendez mansion, which was usually heavily guarded by an elaborate security system. For some reason, on this particular evening the high iron gates had been left open and the security alarm had been switched off. Two young men stepped out of the car and, while one went to take something out of the boot of the car, the other walked up the secluded drive towards the house.

The two men entered the house through the french doors which led into the study. From there they walked down the hall to the family room which was located at the rear of the house. The only light in the room was the flickering from the television set but they could make out the shapes of a man with his legs stretched across the coffee table and a woman lying under a blanket with her head in her husband's lap.

One of the men pointed a shotgun at the sleeping couple and squeezed the trigger. While the first shots immobilised José, one of the men walked round the back and placed his gun against the back of his head and fired at point-blank range. The first shots had woken Kitty, who tried to run away from her attackers, but she was hit in the leg and fell between the sofa and the coffee table. As she tried to stand, the assailants riddled her body with bullets, leaving her severely injured but still trying to crawl away to safety.

By this time the two gunmen had run out of ammunition and were unsure of what to do. They knew they couldn't leave her alive as there was the possibility she could survive and give details of her attackers. One of the men ran back to the car, reloaded their shotguns and came back to finish the job. The two men then carefully picked up all the shell casings from the floor and then left the way they had come in and drove away.

The Beverly Hills Police Department received a distressed phone call at 11.47 p.m. on August 20. It was from a man crying 'Somebody killed my parents!'

Minutes after the emergency call, two policemen arrived at 722 Elm Drive and walked round the outside of the mansion for several minutes. Then they heard the sound of screams and two men ran out of the front door, past the policemen, and then sank to their knees on the grass. The two men were distraught and it was hard for the two policemen to get any sense out of them. When they searched the house they found the bodies of José and Kitty Menendez and understood why the two boys were in such a state.

Detective Les Zoeller was appointed to head the investigation and, on arrival at the mansion, he immediately noticed that nothing appeared to have been stolen and that there was no apparent forced entry. Lyle and Erik were taken down to the police station for questioning but, at the time, neither of them were considered to be suspects. During the questioning Erik became inconsolable, while Lyle managed to stay under control and answered their questions in a methodic manner.

Because the Menendez brothers were not suspects, the police did not carry out any gunshot-residue tests, which determined whether a person has recently fired a gun.

SPEND, SPEND, SPEND

Lyle and Erik organised a splendid memorial service for their parents and then Lyle set about proving that he was worthy of inheriting his father's business. Just a few days after the murder of their parents, Lyle and Erik started to spend, spend, spend. They went on lavish spending sprees all funded by their father's personal life insurance policy of $650,000. They bought designer clothes, new cars, jewellery and Rolex watches.

The two brothers had expected to inherit a vast sum from the death of their parents, somewhere in the region of $90 million. Consequently, it came as a bit of a shock when they learned that they were actually only going to inherit around £2 million each after all the loans and taxes had been subtracted. They felt cheated, as they were both aware that their father's assets were far in excess of $4 million, and they started to arrange meetings to find out what had happened to the remainder of the money. They soon discovered that the life insurance policy on José was not valid as their father had refused to take the medical examination. The two brothers decided that they would not stay in the mansion at Beverly Hills because they were scared that the mobsters who had killed their parents would come after them. Instead, they lived out of luxury hotel rooms, amassing enormous bills, and then rented plush adjoining apartments in the infamous Marina del Rey. Lyle hired expensive bodyguards to travel with him and the spending just went on and on.

HARD CASE TO CRACK

Meanwhile, Detective Zoeller was having a hard time trying to crack the case of the Menendez murders. Although they had pulled in several suspects and had a few theories, they couldn't make any of the evidence stick. The police watched in amusement as the brothers literally threw money around and little by little Zoeller began to suspect that the brothers were behind the murder of their own parents.

The two brothers had started to argue, with Erik complaining about the amount of money Lyle was spending and Lyle complaining that Erik had become just like their father. Although Erik appeared calm on the exterior, inside he was depressed and he knew he needed to talk to someone. He decided to call his psychotherapist, Jerome

Oziel and told him about his suicidal thoughts. During one of their sessions, Erik quite openly admitted, 'We did it. We killed our parents'.

Lyle was furious that his brother had blabbed, even if only to his psychotherapist, and he went to visit Oziel in a flaming temper. He threatened Oziel and told him that if he dared to tell anyone he would kill him too. Although by law Oziel could have gone to the police with this information because he had been threatened, he decided to make notes and tape recordings of his sessions with the brothers instead.

Erik had a friend by the name of Craig Cignarelli. When Zoeller interviewed Craig he told the detective that he had visited Erik at the mansion shortly after the murders and his friend had asked if he wanted to know how *it* had happened. He told Zoeller that he knew exactly what he meant by *it*, and they decided to set up a meeting between Erik and Craig to try and get the story on tape. With Craig heavily wired they met for dinner on the evening of November 29. Unfortunately, the meeting was a failure as Erik told his friend that he had been lying and that they had had nothing to do with the murders.

It wasn't until March 5, 1990, that Zoeller saw a chink in the armour, when he received a call from a woman named Judalon Smyth. Smyth happened to be Dr Oziel's lover and also owned an audiotape duplicating company. She told the detective that Oziel had asked her to listen to a recording of a session he had had with the Menendez brothers in which they had threatened him. Zoeller managed to obtain a search warrant for Oziel's tapes based on the information given to him by Smyth. The tapes incriminated the two brothers, but Zoeller knew he had to tread carefully because of the patient–doctor confidentiality law regarding such matters.

THE TRIALS

The Menendez brothers were accused on March 26, 1990 with murdering their parents, but Erik and Lyle seemed totally unaffected by the ordeal. Throughout the hearing they appeared smug and arrogant, not in the least bit contrite over their actions.

The Menendez brothers spent three years in the Los Angeles County Men's Jail waiting for their trial to begin. The trial eventually took place on July 20, 1993 and, although the prosecution tried to show that they had killed in cold blood, the defence put forward a plea of self-defence after a life of abuse that had transformed the brothers into killers. In the end the jury were deadlocked and the result was a mistrial, which many considered to be a miscarriage of justice.

A second, far less publicised, trial took place in August 1995, and this time, with the flaws of the original prosecution ironed out, Erik and Lyle Menendez were convicted on two counts of first-degree murder, plus conspiracy to commit murder. On July 2, 1996, they were sentenced to life imprisonment without the possibility of parole.

Lyle is currently being held in Mule Creek State Prison, while Erik is in the Pleasant Valley State Prison in California. They have both married since entering prison, but neither are allowed conjugal rights. As the brothers are expected to spend the rest of their lives behind bars, it would appear that they will never consummate their unions, which perhaps is a punishment in itself for the fiendish crime they committed in pursuit of riches.

PART EIGHT

SCHOOL SHOOTINGS

COLUMBINE MASSACRE

For over a year, two boys, seventeen-year-old Dylan Klebold and eighteen-year-old Eric Harris, meticulously planned their attack on Columbine High School. As early as 1997 they had both hatched a plan to carry out a large massacre using guns, knives and hand-made bombs to wreak the maximum carnage. Klebold and Harris were angry young teenagers, who had a general hatred towards humanity. Added to this, they had been bullied mercilessly by their classmates and decided they would get their revenge.

Their trademark, if you like, was a long, black trenchcoat and the other kids at the school gave them the nickname 'the Trenchcoat Mafia'. They were both obsessed with violent video games and paramilitary techniques, and used the internet to find recipes for home-made bombs and other explosives. Their plan was to kill as many people as possible and they decided the best time to launch their attack would be when the first lunch period began, when the maximum number of students would be assembled in the cafeteria. Although on the outside Klebold and Harris appeared to be two fairly normal adolescents, little did the authorities realise quite how deep their anger went.

THE MASSACRE

It was on the morning of Tuesday, April 20, 1999, in the town of Littleton, Colorado, that Klebold and Harris put their plan into action. At 11.10 a.m. the two young men arrived in separate cars and parked in the school car park at Columbine High School. A few minutes later, carrying bags stuffed with explosives, they entered the school using the back door of the cafeteria and placed the bags under two of the the tables. Klebold and Harris then returned to their cars and waited for the explosion. The students started to fill the cafeteria for the first lunch sitting and no one paid any attention to the bags on the floor; they simply lay among the hundreds of other bags that had been brought in by the students as they ate their lunch.

The timers on the bombs had been set to detonate at 11.17 a.m., but when Klebold and Harris realised that it had gone past the allotted time, it was obvious their original plan had failed.

The boys decided to enter the school anyway, wearing their long trenchcoats to conceal the weapons and utility belts full of ammunition. Harris was armed with a 9-mm carbine rifle and a 12-gauge pump sawn-off shotgun, while Klebold carried a 9-mm semi-automatic handgun and a 12-gauge pump sawn-off shotgun. As well as the guns they carried knives and bags crammed with hand-made bombs.

At 11.19 a.m. two pipe bombs exploded in an open field several blocks away, which the boys had planted as a diversion for the police. As they heard the bombs explode Klebold and Harris opened fire on some students who were innocently sitting outside the cafeteria. Seventeen-year-old Rachel Scott was killed outright, while her companion Richard Castaldo lay injured.

Inside the school the remainder of the students and teachers were unaware of what had happened. They had put the noise down to a senior prank, which was a tradition among the older students in the weeks leading up to graduation. Some students who were walking out of the cafeteria actually saw Klebold and Harris holding their guns, but thought they were paintball guns and so just kept on walking. All three were shot and wounded.

Then the two boys swung round and fired at a group of students who were eating their lunch on the grass and only one managed to get away. As Klebold and Harris walked towards the school they started throwing small bombs indiscriminately and it was then that one of the teachers, William Sanders, realised that this was no prank. He yelled at the students in the cafeteria to hit the deck and so when Klebold peered into the window it looked as though it was empty.

The two boys entered the school together using the doors on the west side, firing all the time and yelling and shouting. At this stage a policeman had arrived at the school, having been alerted to the explosions, and for a while there was a brief exchange of fire between the officer and Harris, but Harris managed to hold him off and the two boys ran down the north hallway, laughing.

It was only the students in the cafeteria who were aware there was anything going on; all the others were attending their classes as normal. One student, Stephanie Munson, who was walking down the hall away from her class, was confronted by Klebold and Harris and was hit in the ankle, but managed to hobble away to safety.

As the gunmen ran through the building toting their weapons, students and teachers fled and hid wherever they could. By 11.29 a.m. the two boys had reached the library and this is where they killed the largest number of victims. In the seven and a half minutes they were in the library, they killed ten people and injured a further twelve.

In the meantime police and SWAT teams had gathered outside the school and watched as students poured out of the windows and doors, screaming, with many showing signs of injury. The police tried desperately to evacuate the building as they had found a number of explosive devices and were eager to clear the area before they went off.

Harris and Klebold, however, were now on the second floor continuing with their mission. They hunted down any students who were hiding in the classrooms or bathrooms, and although it all happened so quickly, their actions had a devastating, and what later turned out to be a lasting, effect.

The last shots heard to be fired by Harris and Klebold were at 12.30 p.m., which is when they turned their guns on themselves, thus ending the Columbine massacre. As no one had actually witnessed the two boys taking their own lives, it was not until 4.00 p.m. that the police managed to declare the building a safe area. At the end of the tragedy there were thirty-four casualties, including fifteen deaths.

A TOWN IN PANIC

The district had six hospitals, all of which had been

put on alert as soon as the news of the shooting had been reported. Terrified parents ran to the school, desperate to see if their children were safe, and watched in horror as the students ran from the building. Many parents scanned the lists of children who had been taken to the hospitals, but for many it was a long and agonising wait, often ending in sorrow.

Everyone in the town of Littleton was affected by the frightening events of that day and many people wanted to try and apportion the blame on someone. But of course no one can ever be certain why Klebold and Harris committed such a horrific crime. In fact it took many months of intense investigation before anyone could come up with some possible answers.

As the police investigations continued they managed to build up a picture of the lives of the intelligent, well-mannered young men, who had come from good homes. Bit by bit they uncovered reasons for their intense anger and realised that for quite some time they had been seeking their revenge. Eric Harris had posted a website which quite blatantly expressed his hatred towards the inhabitants of Littleton and, in particular, the teachers and pupils at Columbine High. On this website they also posted detailed accounts of their experiments with pipe bombs.

The police also uncovered a diary in Harris's

bedroom, which gave details of his and Klebold's intention to kill as many as 500 people. From the pages of this diary it would appear that Columbine was to be only the start of their revenge and they listed further atrocities that they would like to have carried out.

Teachers had already expressed concerns about Klebold and Harris who, on more than one occasion, had shown disturbing signs of violence. They openly bragged about getting their revenge on the school that they felt had ridiculed them and treated them like outcasts. The pair had also made a video as part of a school project which showed them running through the corridors, wielding guns and killing everyone in sight. Unfortunately, no action was ever taken and the boys' parents were never informed of the teachers' suspicions. It would appear that both Klebold and Harris had managed to hide their violent tendencies from their parents and so it was hard to apportion the blame in that direction.

AND THE NIGHTMARE GOES ON

Just days after the massacre a letter was sent to the *Rocky Mountain News*, which placed the blame on the teachers and students of Columbine for treating Klebold and Harris as outsiders. The letter ended in a threatening tone with the words:

You may think the horror ends with the bullet in my head, but you wouldn't be so lucky. All that I can leave you with to decipher what more extensive death is to come is '12Skizto'. You have until April 26. Goodbye.

Security was increased in the town for the following Monday, but nothing happened and the note was then believed to be the work of a sick prankster.

A mother of one of the wounded students walked into a gun shop and proceeded to shoot herself in the head, having been so traumatised by the events on April 20. A seventeen-year-old student was arrested when he claimed that he was going to finish the job that Klebold and Harris had started.

Although the shooting at Columbine was the worst act of school violence in America up until that time, it was not to be the last and several copycat attacks followed. It drew the nation's attention to the problem and exacerbated the fear that these events would continue and possibly escalate in severity.

HISTORY OF SCHOOL MASSACRES

Of course, school violence and students with guns are not exclusive to the US educational system and we can go as far back as 16th-century Scotland to see students rebelling against the authorities. The Royal High School in old town Edinburgh, Scotland, had a new teacher by the name of Hercules Rollock, but his appointment was to have major repercussions. Rollock didn't have the skill to control his students and consequently they missed a lot of valuable study time due to disruption during the lessons. These students were the sons and daughters of wealthy politicians and businessmen, and the school board were scared that they would pull their children out of the school. To try and rectify the situation they decided to ban the week-long autumn holiday that was coming up so that the students could catch up on their lessons, but this caused outrage. The students gathered weapons

562

and food and barricaded themselves inside the school as a protest. The school officials called on the magistrate of the town, Bailie John Macmorran, to come to the school to see if he could resolve the situation. Macmorran thought the best way of dealing with the students was by battering down the door and taking them by force. However, as they approached bearing a battering ram, one of the students yelled that they would shoot the magistrate if they came any closer. However, the men ignored the student's warning and rammed the door anyway. William Sinclair, the student who had warned the men, wasted no time in firing at Macmorran, killing him with two shots to the head.

BATH, MICHIGAN

On Wednesday, May 18, 1927, farmer Andrew Kehoe lost control and went seeking revenge. His gripe was because the mortgage on his farm had been foreclosed and he found out that the taxes he loathed paying were going towards a new school building, despite the fact that he was treasurer on the school board.

At 9.40 a.m. just after the Consolidated School of Bath had opened for the day, a bomb exploded in the north wing killing nearly forty students and teachers. A bomb in the south wing was defused before it could do any damage, otherwise many more students would have died.

As worried parents rushed towards the school, Kehoe had got back into his car and drove into the school grounds. He leaned out of the window and beckoned for the school superintendent, Emory E. Huyk, to come over to his car. As Huyk approached Kehoe fired a shot into the back seat of his car igniting the dynamite concealed in the padding, killing himself and the superintendent.

The following morning the police discovered Kehoe's wife lying in a barn on their farm with her skull crushed. Kehoe had also placed dynamite in his home, barn and wagon shed, destroying everything – determined that the mortgage company would not get their hands on any of his precious belongings.

COLOGNE

The Cologne massacre took place on June 12, 1964, in a Catholic elementary school in a suburb of Cologne, Germany, called Volkhoven. The lone gunman was a man called Walter Seifert, who had reportedly broken down when his wife died giving birth to their child. He suffered from tuberculosis and had also been diagnosed as being schizophrenic.

The reason for his drastic action was that, in his

mind, he felt he was being unfairly treated by the government, whom he said were cheating him out of his war pension. To get his revenge Seifert made himself a flame-thrower out of a garden insecticide sprayer and bought himself a lance.

On June 12, Seifert headed for the school armed with his flame-thrower and lance and went into the school playground, after first blocking off the main gate using a wooden wedge. He smashed in the windows of the individual classrooms and then pointed his flame-thrower inside, setting everything on fire. When he was confronted by one of the teachers, Gertrud Böllenrath, he stabbed her with his lance shouting, 'I am Adolf Hitler the second!'

After leaving the school grounds he swallowed a quantity of insecticide E605, which is very toxic when ingested. He had hoped the poison would take effect before the police caught up with him, but he was apprehended quicker than expected, but died in hospital the following day.

The death toll at the school was eight children and two teachers, and a further twenty children and two teachers were treated for severe burns.

DUNBLANE

Dunblane is a sleepy town of just 9,000 people on the edge of the Scottish Highlands, which was taken unawares by a school shooting that left the inhabitants in a state of disbelief. The Dunblane massacre took place on Wednesday, March 13, 1996, and remains to this day one of the deadliest attacks on children in the UK to date. A total of sixteen children and one adult died, as well as the lone gunman, Thomas Hamilton.

Hamilton was a forty-three-year-old local man, who was an unemployed shopkeeper. He had also been a scout master but had recently been sacked by the Scout Association which had left him with several grievances. Although the exact motives for his attack are not certain, there had been several complaints regarding his behaviour towards young boys who had been under his guidance in the scout movement. Letters regarding his behaviour led to further rumours, which resulted in the collapse of his shop business in 1993. He had also had several run-ins with the police and the Scout Association when he attempted to set up a boys' youth club, and it is thought that these were all contributory to his erratic behaviour on March 13.

Hamilton managed to get into the primary school carrying two 9-mm Browning pistols and two Smith and Wesson .357 revolvers. Once inside the school he headed towards the gymnasium and opened fire on a class of five- and six-year-old children, killing or wounding everyone with the exception of one person. Fifteen children and their teacher, Gwen Mayor, all died instantly. Hamilton left the gymnasium via the fire exit and went into the playground, where he fired a few rounds of ammunition into a mobile classroom. Luckily, the teacher in the mobile classroom had had the forethought to tell the children to lie on the floor when she heard the shooting, which meant that no one was harmed. However, Hamilton also fired on a group of children walking down one of the corridors, injuring their teacher in the process.

After this Hamilton returned to the gymnasium where he had caused most damage, and fired his gun into his own mouth killing himself instantly. When the emergency services arrived, a further eleven children and three adults had to be rushed to hospital and one of these children was pronounced dead on arrival.

Stuart McCombie, a teacher who rushed to the gymnasium after the shooting, described the scene – one he says which will always be imbedded on his brain: 'They were looking up at me with their wee eyes, slowing changing colour as the blood drained from their faces and they died in my arms. The room was just awash with blood!'

It later emerged that Hamilton had a gun licence for six firearms, which led to criticism of the police for not questioning why he had so many and what they were used for. The event at the Dunblane school led to a massive campaign being launched asking for tighter gun controls, although many felt it was a little too late.

ERFURT, GERMANY

This school shooting took place on April 26, 2002, at the Johann Gutenberg Gymnasium in Erfurt and resulted in the deaths of thirteen members of staff, two students and one police officer.

Robert Steinhaüser was a former student of Johann Gutenberg, who had been expelled a few months earlier for skipping lessons and forging letters of absence. His parents were still under the misapprehension that their son was attending school, as he would leave home each day on the pretence of attending lessons.

On the day of the shooting, Steinhaüser left home as usual and told his parents that he was sitting for an examination. Strapped to his back was a pump-action shotgun and he also carried a 9-mm Glock 17. When he arrived at the school Steinhaüser went to the lavatory and changed into a black outfit and put on a mask. At about 11.00 a.m. he went from class to class, opening the door and pausing just long enough to shoot the teacher. He did not seem to be aiming at any of the students, even though two did get killed when they got caught up in the line of fire by accident.

Just five minutes after the shooting started, police officers arrived on the scene. On hearing the sirens, Steinhaüser leaned out of one of the windows and fired at one of the police, killing him outright.

The hero of the day was one of Steinhaüser's former teachers, Rainer Heise. He managed to convince Steinhaüser to stop killing and was able to lure him into an empty room and then quickly locked the door. Within minutes Steinhaüser had committed suicide.

BESLAN SCHOOL SIEGE

Although this massacre was not carried out in quite the same vein as the previous events mentioned, it was a major event that rocked North Ossetia, killing 344 civilians, including 186 children.

At 8.00 a.m. on Wednesday, September 1, 2004, a group of Chechen separatists, both men and women, stormed the Beslan No. 1 school, holding more than 1,000 children and adults hostage. After an initial shoot-out, the rebels forced the children and teachers inside and held them in the school's gymnasium, placing several of the children in strategic positions at the windows to try and prevent troops from storming the building. In the initial chaos, around fifty people managed to escape and alerted the authorities.

The rebels made a series of demands, asking to speak to the president of North Ossetia, Alexander Dzasokhov, Ingushetia's president Murat Zyakikov and a famous doctor by the name of Leonid Roshal. What they wanted was the release of Chechen fighters and the withdrawal of Russian troops from Chechnya itself. The militants said that if their demands were not met they would blow up the school and kill twenty hostages for every member of their group who was killed.

On the second day there was very little progress made in the negotiations, but the rebels did release a few of the women and some of the youngest children. They described the conditions inside as bearable, but they had been denied any food or water and had been forbidden to use the bathrooms.

On the third day it appeared that there was renewed hope for the hostages when the rebels allowed a vehicle to enter the grounds to pick up the bodies of the people killed on the first day. However, as the emergency services started to recover them, a series of explosions went off inside the school. Part of the roof of the gymnasium, where the majority of the children were being held, collapsed killing several of the hostages, while others tried to escape during the confusion. Several

Russian soldiers were seen carrying children out of the building covered with blood.

However, the worst carnage came at the start of an attempt to rescue the remaining hostages. At about 1.00 p.m. on the Friday, Russian special troops stormed the building and the rest can only be described as pandemonium.

Children and adults ran to escape the rebel's fire, while the Russian soldiers surrounded a residential building where some of the militants had taken refuge. The floor of the gymnasium was a scene of carnage, while outside, children wandered around dazed and naked, gulping down bottles of water.

By 2.30 p.m., rows of ambulances lined up outside the school, while civilians turned their vehicles into rescue wagons, ferrying people to hospital. The rescue operation was temporarily halted when a new phase of shooting broke out near the line of ambulances. Rocket-propelled grenades and gunfire from automatic rifles sent people retreating away from the school. Bodies of the hapless victims lay covered by white sheets as relatives peered underneath, praying that their child was not among the corpses.

The scene at the hospital was just as chaotic, with the courtyard housing row upon row of stretchers with injured and dazed children.

The battle with the rebels continued well into the

evening and as night fell the school gymnasium was still smouldering, pock-marked with bullet holes and its massive windows blown out by explosions.

Russia declared September 6 and 7 as days of mourning and many questions regarding the siege still remain a matter of dispute. Issues regarding the government's handling of the situation are still outstanding as is the use of such heavy weapons when such young lives were at stake.

VIRGINIA TECH

Thirty-three people were killed on the campus of Virginia Tech on April 16, 2007, in Blacksburg, Virginia. Witnesses on the day described the massacre as 'unimaginable horror', as students were literally lined up against a wall and shot to death.

Seung-Hui Cho had moved to the USA when he was eight years old and was majoring in English at Virginia Tech. In 2005, Cho was declared to be mentally ill after an obsession with two female students whom he had been constantly stalking. One of his professors was so worried about his state of mind that he had constantly pushed Cho to go and see a psychiatrist. However, his advice went unheeded and Cho was left to his own devices.

The tragedy on April 16 took place in two separate attacks on the campus of Virginia Tech. The first attack was around 7.15 a.m. at West Ambler Johnson, a residential building for students that housed around 895 people. Cho, armed with a 9-mm pistol and a .22-calibre handgun, killed a man and woman in one of the dormitories. This attack occurred when most of the students were getting ready for classes and the university let everyone carry on as normal, despite the fact that two people had been killed.

More than two and a half hours later, police responded to an emergency call saying that shots had been fired at Norris Hall, which was an engineering and science building at the opposite end of the campus. When the police arrived they found that the doors had been chained from the inside, preventing any of the students from escaping. The police managed to force their way into the building and followed the sound of gunshots up to the second floor. Lying on the floor was the body of Cho who had taken his own life by shooting himself in the face.

As the police searched the rest of the building, the severity of the scene reared its ugly head. There was carnage everywhere in the nine minutes Cho had been on the rampage he had unleashed 170 rounds, killing thirty people and wounding many many more. Eleven students died in an intermediate French language class in Norris Room 211, nine students died in a hydrology class in Room 206, four students died in a German language class in Room 207 and one student died in a mechanics class in Room 204.

Twenty-five people were also injured as a result of Cho, either by his bullets or when they jumped out of the second-storey windows to escape the attack. Many of the students believed that lives could have been spared if campus officials had taken immediate action when the first two people were shot at 7.15 a.m. However, the first warning the students and staff received was an email at 9.26 a.m., more than two hours after the shooting in the dormitory. The email simply warned the students to be cautious, but the officials did not attempt to stop any of the classes even though the gunman had not been apprehended.

It is not clear exactly what happened between the two shootings – a gap of over two hours. The buildings where the attacks took place were about half a mile apart, a distance that could be walked in about fifteen minutes. The police had cordoned off the dormitory where the first shootings had taken place and were still carrying out initial tests, when they learned of the second spate of shootings.

On April 18, NBC News received a package from Cho which had been time-stamped between the first and second attacks. Inside was a 1,800-word declaration, several photographs and twenty-seven digitally recorded videos in which Cho compared himself to Jesus Christ and expressed his loathing of the upper classes.

ABC News also confirmed that there had been

two separate bomb threats the week before at Virginia Tech, the first being directed at Torgersen Hall and the second at the many engineering buildings. Campus officials evacuated students and staff and sent out emails offering a $5,000 reward to anyone who came forward with information regarding the threats. Virginia Tech had always been noted for its peaceful atmosphere and security, and the majority of the students were under the impression that it was nothing more serious than someone playing a prank. Little did they realise just how wrong they were.